D1078857

Prostitution, Power and Freedom

BW

Library and Information Services

Littlehampton Road site   Tel: 01903 606213
Broadwater Road site   Tel: 01903 606451

This book must be returned to the library, or renewed, on or before the date last entered below.
Renewal can be granted only when the book has not been previously requested by another borrower.

PLEASE PROTECT BOOKS FROM DAMAGE   D.9304

E153730

For 'Desiree'

Prostitution, Power and Freedom

Julia O'Connell Davidson

Polity Press

Copyright © Julia O'Connell Davidson 1998

The right of Julia O'Connell Davidson to be identified as author of this work has been asserted in accordance with the Copyright, Designs and Patents Act 1988.

First published 1998 by Polity Press in association with Blackwell Publishers Ltd.

Editorial office:
Polity Press
65 Bridge Street
Cambridge CB2 1UR, UK

Marketing and production:
Blackwell Publishers Ltd
108 Cowley Road
Oxford OX4 1JF, UK

All rights reserved. Except for the quotation of short passages for the purposes of criticism and review, no part of this publication may be reproduced, stored in a retrieval system, or transmitted, in any form or by any means, electronic, mechanical, photocopying, recording or otherwise, without the prior permission of the publisher.

Except in the United States of America, this book is sold subject to the condition that it shall not, by way of trade or otherwise, be lent, re-sold, hired out, or otherwise circulated without the publisher's prior consent in any form of binding or cover other than that in which it is published and without a similar condition including this condition being imposed on the subsequent purchaser.

ISBN 0–7456–1739–5
ISBN 0–7456–1740–9 (pbk)

A catalogue record for this book is available from the British Library.

Typeset in 10.5 on 12 pt Palatino
by Wearset, Boldon, Tyne and Wear
Printed in Great Britain by T.J. International, Padstow, Cornwall

This book is printed on acid-free paper.

NORTHBROOK COLLEGE SUSSEX

ACC. No.
€153730

CLASS No.
306.74 OCO

SUPP.

DATE
2/09

LOCATION

BW

Contents

Acknowledgements

Licence my roving hands, and let them goe
Behind, before, above, between, below . . .
How blest am I in this discovering thee
To enter in these bonds is to be free
  John Donne, *Elegie to his Mistris Going to Bed*

The views expressed in this book are not necessarily shared by the many people to whom I have become indebted in the course of researching and writing it, and my purpose here is to thank those people, rather than to suggest that they endorse my analysis of prostitution. I want to start by acknowledging the support of the Research Board of the Faculty of Social Science at Leicester University, which funded fieldwork in Thailand and Cuba, and ECPAT (End Child Prostitution in Asian Tourism), which funded field trips to Cuba, Costa Rica, Venezuela, the Dominican Republic, South Africa and India. Particular thanks are due to Ron O'Grady, Amihan Abueve, Martin Staebler, Helen Vietche, Frankie Chissim, Jo Bindman and, above all, Anne Badger, for encouragement, advice and support. I am also grateful to the following people for providing information and/or assistance during field trips: Siriporn Skrobanek, Anjana Suvarnananda, Bruce Harris, Caroline Colaso, Roland Martins, Shifra Jacobsen, Marianne Thamm, Glen Smith, Terry Lacey and Edgardo Garcia. Special thanks go to Inez Grummitt for both distracting and helping us during fieldwork in Jamaica and to my long-time friend and hero Sun Wen Bin for coming to my rescue in Thailand.

A number of people have generously supplied me with insights, assistance, information, photocopied materials, references, contacts and/or general support over the past four years, and I am especially grateful to Matt Clark, June Gregory, Eve Rose, Ruth Knott, Bridget Anderson, Usman Sheikh, Simon Carter, Rohit Barot, Mark Maynard, Shelley Anderson, Kevin Yelvington, June Kane, David

Prosser, Annie Phizacklea, Maz, Lisa and Christina, and, above all, Leigh Pinsent and Della Cavner.

In preparing this book I have been helped by Rebecca Harkin of Polity Press and by the detailed comments of an anonymous reader. I am also grateful to Theo Nichols, who gave me valuable feedback on a draft of Part I, and to Derek Layder, for his insights on issues of power, his comments on the manuscript and his more general camaraderie. Without Jacqueline Sánchez Taylor this book would not exist in its present form: she co-researched virtually all of the material it includes on sex tourism, many of the ideas developed from or were refined through discussion with her, and her work on the commodification of blackness has contributed greatly to my understanding of prostitution. Since it was Laura Brace who pointed out to me the significance of notions of political community for prostitution, drew my attention to the many and varied ways in which the moral philosophy of the sex tourist is informed by a liberal political tradition, supplied me with the references necessary to develop such insights and then critically commented on my attempts to do so, it can safely be said that she is the source of any theoretical merit found in Part II. Finally, John Hoffman has not only given me inspiration and encouragement over the past three years, but also read through an entire draft manuscript and gave me detailed and challenging, but always constructive, feedback.

I am an unrepentant romantic, and I choose to read John Donne's elegie as meaning that the license to discover another person's body confers both subjection and freedom: lovers take on bonds which oblige and commit them in certain ways, and yet simultaneously release them from the spectre of separation, loss, isolation and other existential anxieties. This potential is, I believe, also present in non-sexual friendships, for it lies not in the physical intimacy of sexual acts but in the possibility for mutual recognition implicit in all bonds of emotional intimacy. As a person who is much haunted by existential despair I value this kind of recognition above all else, and for this reason I want to thank Jacqueline Sánchez Taylor, Della Cavner and Laura Brace, who have not only given me constant intellectual and emotional support but also, in so doing, the closest thing to freedom I can imagine.

Introduction

A Canadian tourist once told me a story about his relationship with a young Cuban woman, 'Lourdes'. He had met her in a bar in a Cuban tourist resort in 1992, and 'Brian', the Canadian, said that Lourdes was a 26-year-old doctor, intelligent, educated, beautiful, kind, from a 'good' family. Brian was a 43-year-old divorcee. He occupied a relatively well-paid but unglamorous middle management position back home in Toronto and, with his paunch, his thinning, gingerish hair and his pasty complexion, he could hardly be described as possessing 'film star good looks'. His conversational skills, at least in the two to three hours I spent in his company, also appeared somewhat limited (perhaps because his interests were confined almost exclusively to himself and the houses, boats and cars he possessed). He did not exude charm or charisma, and I could not help thinking it unlikely that an attractive 26-year-old doctor from an equally well-connected, wealthy family in Canada would have formed an erotic or emotional attachment to him. And yet, according to Brian, Lourdes had fallen just as passionately in love with him as he had with her. 'I know there are a lot of Cuban girls who are just looking for a ticket out of here', Brian told me, 'but this was different. Lourdes was *really* in love with me.' They wrote to each other constantly, and Brian returned to Cuba four times in a year in order to spend time with her. He brought with him gifts of clothing, shoes, make-up and other items which are difficult to obtain in Cuba as a consequence of the US economic blockade. He wined and dined her in the best tourist hotels and restaurants, establishments which accepted only hard currency – something to which few Cubans at that time had access. Eventually, he decided to investigate the possibility of marrying Lourdes and taking her back to Canada with him. It was this that ended their relationship, for, in Brian's own words:

> It brought everything home to me. It would've cost me $45,000 to get her out of Cuba [the cost of her medical training], plus she would've had to spend another two years in medical school in Canada before she could have practised, plus the Canadian government would make me sign a guarantee that I'd support her financially for ten years. It was just too much. I'm a realist. What if I paid all that, and then she found herself some young guy? . . . I could've paid all that and she could've just run off with another guy.

Brian's story put me in mind of the tale of Mr Peel, recounted by E. G. Wakefield in 1833, and retold by Marx in *Capital* (see Nichols, 1980). Mr Peel was an enthusiastic colonist who set off for Swan River, Australia, taking with him from England not just 'means of subsistence and of production to the amount of £50,000' (Marx, 1954, p. 717) but also three hundred men, women and children of the labouring classes, intending to set them to work in his small empire. Once arrived in Swan River, however, these three hundred 'labourers' disappeared to eke out an independent subsistence on the land, and 'Mr Peel was left without a servant to make his bed or fetch him water from the river' (Wakefield, quoted in Marx, 1954, p. 717). Mr Peel's story, Marx argues, reveals that 'property in money, means of subsistence, machines, and other means of production, does not as yet stamp a man as a capitalist if there be wanting the correlative – the wage worker, the other man who is compelled to sell himself of his own free-will' (1954, p. 717). Capital is not a thing, Marx continues, but a 'social relation between persons', and Mr Peel had not been able to export English *relations* of production to Swan River. To turn his £50,000-worth of 'things' into capital, Mr Peel needed 'a *class* of labourers – a class of non-owners who had no choice but to labour for those who did own and control the means of production' (Nichols, 1980, p. 74). Given access to subsistence land, the labourers Mr Peel had transported chose not to perform wage labour for him.

Unlike Mr Peel, Brian foresaw all too clearly what would happen if Lourdes ever found herself in a position to refuse, as well as to consent to, his wishes. He understood the truth of Marx's observation that:

> Money's properties are my – the possessor's – properties and essential powers. Thus, what I *am* and *am capable* of is by no means determined by my individuality. I *am* ugly, but I can buy for myself the *most beautiful* of women. Therefore I am not *ugly*, for the effect of *ugliness* – its deterrent power – is nullified by money. (*Marx*, 1959, p. 122)

Brian realized that, if Lourdes had no need of hard currency, that is, if she was in a position to support herself independently in the style to which she wished to become accustomed, his money would lose its miraculous powers. Stripped of his massive economic advantage, he would have to meet Lourdes merely as an individual man, and:

> Assume *man* to be *man* and his relationship to the world to be a human one; then you can exchange love only for love, trust for trust, etc. . . . Every one of your relations to man and to nature must be a *specific expression*, corresponding to the object of your will, of your *real individual* life. If you love without evoking love in return – that is, if your loving as loving does not produce reciprocal love; if through a *living expression* of yourself as a loving person you do not make yourself a *beloved one*, then your love is impotent – a misfortune. (*Marx*, 1959, pp. 124–5)

Prostitution is an institution that allows clients to secure temporarily certain powers of sexual command over prostitutes. These are not the kind of powers that many people wish to transfer indiscriminately to anonymous others. In fact, people will generally surrender such powers over their person to others only under very particular social, political and economic conditions – conditions which effectively limit their 'choices' to a set of alternatives which are not of their choosing. In other words, prostitution, as much as wage labour, is predicated upon the existence of a very particular set of social relations. In some cases these relations present people with a stark 'choice' between abject poverty or prostitution, or between violence, even death, or prostitution. In other cases the 'alternatives' may stretch to include monotonous, low-paid employment, as well as prostitution. I will labour an obvious point. Wealthy, powerful individuals do not typically elect to prostitute themselves. We hear stories about government ministers, senior executives, bishops, movie stars, directors of public prosecution, university vice-chancellors and so on *using* prostitutes. We do not hear stories about them giving up their careers in order to *become* prostitutes.

Those who wish to defend the institution of prostitution often state that there are individuals who enjoy working as prostitutes. There are, for example, some men who say that prostitution represents for them a happy coincidence between their desire for multiple anonymous sexual encounters with other men and their need to make a living (see, for instance, Marlowe, 1997). There are also some women who state that they find fulfilment in prostitution. The American prostitute-cum-performer-cum-self-publicist Scarlot Harlot (Carol Leigh), for instance, describes the laws which criminalize prostitution as curtailing her 'freedom of sexpression' and her 'freedom to do whatever I want with my body' (Bell, 1994, p. 179). There are also prostitutes who describe themselves as 'high priestesses of sacred sex magic rituals', 'professional sexual deviants' and 'sexpositive feminists', and claim to derive certain pleasures from their work (Nagel, 1997, DePaulo, 1997; see also Califia, 1994).

I do not wish to join with those feminists who insist that people who find prostitution sexually as well as financially rewarding are the victims of false consciousness. I think that we can allow for the possibility that these individuals are providing a faithful account of their own subjective experience without this in any sense undermining the more general argument that prostitution is an institution which founders upon the existence of economic and political conditions that compel people to act in ways in which they would not otherwise choose to act. If one or two of the labourers transported to Swan River had taken a special fancy to Mr Peel and elected to remain as his servants, it would not, after all, invalidate Marx's general analysis of this tale. Likewise, there are very probably some individuals who choose to become soldiers because they are attracted to the idea of killing other people. However, if national armies could *only* recruit this kind of psychotic, they would hardly be the massive and powerful institutions that they are. And there may exist some individuals who find the kind of tasks allocated to workers on factory assembly lines challenging and rewarding, but industrial capitalism would not have advanced very far if its enterprises *only* employed those individuals who can take active pleasure in performing mindless, repetitive tasks.

It is equally the case that, if those with the will and the money to enter into commercial sexual transactions had recourse only to the Scarlot Harlots of this world, prostitution would be a small-scale affair indeed. But the fact is that prostitutes' clients do not find themselves constrained in this way. In virtually any city, port or tourist resort of the world, their money can buy them sexual access to a selection of adults and children who will derive no physical, sexual or psychological gratification (and often precious little financial reward) from the encounter. These are people whose entry into prostitution is conditioned by and predicated upon a particular set of *social* relations rather than being a specific expression of their individual selves. They become prostitutes because the economic, political and social circumstances in which they live make it either the best or the only means of subsisting, or they are people who are forced into prostitution by a third party.

This book is not concerned with the tiny minority of individuals who are attracted to prostitution by the intrinsic qualities of 'sex work', but deals only with the experience of people for whom prostitution represents either the best of a bad bunch of options or a condition forced upon them by another person or persons. Its aim is to examine the nature, meaning and consequences of the bonds which prostitutes enter into with clients and with other third parties, and to consider the power relations which are associated with and reproduced by these bonds.

Methodology

The book draws heavily on my own research on prostitution, which started in 1993 with an ethnographic study of a successful, entrepreneurial British prostitute (see O'Connell Davidson and Layder, 1994). This project involved participant observation as a receptionist, in-depth interviews with ten regular clients and four receptionists, a survey of clients' demands and analysis of letters and other documents provided by clients, as well as transcripts of tape-recorded sessions with clients. In 1994 I conducted a small-scale study of the attitudes and motivations of British sex tourists to Thailand (O'Connell Davidson, 1995a) and in March 1995 I undertook a similar piece of research on sex tourism in Cuba (O'Connell Davidson, 1996a). Jacqueline Sánchez Taylor, who is bilingual in Spanish and English, accompanied me on this trip and carried out interview work with women, children and men working in informally arranged tourist-related prostitution as well as interviews with Spanish sex tourists. Jacqueline and I were subsequently commissioned by ECPAT (End Child Prostitution in Asian Tourism) to undertake a series of research trips to investigate the identities, motivations, practices and attitudes of individuals who exploit child prostitutes (ECPAT employs the United Nations definition of a child as a person under the age of eighteen). Between July 1995 and June 1996 we visited Costa Rica, Venezuela, the Dominican Republic, Goa, South Africa and Cuba for a second time. In each research site we used the same basic methods: observation in brothels, bars, clubs and tourist haunts, interviews with sex tourists, prostitutes, pimps, brothel keepers, hoteliers, taxi drivers and others involved in the informal tourist economy, and, where possible, interviews with staff of agencies and NGOs working on issues of child protection, prostitution, child prostitution and tourism. We also used printed questionnaires to gather structured data on sex tourists' background characteristics. In August 1997 we conducted pilot research on male prostitution and female sex tourism in Jamaica.

In all, I undertook fifteen weeks of fieldwork on sex tourism, and, taken together, 230 prostitute users (tourists, expatriates, businessmen, locals and sailors) and 169 people involved in prostitution (adult and child prostitutes, pimps, procurers, brothel and escort agency managers and doormen) were interviewed by Jacqueline Sánchez Taylor and myself in the course of all nine field trips. The sex tourists we interviewed formed a diverse group in terms of age and socio-economic background. The vast majority were white heterosexual men, but our sample does include five African-American and Black British male sex tourists and ten white female and three African-American female sex tourists. We also have survey data from around forty Western female sex tourists.

We did not attempt to measure the scale of the problem of child prostitution, or to produce quantitative data on the numbers of sex tourists, expatriates, businessmen, sailors, locals and others involved in the sexual exploitation of local and migrant women and children. Although the research involved interview work with a fairly large number of individuals involved in prostitution and sex tourism, this was an opportunistic, not a random, sample and any attempt to advance generalizations along the lines of 'x per cent of prostitutes in tourist-related prostitution are under the age of 18' or 'x per cent of their clients are married men' on the basis of such a sample would be entirely inappropriate. Instead, our fieldwork aimed to produce insights into the lived experience of participants in sex tourism by documenting their narratives and lifespan biographies, examining contradictions and tensions in sex tourists' spoken defences of their prostitute use and using observational methods to build on our understanding of prostitute–client inter-actions. We were attempting to achieve what Geertz (1973) has termed 'thick description' of sex tourism as a social practice, and our confidence in the description we offer on the basis of our field research comes from the fact that we were able not only to triangu-late different kinds of research evidence (observation, interviews with sex tourists, interviews with prostitutes, interviews with pimps and brothel keepers, survey evidence, documentary evid-ence) but also to compare and analyse our own very different experiences in the field.

As well as the research already mentioned, I have, over the past four years, conducted interviews with ten British women who work in street and/or massage parlour prostitution, visited court with a probation officer where I observed magistrates sentencing prostitute women for non-payment of fines for soliciting, and attended the preliminary meeting of a prostitutes' peer support group as well as various meetings arranged by agencies which provide services for prostitutes. Five men who knew of my research interests approached me to 'confess' their prostitute use/sex tourism and subsequently agreed to be interviewed in person or to enter into correspondence about their prostitute use. I have also found the Internet to be a useful means of contacting clients (as well as finding various sites, in themselves, to be a source of data on prostitute users' attitudes), and have conducted a number of e-mail interviews with prostitute users contacted in this way. Other published and unpublished documents that I have col-lected, such as contact magazines, small advertisements for 'massage', pornographic magazines and videos, prostitutes' tele-phone kiosk cards and so on, have also contributed to the analysis of prostitution offered in this book. Again my confidence in the validity of the description of prostitution that I offer in the follow-ing pages comes from the fact that I have been able to triangulate data gathered in different ways from a number of different sources. It is important to note, however, that this book presents and analyses data on Western heterosexual prostitute users, most of whom are white and male, and does not necessarily speak to the demand for prostitution which comes from Asian, South-East Asian and African men or from homosexual men and women. Also, my own research has not focused on the social organization of male prostitution, nor have I investigated links between prostitution and organized crime.

There is a long-standing philosophical debate within the social sciences about the relative importance of structure and agency in theory and method which I will not enter into here, but merely note that I subscribe to what might be termed the 'realist' compromise within such debates:

> Realism ... argues that the knowledge people have of their social world affects their behaviour ... However, people's knowledge may be partial or incomplete. The task of social research is not simply to collect observations on the social world, but to explain these within theoretical frameworks which examine the underlying mechanisms which structure people's actions and prevent their choices from reaching fruition. (*May*, 1993, p. 7)

I have therefore borrowed from theoretical analyses of wage labour and slavery and of various forms of erotic domination as well as from theories of consent, contract and community in order to both structure and explain my empirical observations. My aim has been to examine not simply the intersubjectively agreed rules and meanings which guide interaction and the discourses which surround it, but also the structural mechanisms which underpin the everyday experience of participants in prostitution (see Layder, 1993). Even if I were in a position to do so, it would be impossible in a book of this length to provide a detailed exposition of the ways in which every single macro-phenomenon that impacts on the lived experience of prostitutes and clients structures and constrains action (I can, for example, envisage an entire book on the ways in which prostitution is 'racialized' and how this relates to broader structural and ideological factors, and another entire book on age and prostitution). It merely provides selected examples of how legal and institutional structures, patterns of tourist investment, labour market conditions, systems of debt bondage, ideological representations of 'race', sexuality and gender, and so on, shape the experience of prostitution and give meaning to the interactions between adult and child prostitutes and their clients, and I hope that other contributions to a body of realist evidence on prostitution will compensate for its shortfalls.

Definitions and book structure

'Prostitution' is typically defined by both academics and lay persons as the exchange of sexual services for cash and/or other material benefits (see Phoenix, 1995, for a discussion of the limitations of such definitions), for it is widely assumed that, as Overall (1992, p. 716) puts it, 'sex work is by definition the commoditization of sex.' However, both the idea that it is *sex* or *sexual services* which are commodified in prostitution and the notion that prostitution necessarily involves transactions modelled upon narrowly contractual commodity exchanges can be contested.

The assertion that clients buy sex or sexual services from prostitutes raises the same kind of problems that are advanced by the idea that employers buy labour from their workers. As Marxists have pointed out, while it is possible for one person to design a project and then pay another person to it carry out, 'Labor, like all life processes and bodily functions, is an inalienable property of the human individual' (Braverman, 1974, p. 54). Because it cannot be separated from the person of the labourer, it is not *labour* that is exchanged, sold or surrendered (we cannot, for example, purchase ten kilowatts of plumber's labour at a DIY superstore and then take it home to fix our own leaking sink). What workers sell, and what employers buy, 'is *not an agreed amount of labor, but the power to labor over an agreed period of time*' (Braverman, 1974, p. 54, original emphasis) (thus we can pay for an hour of a plumber's time and *direct* that plumber to execute the labour necessary to fix our leaking sink). This distinction between labour and the power to labour is hugely significant. It draws our attention to the fact that labour power is, as Pateman (1988) puts it, a political fiction. She continues:

> The capitalist does not and cannot contract to use the proletarian's services or labour power. The employment contract gives the employer right of command over the use of the worker's labour, that is to say, over the self, person and body of the worker during the period set down in the employment contract. Similarly, the services of the prostitute cannot be provided unless she is present; property in the person, unlike material property, cannot be separated from its owner. (*Pateman*, 1988, pp. 202–3)

For this reason, I would argue that, although prostitution is popularly defined as the exchange of *sex* or *sexual services* for money and/or other material benefits, it is better conceptualized as an institution which allows certain powers of command over one person's body to be exercised by another. The client parts with money and/or other material benefits in order to secure powers over the prostitute's person which he (or more rarely she) could not otherwise exercise. He pays in order that he may command the prostitute to make body orifices available to him, to smile, dance or dress up for him, to whip, spank, massage or masturbate him, to submit to being urinated upon, shackled or beaten by him, or otherwise submit to his wishes and desires.

The social, technical and conceptual organization of this transfer of powers varies. Sometimes it is organized by a third party, who has either enslaved the prostitute or provided her/him with direct or indirect employment. In other cases it is organized by independent, self-employed prostitutes. Within this, the prostitute-client transaction may be formally arranged along the lines of a closely specified, speedily executed commodity exchange (that is, x sexual service for x amount of money), but it can also be organized as an exchange that is more like a contract of employment or indenture (that is, x amount of time being served by the prostitute for x amount of money). Where the prostitute–client exchange takes this latter form, there can be enormous variability in terms of how and where the boundaries of the contract are drawn. The limits to the transaction and the client's powers of command within it may be tightly drawn, but in other cases the exchange is diffuse and loosely specified. The client may even get to command the performance of non-sexual labour as well as sexual services in exchange for a sum of money and/or other benefits which are not explicitly negotiated in advance. The duration of such transactions can also vary widely, sometimes taking place over a number of days, weeks or even months. Taking the 'employment' status of prostitutes and the contractual form of the prostitute–client relation as two major axes of difference in terms of how prostitution is socially organized, it is possible to distinguish at least six different forms of prostitution (see figure 1), each of which represents a different way of organizing the transfer of powers over the person which prostitution entails.

Figure 1: Dimensions of diversity

	Prostitution contract = informal, diffuse	Prostitution contract = formal, commoditized
'Enslaved'		
Directly/indirectly employed		
Self-employed		

Part I of this book is concerned with the variability of prostitution in terms of its social organization, the power relations it involves and the degree of unfreedom it implies for individual prostitutes. It looks at the hierarchies that exist within prostitution and the economic, social, political, ideological and legal factors that structure them. Chapters 1 and 2 explore these issues in relation to the forms of prostitution which occur in the upper four boxes of figure 1 (that is, informal and formal contracts that are organized or controlled by third parties). Chapter 3 examines independent, self-employed street prostitution which involves narrowly contractual, highly commoditized exchanges, while Chapter 4 is concerned with independent but informally arranged prostitution. Chapter 5 considers the experience of self-employed prostitution at the apex of the prostitution hierarchy.

My purpose in examining the diversity of prostitution is not to show that there is no 'fixity' to this institution or to argue that there are multiples of incommensurate prostitutions. Rather my aim is to locate variability within theoretical frameworks that allow us to identify underlying structural mechanisms which shape differences in prostitutes' experience, and to identify what is common to that experience. In particular, I am concerned with links between systemic features of oppression (see Young, 1990) and the organization of prostitution.

Part II of the book turns to questions about the social meanings that attach to prostitution and about clients' motivations for prostitute use. Chapter 6 is largely theoretical and examines what notions of community, contract and consent can tell us about the construction of the prostitute as a debased and degraded sexual 'Other'. Drawing on my own interview work with clients, Chapter 7 then goes on to analyse the dynamics of sexual desire for such an Other, and to develop a typology of clients through reference to the ways in which they eroticize their own prostitute use. Chapter 8 is concerned primarily to explore the highly 'racialized' and racist narratives Western tourists use to justify their acts of sexual exploitation while travelling in poor countries, and develops an analysis of sex tourism as the pursuit of gender honour. The political implications of parts I and II of this book are briefly considered in the concluding chapter.

Finally, I should make some remarks about the term 'child prostitution'. Childhood is, as many authors have pointed out, a socially constructed condition rather than one which can be clearly defined through reference to biological fact or chronological age.

Its perimeters vary cross-culturally and historically, and even within any one nation state its boundaries are often indistinct (see Pilcher, 1995). For the international community to concern itself with the condition and experience of children around the globe, however, it must necessarily employ some universal definition of childhood, and the United Nations and many other international bodies define a child as a person under the age of eighteen. I follow this definition – even though I am aware of the case made by those who hold such a definition to be Eurocentric (Ennew, 1986) – since, for the purposes of my general arguments about child prostitution, it makes no difference whether we draw the boundary of childhood at eighteen, fourteen or even ten, for the vast majority of child prostitutes of whatever age are actually integrated into the mainstream sex industry which serves *all* prostitute users, rather than working in some isolated 'market niche' that caters solely to the desires of 'paedophiles' or child molesters. It follows from this that any group which represents a source of demand for commercial sex can be assumed to supply a significant number of child sex exploiters, many of whom sexually abuse children because they are prostitute users (and/or strip and sex show customers, and/or consumers of pornography) in a world which, on the one hand, places sexual value on youth and, on the other, forces large numbers of children (either through direct coercion or economic necessity) into working in the sex industry. For this reason I do not separate child prostitution analytically from the more general phenomenon of prostitution, but rather treat age as one of several stratifying factors which impact on the degree of unfreedom experienced by individual prostitutes.

PART I

DIMENSIONS OF DIVERSITY

1

Power, Consent and Freedom

What kind of power do clients and third parties exercise over prostitutes? Can human beings freely consent to their own prostitution? For some feminists these questions are relatively clear cut. Carole Pateman (1988), for example, holds that the prostitution contract establishes a relationship within which the prostitute is unambiguously subject to the client's command. The client exercises powers of mastery over her. There is equally little room for ambiguity in Kathleen Barry's treatment of prostitution. Sexual exploitation violates human rights to dignity, she argues, and there can therefore be no 'right to prostitute' and no distinction between 'free' and 'forced' prostitution. People cannot give meaningful consent to the violation of their human rights (Barry, 1995, pp. 304–6).

This kind of analysis rests on certain assumptions about the essential properties of prostitution (that it *necessarily* subordinates the prostitute to the client's will, that it *necessarily* involves inhuman and degrading treatment) and, more importantly, for the purposes of this chapter, on an undifferentiated view of power. There is nothing in the account provided by Barry, for example, which would allow us to distinguish between the kind of powers that are exercised over a debt-bonded child prostitute and those exercised over an adult who prostitutes independently or voluntarily enters into an employment contract with a third party, and it is this which so infuriates those feminists who campaign for legal rights and better working conditions for 'sex workers'. Barry, and the US-based Coalition Against Trafficking of Women with which she has been heavily involved, stands accused of pursuing an underlying moral agenda of 'abolishing prostitution ... by linking all forms of the sex trade with an emphasis on emotive words like "trafficking, slaves, and child prostitution" ' (Perkins, 1995). For most prostitutes' rights activists, it is the laws that criminalize prostitution, rather than anything inherent in the prostitution exchange, which make prostitutes so vulnerable to coercion, abuse and exploitation. Prostitution should therefore be recognized as a form of work that can be actively chosen and prostitutes accorded the rights and protection that is given to other groups of wage workers.

Although 'abolitionist' and 'pro-sex worker' feminists clearly hold divergent moral and political understandings of prostitution, it seems to me that the view of power implicit in both lines of analysis is equally unidimensional. The former offers a zero-sum view of power as a 'commodity' possessed by the client (and/or third-party controller of prostitution) and exercised over prostitutes, the latter treats the legal apparatuses of the state as the central source of a repressive power that subjugates prostitutes. Part I of this book aims to show that the power relations involved in prostitution are far more complicated than either of these positions suggest. I want to start this chapter with some general remarks about power relations in prostitution, and then move on to explore the operation of power within formally organized, third-party controlled prostitution.

The faces of power

The social relations of prostitution vary. To begin with, we can note a distinction between independent, self-employed prostitutes and those who are controlled by a third party. So far as the latter group are concerned, we can further distinguish between those who are subject to what Truong (1990, p. 184) terms 'relations of confinement' (wherein third parties use physical force and/or debt to prevent individuals from exiting from prostitution, even in the event of an alternative means of subsisting becoming available to them) and those who are subject to 'enterprise labour relations' (which involve individuals who are, in a formal sense, free to exit from prostitution and which take a form similar to direct or indirect 'employment relations' in other capitalist enterprises). This means that there is a continuum within third-party controlled

prostitution in terms of the formal freedoms that prostitutes exercise over their own persons and also that there is variability within
prostitution in terms of the extent and degree to which prostitutes
are subject to the *personalistic* power of third parties. Some prostitutes are directly forced into particular kinds of transactions and a
given work rate by one or more individuals. Others are not.

   While the formal social relationship between prostitutes and
third party has an important bearing upon the type and degree of
compulsion to which prostitutes are subject, it is not the *only* external constraint operating on them. Prostitutes are also subject to
materialistic forms of domination; that is to say, economic pressures
operate as another form of compulsion upon them. This is not
simply true of those who prostitute independently. Prostitutes
who are employed and even those who are enslaved are typically
subject to both materialistic and personalistic forms of power. The
degree of economic compulsion operating on prostitutes also
affects the degree of control they exercise over whether, when,
how often and on what terms they prostitute. The contractual form
of the prostitute–client exchange also impacts on the degree of
power that can be legitimately exercised over the prostitute by the
client. Where the contract is tightly drawn and resembles a
straightforward commodity exchange – for x sum of money the
client has a right to exercise x specific powers of command over the
person of the prostitute – there are clear boundaries to the formal
powers which clients can exercise over prostitutes. Often,
however, the contract takes a form more like that of a contract of
indenture – for x sum of money the client can command the prostitute for x period of time – and it may be very difficult for the prostitute to impose limits on the nature or extent of the client's powers
over her within that set time period.

   Next we should note that the relationship between prostitute
and third party, as well as that between prostitute and client, takes
place in a specific legal, institutional, social, political and ideological context, and that this represents another set of external constraints upon those relationships. In many cases, for example,
prostitution is legally regulated in ways which so heavily penalize
independent prostitution that law/law enforcement effectively
operates as a pressure on prostitutes to enter and remain in third-
party controlled prostitution no matter how exploitative the third
party may be. Equally significant in shaping the relative powers
enjoyed by prostitutes and third parties are broader ideological
and political factors. In contexts where certain social groups (for

instance, women, children, migrants or particular 'castes') are
generally devalued, and/or constructed as objects rather than subjects of property, and/or denied full juridical subjecthood and/or
denied independent access to welfare support, their vulnerability
to prostitution and to third-party exploitation and abuse within it
is increased.

In short, there is no single, unitary source of power within prostitution that can be seized and wielded by third party, client or
prostitute. Rather, prostitution as a social practice is embedded in a
particular set of social relations which produce a series of variable
and interlocking constraints upon action. Finally, we should note
that, as Layder (1997, p. 147) puts it, 'power spans both the objective and subjective aspects of social life', and this too has implications for the degree of unfreedom experienced by prostitutes.
People come to prostitution as *individuals* with particular personal
histories and subjective beliefs, and some people's psychobio-
graphies and attitudes leave them far more open to abuse and
exploitation than others. I want to flesh these points out by looking
at some examples of different types of brothel prostitution in the
contemporary world.

Brothels as business enterprises

Prostitution involves the transfer of certain powers of command
over the persons of prostitutes in exchange for money and/or
other material benefits, but the actual prostitute–client exchange is
necessarily surrounded by various other activities, such as soliciting custom, negotiating contracts, providing a setting for executing
those contracts, managing the throughput of customers, and so on.
In brothel prostitution all or some of these functions are undertaken by a third party – the brothel owner or her/his agents. The
dictionary definition of 'brothel' is 'a house of prostitutes', and we
might add to this that a brothel constitutes premises at which
clients can view, select, arrange and execute a transaction with
prostitutes. In many countries of the world the laws surrounding
prostitution make, or have historically made, the operation of a
brothel illegal, and brothel owners often adjust to such constraints
by running their businesses behind the 'front' of another legally
permitted enterprise, such as a massage parlour, sauna, hotel,
night-club, bar, restaurant or barber's shop.

Legal restrictions on operating brothels (as well as the overheads

associated with providing on-site facilities for executing transactions) encourage some third parties to run what might be
described as 'take-out' brothels. In these, facilities are provided for
clients to view, select and arrange a transaction with prostitutes,
but not to execute the actual transaction. A variant of the 'take-out'
brothel is to be found in escort agencies, which do not usually
provide facilities to view prostitutes (at least not in the flesh;
sometimes customers can select a prostitute from a catalogue of
photographs) or to execute transactions, but instead send prostitutes out to clients in their hotel rooms, rented accommodation or
homes.

Whether it does so overtly or covertly, the brothel is an organization which facilitates numerous prostitute–client exchanges and
through which some or all of the activities that surround those
exchanges are brought under the central co-ordination of a third
party. Brothel owners do not bring together a supply of prostitutes
and a stream of custom out of an altruistic wish to further the
interests of prostitutes and clients any more than factory owners
bring labour and capital together simply out of a desire to facilitate
the manufacture of useful products. Instead, they take it upon
themselves to orchestrate prostitute–client exchanges out of economic self-interest, and it is therefore important to consider how,
exactly, the brothel owner can make a profit from these exchanges.

One way in which political economists have examined social
and production relations in various different class societies (slave,
feudal and capitalist) is by asking how, under different modes of
production, an economic surplus is produced, appropriated and
used once appropriated (Dixon, 1988). The idea is that economic
activity can be disaggregated (conceptually if not practically) into
that which is *necessary* for reproduction – either of a given society
or mode of production, or of the individual worker – and that
which is *surplus* to reproduction. At a macro-level the economic
surplus is defined as 'the difference between what a society produces and the costs of producing it' (Baran and Sweezy, 1966,
p. 23), and at a micro-level we are talking about the disparity
between any particular group of workers' output and the costs of
maintaining their output at that given level.

The same basic concepts of 'necessary' and 'surplus' economic
activity can be applied to prostitution. Assume that, in a given
country, the minimum 'rate' for a trick is x and the cost of an individual's daily subsistence is $4x$. In order to live, and so reproduce
herself and her capacity to continue working each day, a prostitute

must therefore enter into four client transactions daily. If she enters into more than four transactions, and/or manages to get clients to pay more than the minimum rate, she will generate an economic surplus. We can also argue that, just as the capitalist labour process is designed to facilitate the production and appropriation of surplus value, so the social relations and organization of third-party controlled prostitution are fundamentally geared towards this same end, for it is only if third parties can get prostitutes to generate a surplus and surrender that surplus to them that they can hope to profit from the prostitution of others.[1] Third parties therefore need to make 'their' prostitutes enter into more client transactions than are necessary to the individual prostitute's daily subsistence (let us say eight, rather than four) and to devise ways of creaming off some or all of the surplus (in this case, some or all of the surplus $4x$) that each prostitute generates.

As the examples provided below will show, brothel owners typically manage to siphon off a profit from prostitution by inserting themselves as intermediaries in the prostitute–client exchange and demanding payment from either the client or the prostitute, or both, for 'facilitating' each exchange. This means that third parties need somehow to exercise control over either a supply of prostitutes or a stream of demand from clients, or both,[2] and it also means that third parties have an economic incentive to a) maximize the absolute number of prostitute–client exchanges that take place and b) ensure that individual prostitutes retain as little as possible of the surplus they generate by entering into large numbers of client transactions. It is towards these ends that brothel owners' organizational and control strategies are directed.

Identifying the essential goals or 'objective interests' of brothel owners does not immediately reveal to us necessary features of brothel organization or facts about the types of power to which prostitutes must inevitably be subject, however. To begin with, brothel keepers, as much as owners of any other capitalist enterprise, have to adjust the organization of their businesses (including their 'employment' practices) to fit the particular market conditions in which they operate. Where there is a consistently high volume of demand, for example, brothel owners have an incentive to devise organizational forms which compel prostitutes to accept a high throughput of custom. Where demand is low and/or fluctuating, they have an interest in organizational forms which force prostitutes to shoulder the cost of running the brothel and to keep trade ticking over. Equally, there are senses in which the social organization of brothels can be viewed as a response to conditions in the prostitution 'labour market'. According to whether this market is slack or tight, different types of 'employment relation' may be more or less economically attractive to the brothel owner.

Yet any explanation of the very different forms of formally organized, third-party controlled prostitution in the contemporary world which focused exclusively, or even primarily, on market conditions would be inadequate for two sets of reasons. The first is that these market conditions are not natural or given. Instead, both customer demand and the supply of prostitutes are critically shaped by a range of economic, social, geographical, ideological, legal and political factors. The second is that the third party's response to any given set of market conditions has to be understood in relation to these same structural factors. As the remainder of this chapter shows, depending upon the broader structural context in which brothel prostitution is set, the brothel owner's essential goals can be pursued in different ways and can imply different configurations of power between brothel owners, prostitutes and clients.

Massage parlours in England

Under the law of England and Wales, 'prostitution itself is not a criminal offence, but public manifestations of prostitution: soliciting, advertising, making agreements with clients, brothel-keeping, and living on the earnings of prostitution are illegal' (Bindman, 1997, p. 14). The law further stipulates that it is an offence 'for men and women to exercise control over prostitutes ... and for men and women to procure' (Edwards, 1993, p. 115), and thus it formally proscribes all forms of brothel prostitution. In England, then, brothels are typically operated behind the front of another business that offers legitimate services/facilities – most commonly massage or saunas. This makes it possible for the owner to contract women legitimately as masseuses, and to argue that 'these legitimate and licit activities comprise the "core" of parlour work. Any prostitution exchange that may take place is extra to this contract; it is negotiated privately between the worker and the client' (Phoenix, 1995, pp. 72–3).

I will describe the social organization of prostitution in 'Stephanie's', a massage parlour in a midlands town in England, since it is fairly typical of this form of brothel. The physical environment of Stephanie's consists of a reception area, a small sauna and a sunbed, and rooms upstairs where transactions are executed. Between four and six prostitutes work in the parlour at any one time, and the owner also employs a receptionist. The prostitutes are not waged employees, but are offered shift work more or less on an 'as and when' they turn up basis. Clients are attracted by advertisements in the local press, which are perfectly legal providing that parlour owners advertise their legitimate business (in this case, massage services), and, since Stephanie's is located in a known red-light district, it attracts some passing trade as well as regular custom.

On arrival, the client pays the receptionist a 'massage fee' of £10. As Phoenix (1995, p. 73) notes, this kind of set fee 'typically acts as protection for the management from charges of brothel running'. The receptionist takes the client upstairs and tells him to get undressed and wait for the 'masseuse', who then negotiates the details of the transaction with him. The prices are, in theory, fixed by the parlour owner, who involves herself in the details of prostitute–client transactions to the extent that she sets prices for oral sex, penetrative sex, hand relief and 'topless' hand relief, and specifies that, for these prices, the client may spend thirty minutes with the prostitute. The owner takes a fee not only from clients but also from the prostitutes in her (indirect) employ. Prostitutes working at Stephanie's have to pay a 'shift fee' of £20 for the privilege of working there at all, and they are then charged a 'punter fee' of £5 for each client that they see. As well as this, they are expected to pay £25 per shift, supposedly for the receptionist's services. In short, they cover the expenses of running the parlour, and by the time they see their first client they will have incurred 'expenses' of £50 (£10 more than the rate for penetrative sex set by the owner).

On a good day, a prostitute at Stephanie's sees seven clients during a shift. If every client pays the full price for the most expensive 'service' – penetrative sex – then the prostitute will end up with £200 at the end of her shift, while the owner will pocket £125. If the prostitute sees fewer clients, say five, and if they negotiate for cheaper services or to pay lower rates, say £25, then she will walk away from the shift with a mere £55. However, since the owner does not vary the punter fee or the shift fee, she will still pocket £95. On days when there is very little custom it is possible for prostitutes to end up owing money to the parlour owner.

Though there may be individual cases in which massage-parlour owners in England imprison women and/or children and brutalize them into prostitution, force is not routinely used by owners to secure a supply of prostitutes. Instead, prostitutes are typically recruited by word of mouth and/or by advertising. It should be clear from the above, however, that recruits are not enticed by an attractive employment package. The deal they are offered is transparently exploitative. It forces the prostitute to surrender a large proportion of the surplus generated by her prostitution, to carry the costs of running the parlour and to shoulder all the financial risk associated with downturns in demand; it provides her with no employment continuity, rights or benefits. What is it, then, that assures parlour owners a steady supply of 'employees'?

To begin with, employment opportunities for unskilled women in England are limited, and those which do exist are usually extremely low paid. Moreover, the English welfare system barely assures a subsistence to single adults, and is even more inadequate in respect of lone parents. The financial situation of many women is therefore so desperate that prostitution often appears to be the best of a poor bunch of economic alternatives (McLeod, 1982, Edwards, 1987). It clearly makes more financial sense for women to prostitute independently rather than allow a third party to siphon off a portion of their earnings, and many do exactly this. But economically vulnerable women are, by definition, unlikely to be in a position to set up their own private brothel (see Chapter 5) and, since law-enforcement practice in England consistently targets street prostitutes rather than brothel owners or pimps (see Edwards, 1993, Smart, 1995), independent street prostitution carries with it legal as well as other risks. In short, there are various factors (not all of which are legal) which constrain the prostitute's choice whether to prostitute independently or enter into an employment relation with a third party. These constraints are not imposed or orchestrated by such third parties, yet serve their interests very nicely.

Having once entered into this kind of 'employment', the prostitute is then further and more directly constrained by the employment relations and practices adopted by the parlour owner. To begin with, the prostitute must relinquish control over her own work rate, which is determined in large part by the parlour owner's decisions about how many prostitutes to employ per shift. When parlour owners operate with a low prostitute:client ratio, each prostitute will have to enter into a large number of transactions per shift, and refusal to do so will place her continued employment at risk. When the owner operates with a high prostitute:client ratio, each prostitute will be restricted in terms of the number of transactions she can enter into. In neither case can she work or earn at a rate of her own choosing.

Massage-parlour prostitutes also find it more difficult to exercise control over the terms and limits of each individual prostitute–client exchange than do independent, self-employed prostitutes. Consider, for example, the situation of women working at Stephanie's. Though, in theory, prices for specific 'services' are set by the owner, she does not actually make any attempt to enforce the rates set for anything other than the 'massage fee'. It is up to the prostitute to negotiate the terms and limits of the exchange once alone with the client, and, in practice, both prostitute and client often haggle over the set rates. As one woman who works at Stephanie's put it, 'If I'm not earning well, I'll do it for less than the rate, but sometimes I'll charge more depending on how much I think I can get out of him.' Since, as was noted above, it is quite possible for prostitutes to end up owing money to the owner at the end of a shift, there is often a very powerful pressure on the prostitute to enter into transactions that are either dangerous or underpriced (or both) in order to cover the shift fee and receptionist's pay. One 21-year-old woman who works at Stephanie's told me that on a couple of occasions, when it looked as if she was going to leave the shift owing money, she has agreed to customer demands for her to play the submissive role in sado-masochistic scenes.

Finally we should note that the massage-parlour prostitute's freedom to retract from contracts made with clients is highly circumscribed. Although the client's contract with the third party explicitly refers only to the parlour owner's legitimate business – his 'massage fee' entitles him to a massage, and any 'extras' have to be negotiated with the prostitute – in accepting his massage fee the parlour owner implicitly contracts to provide the client with a masseuse who will agree to transfer powers of sexual command to him. Though parlour workers can and do sometimes turn away drunk or intimidating clients, a masseuse who consistently refused to provide clients with anything other than a straight massage would quickly find herself both without an income and owing a backlog of 'punter fees' and shift fees to the parlour owner. There are thus heavy economic constraints on prostitutes' freedom to retract from the implicit contracts made on their behalf by the parlour owner.

The **Genelev** *system in Turkey*

In Turkey, prostitution is regulated by commissions for the prevention of venereal diseases and prostitution, which are estab-
lished in each municipality, and prostitutes are controlled as a
distinct class of persons. They are denied free movement and
required to register with the commissions, undergo medical checks
and so on. Once registered, 'they exchange the identity card
carried by every ordinary citizen for special ones identifying them
as prostitutes' (Bindman, 1997, p. 25). Brothel keeping is not illegal
providing it conforms with the 126 articles laid down in the decree
entitled *Statutes Concerning the Prostitutes, Regulations which Brothels
will Comply with, and the Prevention of the Infectious Venereal Diseases
Resulting from Prostitution* (Willey, 1993, p. 15). These articles are
designed, among other things, to ensure that brothel keepers are
licensed, to regulate the physical location and environment of
brothels, to oblige brothel keepers to exercise certain control functions on behalf of the state (such as notifying the police within
twenty-four hours if a prostitute has moved brothel, failed to go
for required medical checks, or failed to register with the commission), to prevent the prostitution of minors in brothels, and to
compel brothel keepers to pay fees and taxes (Willey, 1993, p. 16).
A common form of brothel prostitution in Turkey is referred to as
a *genelev*, which is:

> a walled off complex in or near a town which consists of a
> number of houses where prostitutes work ... These licensed
> brothel complexes are all privately owned, very often by a group
> of proprietors; or a single proprietor may own one or two houses
> within a particular complex. (*Willey*, 1993, p. 9).

In the past, *genelev* prostitutes are believed to have been effectively
confined in brothels by debt, but it is thought that most now enter
them 'voluntarily' and are technically free to leave at will
(Bindman, 1997). *Genelev* proprietors typically exercise close
control over the work rate of the prostitutes they exploit. Women
interviewed by Anti-Slavery International researchers stated that
they worked a twelve-hour day and entered into transactions with
a minimum of ten customers daily and a maximum of fifty or sixty.
They 'are not allowed to refuse a customer unless he requests services which are considered sexually deviant, or is drunk or violent'
(Willey, 1993, p. 13). Rates are generally set by the brothel owner,
and prostitutes receive:

only 40 to 50 per cent of the set price paid at reception. Upstairs, the women bargain for tips, which are also shared with management ... In addition, a significant charge must be paid daily to the management for tea, electricity, water, paperwork and other overheads. It may also be forbidden to bring cigarettes, snacks, etc., into the genelev – these must then be purchased via the genelev servants ... at an artificially high level. (*Bindman*, 1997, pp. 25–6)

Again, the massive asymmetry of power between brothel proprietors and 'employed' prostitutes is a function of a range of social, economic, legal, political and ideological factors. The 'long-standing inequitable social and economic position of women in Turkish society ... severely restricts the average woman's opportunities to earn, especially in times of recession' (Willey, 1993, p. 26), and once a woman has started to prostitute in Turkey, it is not only extremely difficult for her to exit prostitution altogether, but also difficult for her to leave a particular brothel. This is first of all because prostitutes are treated as a distinct 'class' of persons, and as such are excluded from the social security system, and second because 'once a woman is a registered prostitute she will always be regarded as an outcast and if she leaves the genelev and tries to get another job she is bound to be found out as a former prostitute; her record will be checked against police files and she will be sacked immediately' (Willey, 1993, p. 29). The legal regulation of prostitution reflects and reproduces profoundly gender-discriminatory social attitudes and practices, within which women who are deemed sexually 'impure' are completely marginalized. In such a context brothel owners can force prostitutes to accept a phenomenally high throughput of clients when demand escalates and can extract a large proportion of the surplus this policy generates for the quite simple reason that prostitutes are not in a position to leave their 'employ' – except to move to another *genelev*, where the same policies will exist, or to join 'the precarious life of the illegal sex workers' (Bindman, 1997, p. 26).

The bar system in the Philippines

Prostitution is illegal in the Philippines, but since 1972 legal recognition has been given to those prostitutes deemed 'hospitality workers' (Chant and McIlwaine, 1995, p. 212). To attain this status the prostitute has to work from a designated bar or other establishment, and must also register at the social hygiene clinic (SHC), where she will be required to undergo a chest X-ray, smear and blood test. After this:

> she ... receives a card indicating that she is clean and is required to report for a VD smear twice a month and a chest X-ray and AIDS test twice a year ... The workers pay for the tests at the SHC themselves. If a smear is positive, the bar is contacted and the woman must report for treatment and stop working until she is cured. (*Sturdevant and Stoltzfus*, 1992, p. 45)

Bar brothels typically offer prostitutes direct employment, ostensibly as cashiers, waiters, go-go dancers or hostesses. However, the wages paid are either nominal or well below subsistence level, and employees are usually – but not invariably – expected to make up their income by entering into prostitution contracts with the bar's customers. These transactions are not normally executed on the premises of the brothel, but in a hotel room or other location of the client's choosing. The client is expected to pay what is known as a 'bar fine' before taking a prostitute from the bar for the night or a short time, and:

> Women earn primarily by commission on ladies' drinks and bar fines. A ladies'.drink is a mixed drink that the customer buys for a woman when he wants to talk with her ... In both cases, the woman receives a commission of less than half the cost ... If a customer is not satisfied ... he may ask for his money back from the bar fine. If the bar owner agrees, the bar fine is charged to the woman. (*Sturdevant and Stoltzfus*, 1992, p. 46)

Bar owners also impose fines on women for other 'misdemeanours', such as lateness, improper dress, and so on. This kind of close control is not exercised over the details of prostitute–client exchanges. Other than specifying a time limit to the transaction, the bar owner places no boundaries upon what the client can and cannot demand from the prostitute in exchange for the set bar fine. It is up to the prostitute to attempt to negotiate limits to the powers of command that are transferred to the client once alone with him. The loose and open contractual arrangement struck between bar owner and client places the prostitute at a massive disadvantage within her actual transactions with clients. Many clients assume that they have paid for powers of command that are limited *only* by time; in other words they assume that, within the set time period, they can do whatever they choose, as many times as they choose. If the prostitute contests this assumption, she may well find that the client complains to the bar owner and demands a refund. Very similar arrangements and power relations are to be found in bar brothels in Thailand and the Dominican Republic (O'Connell Davidson, 1995a, O'Connell Davidson and Sánchez Taylor, 1996a), and many of the hostess clubs which are to be found in most of the world's major cities are effectively brothels run along much the same lines as those described here.[3]

The control strategies employed by bar-brothel owners in the Philippines provide another clear illustration of the relationship between the social organization of prostitution and the political, legal, social and economic context in which it takes place. A high level of demand for prostitution was created first by the establishment of US military bases in the Philippines and then by a form of tourist development which capitalized on the existence of a well-established sex industry. Chant and McIlwaine (1995, p. 45) observe that , 'as of 1990, the Philippines had one of the lowest per capita GNPs (US$760) in the East Asia and Pacific region and was one of the most heavily indebted countries in the world', and such economic conditions, along with various other structural factors, ensure that a supply of women, children and men exists to meet this demand. Meanwhile, the legal framework regulating prostitution guarantees that it is third parties, rather than individual prostitutes, who stand to gain most from the prostitution economy. Non-registered prostitutes 'are illegal and therefore subject to arrest and imprisonment' (Sturdevant and Stoltzfus, 1992, p. 45), and the criminal law thus helps designated third parties virtually to monopolize the stream of demand, thereby constructing a huge asymmetry of power between prostitutes and 'employers'.

But, as ever, it is not merely economic and legal factors which empower third party controllers of prostitution. Gender ideologies which devalue women in general and denigrate prostitute women in particular and which encourage men to abuse and neglect wives, partners and children help to construct the kind of personal biographies which underpin the entry of women and children into prostitution and their vulnerability within it. As Enloe remarks in relation to prostitution around US military bases in the Philippines:

> local women working in brothels and discos mediate between two sets of men, foreign soldiers and local men ... their relationships with local male lovers and husbands created the conditions that make them vulnerable to the appeals of labor-needy disco

owners. Unfaithfulness, violent tempers, misuse of already low earnings, neglectful fathering – any combination of these forms of behaviour by the local men with whom they were involved became the major launching pad for work as a prostitute. (*Enloe*, 1992, p. 24)

Against this economic, social, legal and ideological backcloth, bar-brothel owners are in a position to adopt extremely coercive forms of 'labour discipline' to force prostitutes to shoulder the costs of clients who refuse to pay for 'services' they have consumed, and so on.

'Confined' brothel prostitution

It is probably true to say that in every country of the world there are instances of third parties who make money by prostituting individuals who are kept in conditions of confinement (by which I mean conditions that prevent exit from prostitution through the use of physical restraint, physical violence or the threat thereof, or through the threat of other non-economic sanctions, such as imprisonment or deportation). But there are also regions of the world where confinement is known to be more systematically used within prostitution. However, we should note that, even in those countries wherein confined brothel prostitution is most wide-spread, it is *not* legally sanctioned, but contravenes the criminal law, usually on several different counts.

Individuals who are confined in brothels may be victims of abduction, entrapment or debt bondage. In many parts of Latin America, as well as South-East Asia and the Indian subcontinent, there are 'recruiting agents' who use the promise of employment to draw young people from impoverished rural areas into their power. Recruits may be promised work as domestics, bar staff or dancers in a city of their own country or abroad; others know that they will be working as prostitutes but do not realize they will be confined and otherwise abused by their 'employers'. Once they arrive at their destination they are either incarcerated and physic-ally coerced into prostitution, or told that they owe the agent a large sum of money for the cost of their travel as well as other expenses which may have been advanced to them, and that this sum will have to be worked off through prostitution. Where indi-viduals have been trafficked into confinement across national borders, their vulnerability in relation to the third party is usually further reinforced by the removal of their identity papers, by their status as undocumented migrants in the 'host' country, and by their complete isolation from all that is familiar.

Loans are also used as a means of securing 'labour', preventing voluntary exit from the brothel and ensuring the continuous production and appropriation of surplus, and this method can be more systematically employed by brothel keepers and procurers in regions of the world where artificially induced indebtedness is more widely used as a means of enslaving the rural poor. Sawyer observes that:

> Debt bondage arises from a pledge, usually made under economic duress, of a man's services, or the services of his dependants. He must work until the interest on the debt, and the capital sum, are repaid. Likelihood of rapid repayment is remote, partly because of exorbitant interest rates but also because, the debtor having mortgaged himself completely, on a twenty-four-hours-a-day basis, he will incur further debts for food and, perhaps, for clothing and shelter. (*Sawyer*, 1986, p. 123)

Debt bondage has historically taken, and today still takes, a number of forms, and while some debt bondees are condemned to what is effectively lifelong slavery (a condition frequently passed on to their children, who 'inherit' the parent's debt), others are bonded for a specified and limited time period, or (at least in theory) are paid wages which go towards the liquidation of the debt. Certainly brothel keepers are more likely to use debt to construct a temporary than a lifelong condition of servitude, for, unlike creditors who own agricultural land or who are involved in, say, rattan cutting or carpet weaving, brothel owners have no interest in securing indefinite control over the individuals they exploit. The 'shelf life' of a prostitute is not indeterminate.

Thailand and India are perhaps the best-known examples of countries where prostitution is one of several economic sectors in which workers may be subject to forms of debt bondage. It would be quite wrong to suggest that all brothel prostitutes in these countries are debt bonded, but debt is nonetheless known to be used within prostitution for purposes of labour recruitment and control. In India brothels are prohibited by the 1956 Suppression of Immoral Traffic Act, and debt bondage is officially outlawed by the 1933 Children (Pledging of Labour) Acts and the 1976 Bonded Labour System (Abolition) Act, yet both the general phenomenon of debt bondage and the more particular one of debt-bonded prostitution persist (Sawyer, 1986, Fyfe, 1989, Singh, 1989). The latter can be viewed as a hierarchy with moneylenders at the apex and bonded prostitutes at the bottom of the pile. Moneylenders, or their agents, typically 'recruit' by visiting areas affected by desperate poverty and offering 'employment' to girls and young women. Cash advances are made to the parents of recruits, who are then bonded until the debt is repaid. Some of these moneylenders own brothels, or shares in several different brothels, and employ brothel keepers (*gharwali*) to manage them, in which case the recruits will be placed therein to work off the debt. In other cases moneylenders do not own brothels but supply women and girls to brothel keepers, who then make them work off the sum for which they were bought. Often brothel owners borrow from the moneylender in order to buy new inmates for their brothels, and the girls/women then have to pay off not just the capital sum advanced for their person, but also the high interest rates charged by the moneylender (Rozario, 1988).

In Thailand both prostitution and debt bondage are also officially outlawed, and yet there are many prostitutes who are bonded to brothel owners through debt. Again, moneylenders or their agents play a key role in recruiting for prostitution, and the girls and young women they buy are either placed in brothels owned by the moneylenders or are sold on to other brothel owners. Agents recruit in the desperately poor regions of Thailand and/or travel across borders into Laos, Burma, China and Cambodia (Phongpaichit, 1982, Asia Watch, 1993, Ren, 1993, Hengkietisak, 1994, GAATW, 1997).

Relations of confinement are most commonly found in brothels which cater to demand from a clientele that is made up predominantly of extremely low-paid local men and/or migrant workers, 'market conditions' which encourage an emphasis on maximizing the volume of customer 'throughput' and minimizing the costs associated with each transaction. There is no single, uniform way in which brothel owners who confine prostitutes organize their businesses, but the following examples should illustrate some general features of prostitution at this most exploitative and coercive end of the spectrum. The brothels in which confined prostitutes are to be found are usually in poor physical condition. Their owners do not tend to invest much, if anything, in their maintenance or decor, and, similarly, every expense is spared as regards the living quarters of the prostitutes detained in them (O'Grady, 1994; see also Phongpaichit, 1982). Such prostitutes are fed and clothed by the brothel owner, who typically spends the bare minimum necessary to keep them alive. The 'cost' of this subsistence as well as other costs associated with survival, such as medical expenses, is passed on to the prostitutes, who must repay the brothel keeper. Either money is deducted from the extremely low wages (if any) that they receive, or survival expenses are added to the 'debt' to the brothel keeper that has to be worked off.

Thus, for example, prostitutes trafficked to brothels in towns near mining encampments in the state of Pará, Brazil, are generally required to pay off the cost of their transportation from their home town, and often also to 'pay off their own "price" charged to the brothel owner by the intermediary, who has effectively "sold" them on' (Sutton, 1994, p. 95). Many girls and women contract malaria while working off their 'debt', and are then not only unable to work, but also compelled to borrow from the brothel owner in order to pay for treatment. Confined prostitutes may also be compelled to shoulder other costs associated with the brothel owner's business, such as bribes to corrupt police officers. Lee-Wright (1990, p. 150) quotes a fifteen-year-old debt-bonded Thai prostitute who states, 'I also have to pay the police 200 baht (£5) every month – all of the 32 girls [in her brothel] have to do that.'

The size of brothels (in terms of numbers of inmates), the prostitutes' working hours and the 'throughput' of clients per prostitute all vary. Where only one or two brothels exist to serve substantial demand, say from migrant workers in a geographically isolated region, prostitutes will work longer hours and 'service' more clients than those who work in an urban red-light area where large numbers of brothels compete for market share. Truong summarizes the findings of research conducted in 1983 on the conditions of child prostitutes who had been confined in Bangkok brothels as follows:

> The working hours of the children depend on the places where they work, and can range from a full day to periods ranging between 6 and 13 hours. On average, they serve three customers per day, or maximally 12 to 15. Fresh and attractive children are paid between 50 and 150 baht per customer of which the owner takes a share. Less fortunate children sold into indentureship get a 5 baht allowance per day or as little as 20 baht per week until the debt has been fully covered. (*Truong*, 1990, p. 185)

For some very obvious reasons it is impossible to obtain detailed, reliable data on the returns that brothel owners can squeeze from prostitutes subjected to relations of confinement. What evidence there is (see, for example, ECPAT, 1997, p. 5, Sutton, 1994, p. 100) suggests that exploiting prostitutes in this way is highly profitable.

In terms of how prostitute–client transactions are organized, brothel owners generally 'sell' access to confined prostitutes on a time, rather than a 'piece', basis, that is, the client is allowed x amount of time with the prostitute in exchange for x sum of money. The amount of time that can be bought varies hugely. Sometimes clients can purchase only thirty minutes or an hour with the prostitute, and this time has to be spent in a cubicle or room in the brothel, but other brothel keepers allow clients to spend longer with prostitutes and some allow clients to take prostitutes off the premises for a night, or even a number of days. Brothel keepers rarely specify or delimit the powers of command over the person of the prostitute, which are transferred during the set time period. Where clients take prostitutes away from the brothel for a short time or the night, the costs associated with enforcing the contract are generally borne by the prostitute and not the brothel keeper, who simply fines the prostitute if she returns late from a night off the premises with a client.

So far as 'labour' discipline goes, the available evidence on confined brothel prostitution suggests that physical force is routinely used by owners and/or managers to ensure the production and appropriation of surplus. Confined brothel prostitutes variously report being starved, beaten, deprived of sleep, shackled or locked into confined spaces and prevented from freely leaving the brothel; rape is widely employed as a form of violence/torture to 'break in' newly captured victims (O'Grady, 1994, Lee-Wright, 1990, Sawyer, 1986, Truong, 1990, Ren, 1993, Whitehead, 1997). However, physical force is generally used in conjunction with economic sanctions and 'incentives'. Thus, for example, an ECPAT report cites the case of some Filipino procurers who brought rural women and children aged from twelve years to Manila on the promise of work as housemaids. Once in the city the women and children were locked into rooms above beer houses and physically forced to accept an average of six clients a night. However, the women and children were then paid a (nominal and paltry) sum per client – US$1.40 (ECPAT, 1995a, p. 4). Debt-bonded prostitutes are also often controlled through economic as well as non-economic forms of compulsion, as a fifteen-year-old Thai girl's description of her life as a bonded prostitute shows:

> I was sent here from my home village two years ago. My parents
> received 10,000 baht (£250) as a loan in advance, and then I had
> to pay back 20,000 baht, which I have now paid off. I got half the
> 5,000 baht fee for the loss of my virginity; and have sent home
> most of my earnings and tips since . . . I have been well treated in
> the brothel, but now my father wants me to give up this work, so
> I hope to be going home in December. First I have to work off a
> new debt of 7,000 baht (£175), which I got from running off to
> discos – they fine me 500 baht for every time I run away from
> work. (*quoted in Lee-Wright*, 1990, p. 150)

In Indian brothels bonded girls are often kept in a state of imprisonment (they are not allowed to go out of the brothel unless
accompanied by the owner or his agent) and required to work
without payment until the debt is paid off. After this they are permitted to work 'independently', but expected to pay a sizeable cut
to an intermediary upon whom they are dependent for soliciting
custom (Rozario, 1988).

Individuals who are subject to relations of confinement within
brothel prostitution are not only unfree in relation to their 'owner',
but also lack power and control within the transactions they are
compelled to have with clients. It is the brothel keeper and not the
prostitute who sets the terms of the transaction, and the confined
brothel prostitute cannot freely retract from a contract made
between client and brothel owner. Economic sanctions and physical violence are used to enforce the prostitute's compliance. Her
position is made more vulnerable still by the fact that the brothel
owner has specified no limits upon powers of command over her
person that are conferred upon the client by the contract. He has
not told the client, for example, that the prostitute's vagina, but not
her anus, may be used; nor that the prostitute can be vaginally
penetrated once, but not twice; nor that the prostitute can be com-
manded to whip the client, but not to submit to being whipped by
the client. Once alone with the client, a prostitute can attempt to
negotiate such limits, but, should the client refuse to recognize
them, her powers to restrain him are negligible. Consider, for
example, the fate of one thirteen-year-old Filipino girl forced into
brothel prostitution who attempted to refuse to allow a client to
penetrate her for a second time without paying her a second fee.
The client stabbed her, and the brothel keeper subsequently forced
the child to pay for her medical treatment from her own earnings
(ECPAT, 1995a). A passage from a 'guide' to Bangkok describing

hotel-based brothels, written by a prostitute user for other prostitute users and broadcast via the Internet, also provides an insight into the terrifying powerlessness of bonded prostitutes:

> You can visit a short-time hotel ... A group of girls, roughly corresponding with your wishes, are led into the room for your inspection. You pay the attendant, then withdraw to another room (or a cab) with your girl. The hotel girls are usually younger than most other 'available' girls in Bangkok, 14- and 15-year-olds being rather common. They are in effect 'owned' by the hotel, which means that you can treat them more or less any way you want – and many men do. Hotels like this should be like paradise for those of us who are into S&M.

Where brothel owners allow clients to take prostitutes off the premises for a night or for several days in exchange for a set fee, the prostitute is, in effect, the client's temporary slave, and can, at his whim, be forced to submit to any form of sexual use not just by the client himself, but also by his friends. In poor countries it is, on the whole, foreign clients – tourists, businessmen and expatriates – who make use of 'take-out' services offered by brothels, and reports of groups of sex tourists 'sharing' one unfree brothel prostitute for a night are not uncommon. A further indication of the extent of forced prostitutes' powerlessness in relation to clients is provided by the list of physical injuries and illnesses suffered by child prostitutes in Thailand which was compiled in August 1984 by the United Nations Working Group of Experts on Slavery. The list included 'rectal fissures, lesions, poor sphincter control, lacerated vaginas, foreign bodies in the anus or vagina, perforated anal and vaginal walls, death by asphyxiation, chronic choking from gonorrhoeal tonsillitis, ruptured uteruses, bodily mutilation and death in childbirth' (cited in Sawyer, 1986, p. 97).

Power, oppression, the subject and the law

The above discussion does not begin to provide a comprehensive review of all forms of brothel prostitution in the contemporary world. My purpose has been to provide a series of examples which highlight the fact that brothel prostitutes can be subject to a range of different types of compulsion to conform to brothel owners' wishes, that within this they can be subject to those pressures to different degrees, and that the types and degree of compulsion to which prostitutes are exposed are powerfully affected by broader, structural features of the society in which they are prostituted. Here, I want briefly to make some more general points about power and oppression in prostitution, points that will be developed in the chapters that follow.

Idioms of power

It has been seen that brothel owners who control confined prostitutes can and do exercise direct forms of personalistic power over those they exploit, and very often physical force, or the threat of it, is used to subjugate prostitutes to their will. However, those who exploit confined prostitutes also often include economic sanctions and incentives in their repertoire of 'labour discipline', and this, I would argue, tells us something about the relational nature of power. A number of theorists have pointed out that, even where huge asymmetries of power between two people or groups of people exist, other than by murdering them it is impossible for the powerful party *actually* to transform their subordinates from subjects to objects or to eradicate their free will (see Sartre, 1966, Giddens, 1984, Layder, 1997). The human subject of power can, in the final instance, (almost) always choose death in place of submission. This fact is, of course, of small comfort to those who are the victims of the most extreme forms of oppression, but it *is* significant for the oppressor in terms of the control strategies he or she chooses to adopt.

Given that psychological responses to the trauma of being either sold or kidnapped or held hostage, then serially raped include extreme forms of anxiety and withdrawal, thoughts of suicide, and so on, it is reasonable to assume that brothel owners use economic sanctions and 'incentives' partly because of the normalizing and legitimizing effect they can have upon abuse. If a person is told that they are working off x sum from their debt or that they will receive x sum every time they submit to sexual violation, then their desire to be free of debt or to have money on which to live or perhaps escape starts to take on the appearance of consent to their sexual violation. Equally, the relationship between captor and captive takes on a new aspect when the captor apparently pays, charges and fines the victim according to set rates, rather than abusing in an arbitrary and wholly unpredictable fashion. It begins to seem that the victim has some control, no matter how minuscule, over her fate: she begins to feel that, so long as she does a and b and refrains from doing c, her oppressor will do x and not y.

Clearly, it is in the brothel owner's interests to manipulate the subjective experience of captive prostitutes in this way. If such prostitutes accept their condition as a legitimate form of servitude or work, they are less likely to resist through escape or suicide and so require less surveillance, and they are more likely to co-operate with the brothel owner's attempts to maximize the throughput of clients. This reduces the costs associated with the process of generating and extracting surplus. To guard a number of women and children twenty-four hours a day and physically coerce them into every single transaction with clients would be costly in terms of overheads (as well as potentially having an adverse effect on demand). Far better to induce both hope and despair in proportions that encourage compliance, to offer hope of redemption in the form of remuneration for co-operation, then claw back some or all of the payment in the form of charges for subsistence, fines for 'misbehaviour' and the like.

Just as it is important to recognize that confined prostitutes are subject to power in both its materialistic and personalistic idiom, so we should note that those who are not technically confined by brothel keepers can sometimes be physically coerced, as well as being under an economic compulsion, to conform to a given regime. It is known, for example, that Mafia-like criminal organizations are involved in trafficking women from Eastern to Western European countries, and, though brothels in the latter are not usually operated by these organizations, women exploited therein can be under Mafiosi control. They may therefore be compelled to work by the threat of violence, even death (Eurofile, BBC Radio 4, 22 November 1997, Butler, 1997). My own interview work with women who work at massage parlours in England and bar brothels in the Dominican Republic, Costa Rica, Venezuela and South Africa also suggests that some 'employed' prostitutes are controlled by pimps who use physical violence to pressure them into working a given number of shifts and into surrendering a large percentage of their earnings. Such arrangements may not be orchestrated by brothel owners, but they are nonetheless extremely convenient for them inasmuch as they help to ensure the brothel owner a regular supply of labour. Moreover, there are contexts in which the employed prostitute's dependence upon one particular employer is so great that the employer's freedom to employ various violent and/or intimidatory tactics of control is almost as great as it would be if the prostitutes were formally bonded to them in some way.

Although some brothel keepers provide prostitutes in their employ with a degree of protection from abusive clients, they do not always take precautions or action to protect the physical safety of the prostitutes they exploit. *Genelev* prostitutes report frequent incidents of being beaten up by clients (Willey, 1993), something which could easily be avoided if the brothel owners took even elementary steps to protect them; escort-agency workers report agency owners who fail even to keep records of violent or abusive clients; and the organization of many English massage parlours leaves prostitutes vulnerable to attack.[4] Nor can brothel keepers be relied upon to insist that the client fulfils his obligations to the prostitute or to intervene to ensure that the client respects certain limits to the contract or that clients observe safer sex precautions. Prostitutes who are most exploited and most unfree in relation to third parties and clients are the least able to insist upon condom use as a condition of contract, enforce that condition and freely retract if the client refuses to comply, and are therefore the most at risk of contracting AIDS and other STDs. This helps to explain the findings of research which concludes that 'Thirty per cent of Bombay's 100,000 prostitutes, who serve a combined average of 400,000 clients per day, are HIV positive. Thirty per cent of Thailand's 800,000 prostitutes are infected with HIV' (Le and Williams, 1996, p. 244). Figures from UNAIDS (1996) suggest that HIV seroprevelance is possibly even higher among these same groups.

Power and the subject

'People are constantly subjected to the effects of power, but to varying degrees they themselves also have powers that they deploy to greater or lesser effect' (Layder, 1997, p. 147). I want to follow Layder in distancing myself from both the Foucauldian model of 'discursively constituted subjectivity' and Giddens's idea of 'the active subject', and yet still retain a sense of the importance of subjectivity for understanding the actual power relations that exist between individuals. In particular I want to make use of a notion of subjective power which 'refers to variable capacities of specific individuals – their abilities, inclinations and ambitions, as well as their psychological abilities to express whatever powers they possess and to take on power roles' (Layder, 1997, p. 176) – which recognizes that human beings necessarily interpret, give meaning to and engage with the effects of power, and that the way in which they do so also impacts upon their ability and desire to express and deploy power.

Let me start by noting that many (though not all) prostitutes have personal biographies which include various forms of sexual, physical and/or emotional abuse. This is true of both male and female prostitutes, and such histories often leave people psychologically ill-equipped to deploy the powers they do have to positive effect. It is, for instance, not uncommon for prostitutes to express their subjective power through acts of self-harm (such as drug use, various forms of risk taking and self-mutilation) which replicate but transmute the harm done to them by others (see, for example, the collection of life stories by Gibson, 1995, from boys who sell sex). While this allows individual prostitutes to display and attain a level of control over their own bodies and psychological state, it rarely represents resistance to the power exercised over them by third parties, and is hardly likely to alter the balance of power between them in their favour.

It is also the case that individual prostitutes' experience of social constraints – the degree to which they experience them as a form of compulsion – is often mediated by that individual's psychological disposition and subjective beliefs about sexuality, gender, honour, filial duty and so on. For instance, prostitutes, like many other members of society, often buy into discourses about gender and sexuality which attach stigma and moral blame to prostitutes, rather than to their third-party exploiters or clients. Consider, for example, the following passage from a Filipino woman's account of her own experience as a prostitute:

> When I was small, if a man had sex with a woman and they weren't married, I thought that was bad. In the province ... if you have sex outside of marriage, it's as if you're a bad woman who has ruined her life. You're repulsive to look at. I think I'm still conservative in my thinking. I still feel the same toward the women who work in the clubs. (*Sturdevant and Stoltzfus*, 1992, p. 296)

Such attitudes are not uncommon among prostitute women. They often induce a sense of fatalism with regard to the powers exercised by employers and clients and/or encourage the deployment of subjective powers in ways which actually serve the brothel owner's interests, such as taking a fastidious interest in personal appearance or cleansing and ordering the work environment. The internalization of such stigma also means that many women prefer to tell themselves that their own prostitution is a short-term expedient and that they are 'not really prostitutes' and encourages them to treat prostitution as an instrument to achieve very specific and limited economic objectives (to pay a gas bill, to save up for Christmas, etc.). This helps to construct a supply of labour for third-party employers, since employed brothel prostitution offers a flexible, non-committed alternative for women who do not view either setting up a private brothel (which implies a long-term investment in prostitution) or independent street prostitution (which is the stereotypical domain of the 'real' professional), as possible options. As one 22-year-old woman who had been taking occasional shifts at Stephanie's for three years said to me, when I asked why she did not set up independently, 'I know this is a rip off, but I'll not be doing it for long, so it's not worth it. It's not like I want this for a career or something, it's just when I need the cash.'

Finally, we should note that, where children and young women have been debt bonded, a sense of loyalty and obligation towards the family that has benefited from the loan which bonds them can lead them to accept, rather than resist, the brothel keeper's authority.

Power and the law

This chapter set out to show that, while the types and degrees of compulsion which operate on brothel prostitutes vary, formally organized, third-party controlled prostitution always and necessarily implies constraints upon prostitutes' freedoms. I hope that enough has also been said to convince the reader that prostitution laws and law-enforcement practice typically discriminate against prostitutes and, in so doing, either directly or indirectly enhance brothel owners' powers over them. It is precisely for this reason that prostitutes' rights groups focus their political campaigns heavily (though not exclusively) on legal reform. As Alexander puts it:

> Human-rights violations are not individual crimes committed by 'bad guys' outside on the street, be they clients, lovers, pimps or vigilantes; they are crimes of commission and omission perpetrated by bad guys inside legislatures, police departments and sometimes public health departments and ministries (*Alexander* 1997, p. 93)

The politics of prostitution are examined in more depth in the final chapter of this book, but here I want briefly to conclude by noting that, vital as it is to campaign for an end to legal discrimination against prostitutes, such campaigns cannot and will not put a stop to the oppression involved in prostitution. Iris Young's more general comments on oppression are pertinent here: 'We cannot eliminate ... structural oppression by getting rid of the rulers or making some new laws, because oppressions are systematically reproduced in major economic, political and cultural institutions' (1990, p. 41). As I hope to show in the remainder of this book, prostitutes are generally subject to all or most of the five faces of oppression Young identifies, that is, 'exploitation, marginalization, powerlessness, cultural imperialism and violence' (1990, p. 64), rather than being merely oppressed by the bad laws of 'bad guys'.

2

Patterns of Pimping

The definitional problems associated with the term 'pimping' are at least as great as those which surround the term 'prostitution'. Commonsense understandings of the term 'pimp' tend to assume that it refers to an individual who controls the prostitution of one or more other people, but this is imprecise. How actively does an individual need to pursue control over a prostitute and what forms of control does an individual need to exercise in order to be defined as a pimp? The legal regulation of pimping tends to include certain passive beneficiaries of prostitution as well as its active promoters. In many countries of the world the husband or boyfriend of a woman who works as a prostitute will be deemed to be committing the offence of 'living off immoral earnings', whether or not he actively seeks to control or otherwise encourages her prostitution. At the same time, however, the simple fact of benefiting from prostitution is not enough to make a person into a 'pimp' in the eyes of the law or the general public, for there are many passive beneficiaries of prostitution who escape legal and social censure. I am thinking here of tour operators, travel agents, hotel operators and airlines who benefit from tourist-related prostitution without ever explicitly condoning it, bar owners and hoteliers who 'turn a blind eye' to prostitution rather than actually orchestrating it, tabloid and local newspapers which derive an income from advertisements placed by prostitutes and massage parlour and escort agency owners, company executives who arrange 'hospitality' in the form of 'escorts' for visiting colleagues, and so on. Indeed, in countries where street prostitutes are routinely picked up by the police and fined, the state itself is a passive beneficiary of prostitution.

Ken Plummer's comments on the definitional problems associated with paedophilia are useful here. He observes that 'pedophilia is so often hived off from its social context that it becomes the property of people rather than a form of experience. *Activities* become *beings* and the talk is no longer of pedophilia but *the* pedophile' (1981, p. 228, original emphasis), and the same kind of points can be made about 'pimping'. In the popular (and legal) Western imagination, 'pimping' refers not so much to a clearly specified set of *activities* as to a property possessed by an individual ('the Pimp') or found within a particular relationship (that between a prostitute and a prostitute's lover). This book is concerned with the range of unfreedoms experienced by those who work as prostitutes, and it is therefore important to consider how the phenomenon of pimping impacts on questions about power and consent within prostitution. To do this, however, it is necessary to focus on activities which can be termed 'pimping' and to try to locate those activities in their specific social context, a project which in turn requires us to disengage the general phenomenon of pimping from the specific Western stereotype of *the* pimp.

The stereotypical pimp

Western stereotypes of pimping are strongly associated with street prostitution. This form of prostitution is popularly imagined to involve gullible young women whose pathetic yearning for affection and/or glamour has led them into the clutches of a male pimp who first promises them love and then proceeds to manipulate, control and brutalize them into prostitution, using extremes of violence to prevent them from exiting 'the life'. Pimps, in this scenario, generally command far more public indignation than do clients, and I think there is a very real sense in which this stereotype of 'the Pimp' represents a kind of folk devil constructed out of both misogynist and racist fears. Pimps are not only pictured as men who 'live off' women (thereby inverting the 'proper' order between the sexes) but they are also often imagined as Black males who control the sexuality of several 'fallen' women, usually white women, and thereby invert the 'proper' racialized order. Such stereotypes are not merely the province of tabloid newspapers and politicians of the moral right, but are also articulated in what purport to be academic works. A study of prostitution in the United States published in 1985, for example, tells us that:

> The relationship between pimp and prostitute is . . . an interesting reversal of traditional roles – she is the breadwinner . . . Most pimps are black, while their women may be white or black . . . When [the pimp] spots a likely candidate in one of his haunts – a bar, or night club, or at a party – he of course does not disclose his profession. Rather he begins the relationship with *the black male's standard rap for securing his ends* in conventional male–female scenarios. He turns on the charm. He glows. He is cool. He is gentle. He jives. He entertains. He woos. He flatters . . . *He goes 'apes and bananas'*. (*Diana*, 1985, pp. 3–5, emphasis added)

This passage is an example of the kind of sexualized racism which informs popular representations of street prostitution in Britain as well as in the USA. 'The black male' is assumed to have a sexually manipulative and economically instrumental 'standard rap' which is used not just for purposes of grooming potential prostitutes but also in 'conventional' scenarios. The assumption that Black men's heterosexual encounters are all based upon this kind of manipulative and instrumental behaviour is not only racist in and of itself; it also serves to reinforce other popular racist ideas about both Black men and women as well as to police 'interracial' sexual relationships. In the same way that white racism constructs pimps as Black men and Black men as pimps, ideologies which 'Otherize' prostitute women make it impossible to distinguish between pimps and boyfriends. Prostitution is assumed to be so degrading and dehumanizing that a man could not possibly want to enter into a sexual relationship with a woman who worked as a prostitute except for instrumental reasons, and thus any man who forms a relationship with a prostitute becomes, by definition, a pimp. Certainly he is legally deemed as such in many countries (Edwards, 1993, Jaget, 1980, Høigård and Finstad, 1992), and some feminist commentators concur with the sentiments behind laws which criminalize men who enter into non-commercial sexual-emotional relationships with prostitute women. Kathleen Barry, for example, opposes moves to change laws which currently penalize boyfriends and husbands for 'living off immoral earnings' whether or not they actively promote or organize prostitution, stating that:

> all prostitution is sexual exploitation, so every relationship that sustains it is abusive: with a customer, with a pimp or 'my man',

or with a boyfriend or husband. While degrees of abuse and ranges of affection may vary in these relationships, they all promote, aid, and encourage the sexual exploitation of women through prostitution. (*Barry*, 1995, p. 218).

This all-encompassing definition of 'pimping' allows Barry to state that between 80 and 95 per cent of all prostitution worldwide is 'pimp controlled' (1995, p. 198), but it also renders that estimate quite meaningless. People who work as prostitutes, like other human beings, are of course 'sustained' by various relationships with significant others, some of whom may be economic dependants, some of whom may be abusive, some of whom may be both, some of whom may be neither. If all adult significant others are to be defined as pimps, it is neither surprising nor helpful to be told that the vast majority of prostitutes are 'pimped'. Claims about the percentage of prostitutes who are pimped are not reliable unless they are based upon a clearly formulated definition of pimping which has been consistently employed in data collection around the world, and since this kind of research has not been undertaken to date, no one is in a position to play the numbers game in relation to the issue of pimping. On the basis of the kind of research that *has* been done on non-brothel-based prostitution (observational and interview-based studies of street prostitution in particular red-light districts, collections of oral histories and testimonies from non-random samples of prostitutes and ex-prostitutes, etc.), all that can be said with certainty is that some prostitutes are subject to the control of pimps and some work independently.

Towards a definition of 'pimping'

Those who conduct interview research with prostitute women hear, with depressing regularity, reports of sexual-emotional relationships with men who are physically, emotionally and/or sexually abusive towards them. Very often these men are also, to some extent, the prostitute women's financial dependants. Having myself listened to many such stories, I can understand the temptation to lump prostitute's lovers/husbands into some general category of prostitute abusers/exploiters. The problem, however, is that, without access to information about the experience of a matched control group of women who do not work as prostitutes, we cannot claim that the abusive behaviour of prostitute women's male partners   is designed to sustain *prostitution*. I know non-prostitute women, for example, whose economically inactive male partners expect them to work two or three part-time cleaning jobs, as well as to perform all the domestic tasks in their own household, and who will use physical violence or the threat of it to ensure that they meet these expectations. I have also known non-prostitute women who have been manipulated into performing unpaid sexual acts with acquaintances, strangers, even dogs, for the sexual and psychological pleasure of their male partner. I would define the men concerned as abusive, but to call them 'pimps' is to detach the idea of pimping from its specific connotation with prostitution. By the same token, where a person's sexual-emotional partner makes no demands that she or he begins or continues prostituting (and may even express a desire for her or him to stop working as a prostitute), and has no practical involvement in her or his prostitution, it is unhelpful to refer to that partner as a 'pimp' even if gifts, food or accommodation bought from the proceeds of prostitution are accepted by that partner (see also O'Neill, 1996, p. 136).

For analytical purposes, it is better to restrict the use of the term 'pimp' to refer to individuals who secure a benefit from prostitution either because they exercise some form of direct control over one or more person's prostitution (articulating specific demands that she or he prostitutes and surrenders some or all of the proceeds from prostitution) or because they perform some identifiable function on behalf of one or more prostitutes and receive payment in exchange for these 'services', or because they combine the two. I would therefore define a pimp as an individual who plays an active and identifiable role in the daily reproduction of one or more person's prostitution, and pimping as the activities carried out in pursuit of that end. Pimping can thus involve a scaled-down version of the brothel/escort agency owner's 'business', with the pimp performing various functions within prostitution such as soliciting custom, providing a setting for the execution of contracts and so on, but it can also involve activities which amount to little more than systematic extortion. It is also important to recognize that, in some contexts, pimping is embedded in customary relations. All this means that, rather than thinking of pimping as a singular set of activities, it is perhaps more useful to consider different *patterns* of pimping, each of which is distinguished by the way in which the following factors are configured:

• the kind of relationship which exists between prostitute and pimp, or into which the pimp draws the prostitute or prostitutes (short or long term, narrowly instrumental or diffuse and affective)

- the mode of exploitation/surplus extraction (opportunistic/*ad hoc*, or systematically structured along either bureaucratic or customary lines)
- the mode of enforcing prostitute compliance (confinement, force, tradition/obligation, the threat of withdrawing 'benefits' or 'protection' or the supply of drugs).

Some examples of specific patterns of pimping are discussed below.

Pimping as a form of 'street hustling'

Though distorted, racist and oversimplified in content and exaggerated in incidence, the Western stereotype of pimping discussed at the start of this chapter is not entirely without basis. There are pimps – usually male – who play an active role in the daily reproduction of – usually female – street prostitution. Journalistic accounts of prostitution, academic studies and accounts of criminal proceedings against such pimps all suggest that in some cases these are men who take a calculating and instrumental approach to pimping, and deliberately prey upon the most emotionally vulnerable women and children in order either to operate a 'stable' system or to exploit one or two women or girls on a serial basis (Høigård and Finstad, 1992, Boyle, 1994, Sandford, 1975, Edwards, 1993, Faugier and Sargeant, 1997). But there are also pimps (some of whom are women) whose involvement in street prostitution is rather more complex than the stereotypes imply. Often, as Høigård and Finstad note, street prostitutes and their pimps 'in many ways share similar lives' and sometimes '*are* each other's lives, intertwined as sweethearts, lovers, enemies and friends, supporters and adversaries, close to each other through the shifting emotions and their shifting roles' (1992, p. 161, emphasis original).

The same authors observe that both street prostitutes and their pimps depend upon an illegal economy to support themselves (Høigård and Finstad, 1992, p. 160), and one distinct pattern of pimping found in many urban cities around the world can be viewed as a form of 'street hustling'. As such, it is often mixed with other marginal and/or criminal economic activities, such as small-time drug dealing, gambling or fraud, and the degree to which any given individual is economically dependent on pimping varies, as does the degree to which pimping is treated and arranged as a form of 'business' or 'work'. Pimping can even be combined with prostitution as a source of income. We interviewed several men in Cuba, the Dominican Republic, Jamaica and Venezuela whose hustling activities included both selling sex to tourists and extorting money from 'girlfriends' who worked as prostitutes.

Because violence against prostitutes by street-hustling pimps is widely reported it is often assumed that the latter rely primarily upon the use of physical force to control 'their' prostitutes. In practice, however, not every single street-hustling pimp is violent, and those who are rarely secure control over prostitutes through means of violence alone. In the previous chapter it was observed that, though brothel keepers often use violence against confined prostitutes, this is seldom their only strategy of labour control, for the fact is that brute force, on its own, is not a terribly effective means of controlling human beings. (Even in concentration camps, for example, captors usually complement the use of violence with other forms of physical torment and psychological devices designed to debase, humiliate and destroy the sense of self to the point that even passive resistance becomes all but impossible; see Bettelheim, 1960.) The same point can be made in relation to pimps. Even those who appropriate surplus by simple means of extortion generally find that their power over prostitutes is far better secured through the forging of a relationship which the prostitute subjectively perceives as consensual, at least at some level, than through the continuous use of violence. Thus force may be used to 'break' a woman or child into prostitution and to keep her 'in line', but this strategy will usually be complemented by non-violent means of persuasion, such as supplying drugs, declarations of love or affection and so on.

Where pimping constitutes a form of street hustling, prostitute and pimp will often share a common sense of exclusion from 'mainstream' society, and this can, in and of itself, lend a certain legitimacy to the relationship, regardless as to whether the pimp uses violence against the prostitute. Above all, however, the relationship will be viewed as consensual, even reciprocal, if the pimp is perceived to give some combination of material and emotional sustenance to the prostitute, and this will be the case if the pimp can offer some tangible 'benefit' (a supply of drugs, protection, an ability to bail her out of police custody, friendship, physical affection, love, or care). Høigård and Finstad (1992, p. 161) draw attention to an important point about the impact of legal regulation and law-enforcement practice upon the kind of relationships that pimps forge with prostitutes when they note that, where street prostitutes are routinely arrested and taken into police custody, 'the pimp automatically has an important function', that of posting bail. Yet we should also note that the relationship between the legal framework regulating prostitution and the level of pimp involvement in street prostitution is by no means a determinant one, for the extent of pimp involvement varies even in different cities of the same country. It is rare in Glasgow, but fairly common in Birmingham, for example (see McKeganey and Barnard, 1996, Boyle, 1994).

The street prostitute's need for physical protection is greater in some settings than in others, however. This is not because the risk from clients varies (pimps do not often offer prostitutes much protection from violent clients in any case), but simply because it is more dangerous to stand on the streets at night in a city like San Jose or Durban than in Oslo or Glasgow, and pimps can offer 'their' women and girls protection from attack by junkies, muggers and, where gangs operate, rival gang members (in a number of countries, many children and young women involved in street prostitution are controlled by male gang members).

Though street-hustling pimps may themselves be marginalized, abused and vulnerable individuals, the relationship between a pimp and a street prostitute is never genuinely reciprocal. Even where pimps do provide 'their' prostitutes with protection, this hardly justifies the cut (as much as 80 or 90 per cent in the case of some prostitutes I have interviewed) they take from the prostitute's earnings, especially given that in many places the only protection which street-hustling pimps provide is protection against other men like themselves – hardly a cause for thanks or congratulation. Moreover, no matter how pimps exact surplus, whether through force, by overcharging for drugs supplied, or through explicit or implicit threats to withdraw protection, affection and group inclusion, their demands for money mean that prostitutes are compelled to enter into more transactions than are necessary for their own subsistence and/or are prevented from retaining the surplus they generate. On its own, this kind of economic exploitation acts as a constraint on prostitutes' freedom over their own person (they cannot save enough to exit from prostitution; their freedom to reject clients and to retract from contracts is restricted by their obligations to the third party). Where it is coupled with physical, sexual and emotional abuse, this form of pimping can serve to deny completely the prostitute control over her/his person, and so can resemble a form of enslavement.

Child 'pimps' and 'survival sex'

The number of abandoned, orphaned and runaway children in the contemporary world who are forced to live on the streets runs into several millions (it is estimated that there are between seven and eight million street children in Brazil alone; Dimenstein, 1991). Though these children do not necessarily make systematic use of prostitution as a means of subsistence, many of them are forced to surrender their bodies to others for sexual use in order to survive. 'Survival sex' takes a number of forms, and usually occurs not just in the context of very extreme poverty and privation but also in settings in which very extreme forms of violence are commonplace. I am going to use the situation of street children in South Africa to show how activities that constitute a form of pimping similar to that described above are carried out by children, and to argue that their involvement in pimping can be understood only through reference to the broader structural context in which it takes place.

Habituation to and fear of violence is an all-pervasive and brutalizing aspect of life for many South Africans, and, perhaps as a consequence of apartheid's extraordinary and barbaric focus on the body, a great deal of this violence is highly sexualized. As ever, it is women and children (and, more particularly, it is Black and 'coloured' women and children) who are the prime focus of this sexual violence. The statistics are staggeringly horrible. The number of reported rapes of children under eighteen years of age rose from just under 5,000 in 1993 to 10,037 in 1995, and in the first month of 1996 there were 2,321 reported child rapes (SAPS, 1996). These figures are unlikely to represent anything more than the tip of the iceberg, since rape victims are hugely stigmatized and thus have a strong incentive not to report sexual crimes perpetrated against them. Sexual violence is also endemic in South Africa's penal institutions, and, though the government is currently taking steps to reform this situation, it has long been the practice (and still is in some prisons and police stations) to place juveniles in holding cells with adult prisoners. We interviewed one young man who, at the age of eighteen, had spent a year in prison in Cape Town between 1993 and 1994. He described to us details of the extremely vicious rapes perpetrated in prison by older prisoners against children as young as ten years old, as well as against teenagers such as himself. These rapes are not usually simply random, arbitrary expressions of brute violence, but constitute an initiation into a relationship of dependency upon an adult or group of adults for protection and survival within the prison. The knowledge that many street children have, at some point in their lives, been incarcerated, subjected to what amounts to sexual torture and then drawn into a relationship in which sex is traded for immediate survival may perhaps help to explain the frequent reports of older street children replicating this kind of abusive relationship with younger street children, as well as becoming involved in gang rapes of older women.

The economic situation and living conditions in the townships and peri-urban areas surrounding major cities such as Cape Town and Durban are truly desperate. These are settings in which the majority of the population is effectively excluded from South Africa's formal, free-market economy and yet at the same time lacks access to land and a more informal subsistence. In such a context people will exchange almost anything that they can for the basic necessities of survival, and often the only thing that they can trade is sexual access to their children's bodies. It is against this backcloth of poverty, abuse and violence that street children's involvement in pimping must be understood. Children come to the cities because they are orphaned or abandoned or because they are attempting to escape conditions in the townships, but to obtain the things necessary for bare survival on the streets (food, items of clothing, sometimes glue to dull the misery) children are forced to steal, beg and offer up their bodies for sexual abuse in exchange for a few rand. Even children of four and five years old endure such violations in order to survive.

Because life on the streets is violent as well as hard, most newly arrived street children (male and female) attempt to join a group of other, older street children for protection as well as some kind of kinship. Sexual interaction between street children is not always or necessarily violent, indeed it sometimes represents the only positive human touch in their experience,[1] but obtaining protection from older and/or more 'experienced' street children can involve younger children allowing themselves to be sexually abused and/or surrendering a portion of proceeds from prostitution to their older compatriots. Without such protection they will most probably be beaten as well as raped anyway. Then there are some street children who end up taking a more systematic and instrumental approach to pimping younger street children, often employing the tactics used by adult street-hustling pimps (violence and/or the offer of protection, affection, drugs, etc.) to obtain compliance. In light of what they have endured, and must continue to endure, it is more surprising to discover that there are many street children who are not sexually and emotionally abusive of those more vulnerable than themselves than to find that some engage in a variant of pimping.

Pimping as an extension of sexual abuse

Though pimping is, on the whole, motivated by economic need or greed, there are some individuals for whom the financial gain associated with pimping is of secondary importance. I am thinking here of those whose activities as a pimp are best understood as an extension of their own personal abuse of another human being or human beings. The case of Freddie Peats provides an example of this type of pimping. Between 1984 and 1991 Peats ran a boarding house for children in Goa which gave him more or less absolute authority over the daily lives of the inhabitants. He actively and successfully sought respect from the local community (through his charity work, by claiming to be a doctor, etc.), but in 1996 was found guilty of having sexually abused and prostituted children in his care. The prosecution showed that Peats had confined children in his flat in Fatorda, 'photographing them in unnatural and obscene postures ... transmitting obscene photographs abroad ... having sexual intercourse ... with the children ... [procuring] children ... for purposes of prostitution ... sponsoring the boys under his care and control with those who called on him, especially foreigners, in order that they could abuse them sexually' (*Navhind Times*, 1996). The case of Andrew Mark Harvey, arrested in the Philippines in 1988, provides another example of this type of pimping (Lee-Wright, 1990, pp. 226–32), and similar cases of expatriate involvement in child abuse and prostitution have been reported in Costa Rica (Aguilar, 1994). This pattern of pimping typically involves constructing relatively long-term and diffuse relationships with those who are prostituted, relationships in which the extremely corrupt form of 'care' that is extended by the abuser/pimp becomes part of the mode of enforcing compliance.

The motives of abusers involved in such activities are probably best understood through reference to the desire to either 'normalise' their own behaviour by developing contacts with others like themselves, or to obtain sexual and psychological gratification from behaviours that are risky, secretive and manipulative, and thus demonstrate the abuser's power to control others as well as to master his own fears. The commercial benefits for individuals operating this kind of 'paedophile ring' are generally believed to be negligible, but in the cases mentioned above the financial rewards of pimping were sufficient to make the perpetrator's own abuse into a kind of self-funding activity. It seems probable that there are also men who wish to prostitute their adult wives/girlfriends not because of the financial benefits that attach to so doing, but because they are sexually excited by the idea of her 'public' use. I have not researched this phenomenon, but on the basis of pornographic accounts of this kind of pimping as well as my own acquaintance with a well-paid, professional man who wanted to set his girlfriend up in prostitution, it seems to me that it is probably best understood as grounded in extreme forms of ambivalence and hostility towards the women concerned.

The man in question, 'Augustus Large', did not actually succeed in arranging his girlfriend's entry into prostitution, but he certainly devoted a great deal more thought and energy to the project than he ever expended upon encouraging her towards any other 'career'. Considered in the light of his obsessive and almost preposterous anxieties about his own gender identity (the size of his penis and his ability to command and control women as sexual beings were his two main preoccupations in life), Augustus Large's wish to pimp a girlfriend whom he perceived as 'highly sexed' is not difficult to psychoanalyse. Greenwald's comments on pimps are peculiarly apposite in this particular case: 'The role of pimp ... is rich in possibilities for a whole variety of reaction formations. For example, the pimp is able to deny his homosexual drive by the fact that he is satisfying a woman who has so many other men. He proves himself a man in competition with the hundreds of johns his woman sees' (1958, p. 157). Equally important in Augustus Large's case, by orchestrating his girlfriend's sexual encounters with other men he could simultaneously control that which terrified him most, namely the idea of her sexual and emotional autonomy, and 'disarm' her of her power to reject him by turning her into an object rather than recognizing her as full, human subject.

Entrepreneurial pimping

In many countries around the world there are individuals who take what might be termed an entrepreneurial approach to pimping. Unlike the pimps discussed above, they do not enter into pimping because they derive sexual and psychic pleasures from it, and they can also be distinguished from street-hustling pimps in the sense that they perform clearly identifiable functions within prostitution. These people either operate what are often referred to as 'working flats', or else they act as 'agents' for prostitutes, providing various services, such as placing advertisements and otherwise soliciting custom, or finding prostitutes work in hostess clubs or escort agencies. Working flats are essentially small-scale, private brothels and they are to be found in most of the world's major cities. In some cases they are located in red-light districts and attract a certain amount of passing trade by means of displaying the prostitute or prostitutes who work there in the window. Clients are also often recruited by means of advertising in the massage columns of newspapers, and/or in contact magazines, and/or by distributing cards.

Sometimes pimps own/control one or more such flats and employ receptionists and prostitutes to work in them. In other cases it is the 'maid' who controls the business, for many maids are, in effect, entrepreneurial pimps. Almost the entire spectrum of prostitution, in terms of prices, pay and conditions, can be found within working flats. At the 'classier' end of the market the entrepreneurial pimp either owns or rents the apartment, rents telephone lines and arranges marketing, and then offers the prostitute regular employment in exchange for a very large percentage cut of her takings. In working flats in London, for example, it is not uncommon for 'maids' to take 50 per cent of the prostitute's earnings as well as to insist that she or he pays the 'card boy' (who places cards advertising the brothel in telephone kiosks), as well as other business costs, such as supplying condoms, lubricants and tissues. At the opposite end of the continuum, adults and children are worked from dilapidated rooms in tenement blocks, serving much poorer clients for relatively small sums of money, and there can be several layers of third-party involvement in their exploitation (see O'Connell Davidson and Sánchez Taylor, 1996b).

Many of those who are involved in entrepreneurial pimping (at both the 'classy' and the 'down-market' end of the spectrum) have previously worked as prostitutes themselves, for there is a sense in which such pimping can be understood as a form of 'career progression'. One South African pimp, a 22-year-old man who had entered into prostitution at the age of fifteen (having run away from sexual and physical abuse in a foster home), told us that over the past two years he had moved from prostituting himself into various forms of small-time pimping and procuring. He was currently acting as a recruiting agent for a hostess club on a self-employed basis, and also soliciting custom for several women who were prostituting themselves from privately rented accommodation. He explained:

> Sex work takes your dignity and your self respect, but it's like an addiction, you can't get out of the life ... I've tried to get out, but I always go back ... It's the only thing I know. I've got no education. I've got no skills. I'm a drug addict. What am I going to do? I know the sex business, I know everything there is to know about sex work ... sex work, it's like family. Everyone understands the scars. You can get high together, you know everyone's been through the same thing ... I don't exploit the girls, they're like family, but I have to make a living.

'Making a living' included placing advertisements in newspapers that were designed to lure young women to Cape Town on the promise of work as dancers and then entrapping them into prostitution, and this illustrates very clearly how a 'career progression' from prostitution through to entrepreneurial pimping (possibly then on to brothel owning proper) is a process through which the abused can become abusers in their turn. The case of Vicki, a 32-year-old British woman I interviewed in 1994, provides another such example. Vicki had been working for several years as a self-employed prostitute from her own private brothel, and saved enough money to buy another property from which she wanted to work one or two prostitutes. Her ultimate aim was to make enough money to set up a massage parlour such as those described in the previous chapter. Vicki continued to prostitute herself, but engaged a maid for the second flat and recruited two women to work there by placing an advertisement in a newspaper.

The contrast between the way in which she organized these women's work and the way in which she arranged her own prostitution could not have been more marked. Where she charged a minimum of £60 for penetrative sex and specialized in domination in order to attract a low volume of high paying clients, Vicki wanted to ensure that the women she pimped would service a high volume of clients and so instructed them to charge a mere £30 for penetrative sex. The women she pimped were further required to pay the maid's wages and to surrender both a 'session fee' and a 'punter fee'. Vicki was well aware that she was exploiting the women she recruited, but rationalized it using 'survival of the fittest' arguments – 'If they're too thick to get it together for themselves, why shouldn't I screw them? There's plenty of bastards out there who'd screw me the same way if I gave them the chance.'

Children and women who are confined in working flats are subject to the total and arbitrary powers of the pimp, while those who enter into an 'employment relation' with pimps like Vicki are restrained by more materialistic forms of power. Either way, this kind of pimping operates as a constraint on the prostitute's freedoms within prostitution.

Customary pimping

In recent years feminists have raised our awareness about the ways in which fathers, brothers and other male relatives can be implicated in the sexual exploitation of children (Russell, 1986, Kelly et al., 1995). Less has been said about the role of female relatives in prostitution, and yet there is good reason to believe that mothers, aunts, grandmothers and/or sisters are among those who exercise powers of direct control over (usually child) prostitutes. Mothers, as much as fathers, are known to 'sell' or 'lease' their female children into brothel prostitution (Ekachai, 1990); NGOs, journalists, and human rights lawyers and activists have documented cases in which female relatives have actively taken the role of pimp in relation to girl children (see Kristof, 1996, Dunham and Carlson, 1994, O'Grady 1994). Furthermore, in those countries of the world where prostitutes are forced to work in geographically and socially isolated brothel districts (districts which call to mind images of leper or penal colonies), it is not uncommon for prostitute women to initiate their daughters into prostitution and to live off their earnings (see Radda Barnen, 1996, on this phenomenon in one Bangladeshi brothel area).

In red-light districts in Goa, for example, a girl's entry into prostitution is often arranged by her own mother, grandmother or aunt. While undertaking research for ECPAT, we visited one such district in which all those working as prostitutes were migrants from neighbouring, and much poorer, Indian states. Women in this district work from small rooms which serve both as living and 'business' space for themselves and their children, so that, at night, the children sleep beneath the bunk on which their mother is used by clients. Their mother's status as migrant, as low caste and as 'whore' excludes these children not just from educational opportunities (other than those provided by special projects set up to help the children of prostitutes) but also from contact with a world outside prostitution. They are entirely immersed in the subculture of the brothel district, and we interviewed girls of nine and ten years old, daughters of migrant prostitutes working in Goa, who already earned money in bars used by prostitutes for soliciting by performing highly sexualized dances to the tunes of Hindi film songs, then begging for coins from the sailors and other clients who have watched them. This practice is widespread in Goan red-light districts (INSAF, 1995). When the daughter of a prostitute starts to menstruate it is a cause of celebration in the family, for at this point she will enter into prostitution proper and so earn more. The girls' incremental inclusion into prostitution, it seems to me, must contribute to the sense of inevitability with which these children regard their future condition.

Where prostitution is so profoundly stigmatized and women's general political and social status so low that a child's entry into prostitution is conditioned by the mere fact of her mother's prostitution, and where poverty is so intense that prostitution is the sole means of subsistence available to mother and child, it is unlikely to be necessary to seduce or brutalize that child into prostitution. Her entire childhood socialization 'grooms' her for the economic role she is destined to play (see also Cox's 1993 study of prostitution among the Nepali untouchable Badi caste, cited in Shrage, 1994). In other words, the prostitute mothers of child prostitutes in such settings do act as pimps, but the relationship between them, as well as the mode of securing compliance from the prostitute, is very different from stereotypical images of pimping.

The social relations of prostitution in districts like this are further complicated by the fact that the mother may herself be supporting another pimp – a husband or male relative who has migrated from the same region as herself and plays a direct role in prostitution by soliciting 'on behalf' of the woman. The general status of women in Indian society makes it virtually impossible for female prostitutes to leave the red-light district in order to solicit by the docks or in the town centres, and pimps (known as 'pilots') therefore drive down to such places, tout for business, and bring clients back to the brothel area (occasionally pilots drive girls/women to clients in hotels which tolerate prostitution). NGOs working in the area believe that few women or girls in Goan red-light areas work independently. Even if they are not controlled by *gharwalli* but rent their own rooms, some form of control will be exercised over them by pilots, who either take a cut from the women or negotiate transactions with the clients and take payment from them, then give a small percentage to the woman/child.

This kind of pimping rests upon a kinship relationship between pimps and prostitutes (mother and daughter, husband and wife, or extended family members who have migrated from the same area), takes a structured and systematic approach to appropriating surplus, and relies on customary relations (supplemented in some cases by the use of violence) to enforce compliance.

Pimping and prostitution: some general remarks

As well as noting that the prostitute–pimp relationship can take a number of different forms, it is important to recognize that pimps may themselves be enmeshed in social relationships not just with prostitutes, but also with other third parties involved in prostitution. This is true not only in the traditional or customary forms of prostitution discussed above, but also where prostitution is highly commercialized.

For example, some pimps operate as intermediaries in the formally organized sector of prostitution, supplying prostitutes to brothels, hostess clubs or agencies. Pimps can also be of service to the owners of sex clubs, night-clubs and bars which do not 'employ' prostitutes (either directly or indirectly) or otherwise organize prostitute–client transactions, but instead simply provide a setting in which prostitutes can solicit. Ostensibly these establishments make money from entrance fees and the profit on drinks alone, but, like bar brothels described in the previous chapter, their profits hinge on prostitution. They cater to a clientele in search of prostitutes, and if no prostitutes were to be found on the premises the customers would quickly move on. The owners of such establishments thus require a supply of prostitutes and, while some of the people who solicit in these settings will be working independently, some will be pimped. The pimp may have a financial arrangement with the bar or club owner, or may simply demand money from the prostitute or prostitutes after they have solicited custom and executed a transaction. Though some pimps are involved only in street prostitution and others are involved only in supplying brothels and/or clubs in the formal sector, they can be associated with both formal and informal sector prostitution, or move between the two.

It is also important to note that pimps are sometimes identified with organized criminal networks and that the terror inspired by Mafia-like organizations operates as an almost complete constraint on prostitutes' freedoms (see Butler, 1997, Whitehead, 1997). Whether they have links with organized crime or not, pimps may be involved in trafficking women and girls from poorer to richer countries. As (often illegal) migrants, such prostitutes are made particularly vulnerable by their unfamiliarity with their surroundings, by their status as undocumented workers and by 'debts' to traffickers. Thus, for example, an International Organization for Migration study of trafficking in women to Italy found that:

> Trafficking from Nigeria seems to be especially well organized, and centres around a female figure called 'Mama' who plays a key role in persuading young women to leave their homes for Italy. Recruitment is achieved by means of deception, physical threats or payments made to the women's families. In Italy, the Nigerian women are easily controlled because they and their families are forced to pay back huge debts to the trafficking organization for the cost of their trip to Europe and related expenses. It can take several years before such debts are paid off. (*IOM*, 1996, p. 1)

Whatever form the pimp's involvement takes, it is exploitative. This said, I want to reiterate the fact that analyses of prostitution which accord pimps a central role in prostitution and/or which treat pimping as a form of *male* violence against women are theoretically as well as empirically limited. Not only is it the case that women and children can be and are pimps, but also to speak of pimping as a ubiquitous feature of prostitution is to encourage people to view prostitution as necessarily an aspect of the criminal underworld rather than as a phenomenon predicated upon economic, social and political inequalities. Furthermore, to treat a single pattern of pimping, that associated with street-hustling pimps in Western countries, as paradigmatic of all forms of third-party involvement in prostitution is politically dangerous. The entry costs of (and the returns on) this form of exploitation are very low and it is therefore to be predicted that people from economically disadvantaged and politically disempowered groups (working-class, Black and migrant people) will be over-represented in it. If generalizations were instead based upon forms of pimping into which the entry costs are higher (such as pimping in private brothels), or upon the many indirect and so legal modes of benefiting from prostitution (from which the returns are far higher), then a very different picture of the 'racialized' and class identity of exploiters would be produced. Finally, it is important to recognize that the Western stereotype of 'the Pimp' does not even begin to grasp the moral complexities associated with the many and varied patterns of pimping which exist in the contemporary world. Often people's entry into pimping is predicated upon exactly the same kind of poverty, abuse, neglect, deprivation and despair that underpins entry into prostitution.

There is no doubt about the fact that many prostitutes, both male and female, adult and child, are controlled and exploited by pimps, and that this form of third party control forces prostitutes to enter into more transactions than they otherwise would (because they must generate enough surplus to support one or more layers of financial exploitation) and operates as a restraint on the prostitute's freedoms, just as third-party employers' control in the formally organized sector of prostitution disempowers the prostitute in a number of ways. But, as the following chapter shows, the presence or absence of a pimp is not the only factor which affects the degree of unfreedom the prostitute endures in relation to her/his person, and analyses which give centre stage to pimps as agents in prostitution deflect attention from the fact that many adults and children are driven to prostitution by economic desperation rather than forced into it by any third party.

3

Independent Street Prostitution

Many prostitutes solicit independently from informal settings, such as streets, hotel foyers, bars, night-clubs, beaches and parks. This chapter is concerned with independent street and hotel prostitution and aims to show that the experience of prostitution in this 'informal sector', as much as the experience of prostitution in the formally organized sector, varies according to a range of economic, social, political and legal factors, as well as being critically shaped by the individual prostitute's age, experience and personal history.

Contract and control

Whether they work from formal settings such as brothels and massage parlours or informal settings such as streets and hotels, prostitutes in the Western world typically enter into closely specified, narrowly circumscribed, highly commodified exchanges with clients. Both prices and the limits to the transfer of powers over their persons are thus usually negotiated with the client in advance of the sexual transaction itself. So far as informal-sector prostitution is concerned, the contract may then be executed in one of a number of settings, including the client's car or his hotel room, a rented room above the bar, the prostitute's own home or an apartment that she or he has use of, a park, back street or car park, or any other convenient and secluded spot. In theory, where the prostitution contract takes a highly commodified form, it operates as a constraint upon the client's 'freedoms' within the transaction. Indeed, this is the whole point of close contractual specification. By stating that a given sum of money entitles the client to command use of the prostitute's mouth for purposes of fellatio, but not for kissing, for example, the contract simultaneously confers rights upon and restrains the client. Even where specification refers only to the amount of time a client may spend with a prostitute, this still represents a constraint upon his freedoms. If he agrees to pay a given sum for thirty minutes with the prostitute, then his right to exercise powers of command over that prostitute's person ends when those minutes expire, regardless of whether or not he has attained full sexual and psychological satisfaction. It might be assumed that power and control within prostitute–client transactions are zero-sum, and that, where clients are restrained by the form of contract, prostitutes necessarily enjoy greater freedoms. In practice, this is not always the case.

For many adult women in both economically developed and underdeveloped countries who are experienced and skilled in prostitution and who work independently, street prostitution and/or independent bar and hotel prostitution is preferable to 'employed' prostitution in brothels or massage parlours. The economic advantages are obvious – since no third party is siphoning off an income from their labours, these prostitutes get to keep the full amount of money that each client is willing to pay for each transaction. As one independent British street worker put it, 'I'd sooner do street work than parlour work any day. There's no worrying about the shift fee, I'm not paying a receptionist, I'm not paying a punter fee. Whatever I get, it's mine at the end of the night.' Equally important, these women control their own work rate, working hours and days of work. They are not under any form of compulsion to continue to enter into transactions once they have earned what they need for the night, week or month.

Because experienced adult prostitutes are not answerable to any third party in terms of the prices they charge or the degree of 'customer satisfaction' they provide, they are also in a position to vary the terms of the transactions they enter into. Clients often haggle over prices, but experienced prostitutes are usually skilled at such negotiations, as well as in using a highly commodified form of contractual relation to obtain the maximum payment possible from each individual client. If a client appears to be naive, nervous or credulous, they will build upon an agreed price for, say, a hand job, by adding charges for 'extras' – x amount more to undo or remove her top, x amount more to touch her breasts, and so on. Although the same techniques can be adopted in the setting of a sauna or massage parlour, the fear of losing a client and yet still having to pay a 'punter fee' operates as a constraint. In short, independent street prostitution offers a certain flexibility, and a sense of control over their own working lives is identified by independent adult prostitutes around the world as a benefit of working in the informal prostitution sector.

Enforcing and retracting from contracts

As well as enjoying a fairly high degree of control over their work routine, the highly commodified form of the exchanges they enter into should, according to liberal theories of contract, accord such prostitutes a good deal of control over the kinds of powers over their persons which are transferred to clients within the transaction. However, for a number of reasons independent street and bar/hotel prostitutes are limited in terms of their powers to enforce or to retract from contracts. The first, and most obvious, factor which constrains them is their physical vulnerability in relation to the client. In order to execute transactions street prostitutes often enter a physical environment which they do not themselves control (the client's car or hotel room, a back street or park) and are usually completely alone with their clients. They are consequently at great risk not only of both opportunistic and premeditated attack, robbery, rape, kidnap or murder by all manner of thugs and psychopaths, but also of violence from clients should they attempt to retract from a contract, and they are at a massive disadvantage in terms of being able to enforce the contract should the client attempt to renege on it.

One consistent research finding is that levels of violence against prostitutes in the informal sector are very high (McKeganey and Barnard, 1996, O'Neill, 1996, Høigård and Finstad, 1992, Scambler and Scambler, 1997), and that experienced independent adult prostitutes, being conscious of these risks, take a variety of precautions to reduce the likelihood of assault. McKeganey and Barnard's (1996, pp. 74–9) summary of the strategies adopted by street prostitutes in Glasgow (a city in which six prostitute women were murdered between 1991 and 1997; Nelson, 1998) includes taking control of the encounter, using their intuition, adopting certain working rules – such as never going with more than one client at a time, checking the rear seat of cars before getting into them, etc. – working with other women and carrying weapons. This list appears to hold good for prostitutes working in other cities and countries, and adopting such strategies gives prostitutes a sense of control. In my own interview work I have found that women who have never been attacked often attribute this fact to their routine enactment of certain precautions, while women who have been attacked blame themselves retrospectively for having deviated from their own self-imposed safety procedures.

However, as McKeganey and Barnard observe, none of the strategies employed by street workers *ensure* the women's safety; they merely give them the confidence to continue with such dangerous work. In cases where assailants are carrying out premeditated attacks on prostitute women, the only way to guarantee safety would be not to work at all, a choice which, for economic reasons, is not open to them. Meanwhile, though the use of intuition, the imposition of rules such as never accompanying two men and so on may provide some protection against clients who plan violence against prostitute women, they are unlikely to protect against opportunistic attacks by men who wish to retract from contracts. The only real defence in such situations is submission, as a quote from an Oslo street prostitute shows: '[A client] threatened me with a knife because he wanted sex several times. You're supposed to pay for each time. But I like my life better than money, so the only thing to do was roll over on my back. He raped me several times in a row' (Høigård and Finstad, 1992, p. 59).

Plumbers, television repair persons, meter readers, estate agents and other sales people, as well as prostitutes, often have to enter into physical environments which they themselves do not control. Although there have been cases of such workers being raped, attacked or abducted, for a number of reasons, the risk they run is negligible by comparison to the risks faced by prostitutes. Leaving aside the fact that calls made by such tradespeople can generally be traced, so that crimes against them would usually be easily detected, the fact is that there is no ideology which identifies plumbers, for example, as social outcasts and so a legitimate focus for hostility, violence – even murder. No matter how displeased customers may be with the service provided and the prices charged, they are not going to feel that punching the plumber in the face is justifiable simply on the grounds that he or she *is* a 'dirty plumber'. Furthermore, because clients' hostility towards 'dirty whores' is grounded in a popular, conservative moral ideology, those who attack prostitutes can feel reasonably confident that the consequences of so doing will be minimal or non-existent. Their confidence is not misplaced, for it has been repeatedly proven that women who work as prostitutes find it difficult to press charges successfully against men for rape or battery (Alexander, 1988, Human Rights Convention, 1994).

Even in countries where brothel prostitution is legal or tolerated, soliciting in informal settings is usually illegal, and this makes prostitutes in the informal sector extremely vulnerable to harassment and extortion. In some cases money is extorted through legal channels. Edwards (1993, pp. 115–17) observes that, although the law in England and Wales criminalizes third-party control and involvement in prostitution, 'the overwhelming number of prosecutions are of women for loitering and soliciting ... the weight of the criminal law has ... been directed toward ... streetwalkers.' In other cases it is corrupt policemen who must be paid off, either in cash or in the form of sexual 'favours' (this kind of corruption was reported to Jacqueline Sánchez Taylor and myself by women working in the informal prostitution sector in the Dominican Republic, Venezuela, Cuba and South Africa). The fact that the law is invariably used to punish, exploit and control street prostitutes rather than to protect them from exploitation and violence, and that law-enforcement agents in many countries are among those who physically and sexually abuse prostitutes, further undermines the prostitute's power to enforce or retract from contracts. Policing policies can also impact on the street prostitute's control over health and safety issues. In the past, in Britain and America, being in possession of condoms has been used as evidence that a woman is loitering for purposes of soliciting, for example (Alexander, 1988, Lopez Jones, 1990). Clearly, where such a policy is in force, it acts as a disincentive to practice safer sex. It should also be noted that migrant women involved in independent street prostitution are made more vulnerable to all these forms of harassment by their undocumented status.

Next, we should note that, even where prostitution involves independent, experienced adults, the prostitute's freedom to impose limits upon the kind of powers over her person which are transferred to the client is powerfully affected by her economic situation. The more financially desperate she is, the less freedom she has to dictate the terms of the exchange. Take the case of Maria, a 45-year-old Costa Rican woman interviewed during the course of research for ECPAT. Maria's husband was paralyzed in an accident ten years ago, and receives a pension of 8000 *colones*

(about US$45) per month. This paltry sum is all that Maria, her
husband and the three-year-old grandchild who lives with them
have to live on, and since her husband's accident Maria, who
cannot find any other paid employment, has worked as a prostitute. She lives in a small port town in one of the poorest states of a
country in which 10 per cent of the population are living in
absolute poverty, 25 per cent of mothers have their first child
between the ages of fifteen and eighteen, 41 per cent of births are
to single mothers, and what welfare provision there was in the
past is presently being dismantled as part of the austerity measures introduced by the government as a response to massive international debt (Barry, 1991). The prostitution 'labour market' is well
stocked, and competition for clients is intense. Demand for prostitution comes predominantly from sailors, and thus fluctuates with
the arrival and departure of ships. On Tuesdays, when ships dock,
Maria, along with other women and children as young as eleven
years of age, goes to bars near the dock to solicit. If she is lucky she
will manage to get a client and take him to a room above a bar, for
the use of which, she (not the client) will pay 200 *colones*. If she is
luckier still she will get the client to pay 2000 *colones* for an hour
with her, during which time he can use her body for penetrative or
oral sex. If she can do this three times, so that she retains around
5400 *colones*, she can manage to subsist for the week, providing
that there are no medical expenses for her husband, that her
grandchild does not need new clothes, etc.

But Maria is a 45-year-old woman, and she has to compete with
children and crack-addicted young women who will enter into
transactions for the price of a rock – around 500 *colones*. Often she
is not lucky and therefore has to transfer powers of command over
her person on terms which are not of her choosing:

> [The clients] always try to beat you down. 1,000 *colones*, 500
> *colones* even. If I've had a bad week, I'll take what they offer.
> What else can I do? . . . One time a man, he was a Tican, a busi-
> nessman, he offered me 10,000 *colones*. He wanted to whip me. I
> was afraid, but 10,000 *colones* is a lot of money. He took me to his
> hotel, he tied me . . . arms and legs, he hung me from the door
> and whipped me. He didn't even want to fuck, just wanted to
> whip me . . . But 10,000 *colones*, what else could I do?

Experienced adult prostitutes generally have a very clear set of
boundaries in their own minds as to the powers they will and will
not transfer to clients. Refusing to contract to be the submissive

party in sadomasochistic sex or to transfer the power to command unprotected sex or use of the mouth for kissing were the most commonly identified boundaries among the experienced prostitute women I interviewed, and these boundaries are designed to protect them from both physical and psychological harm. Clients, however, often seek to negotiate transactions which transgress these boundaries, and under economic duress prostitutes will sometimes feel that they have no choice but to breach their own rules and limits.

Finally, prostitutes' capacities to control transactions with clients are affected by their individual histories and psychologies. All of these points are pulled together in Vanwesenbeeck's (1997) work. She notes that 'every prostitute wants to use condoms, and giving in on that points to a lack of control', and in her research with prostitutes in the Netherlands she found that women who gave in relatively often on condom use differed significantly from other prostitutes:

> They worked under more stressful conditions, both in terms of financial need and in terms of working routines ... More of them were drug-users and their level of well-being was lower on a range of different criteria ... they had experienced more victim-ization, both in childhood and in adult life, both off and on the job. They were also younger and more often born outside the Netherlands. (*Vanwesenbeeck*, 1997, p. 173)

Children and independent street prostitution

Whether children's entry into prostitution is predicated upon eco-nomic desperation or forced upon them by a third party, and regardless of the contractual form their prostitution takes, those who enter prostitution as children are *necessarily* vulnerable (and continue to be vulnerable even as adults) in ways that those who enter prostitution as adults are not. This is well illustrated by the case of 'Marlene', a woman I interviewed in 1995.

Marlene is a twenty-year-old white British woman who has been involved in prostitution since the age of fourteen. Unlike many British child prostitutes, she was neither in local authority care nor a runaway at the time she entered prostitution, but she was placed in a children's home for six months at the age of fifteen, and during this time she began to prostitute herself on a more regular basis. Her mother had a long history of psychiatric illness and had been hospitalized several times during Marlene's early childhood. When she was fourteen Marlene started to 'hang around' at a community workshop in the town's red-light district, and one of the young men who 'befriended' her, 'Tony', pressurized her into her first trick. Tony did not involve himself in the sense of advising her how to go about prostitution, the prices to charge, or how to protect herself, nor did he supervise her in any way. He simply told her that he wanted money, said that she could get it by prostituting herself in the fashion of other street workers, and threatened to 'rip her heart out' if she did not comply. Marlene did as she was bidden, and after this she was periodically subject to the same kind of demands, made in the same manner, by Tony and a male friend of his, both of whom were aged eighteen at the time.

Marlene did not start working for these men on a regular basis, nor did they seek any systematic control over her; they would simply demand money with menaces on an *ad hoc* basis. Still aged only fourteen, Marlene stopped attending school and spent most of her time roaming around various red-light districts and city centres in the region. She continued to be preyed upon opportunistically by men like Tony and was subjected to a series of rapes:

> It isn't all rosy this game, it's not just money. I was kidnapped . . . I was only fourteen years of age . . . I was in Birmingham walking with my friend, and some Black guys pulled up and they had a gun. Probably fake, I don't know, but they said 'Get in the car' . . . [One man] said 'Have you got any money?' I'd got £20, so they took that. Then I says, because there was this Indian bloke as well, and they took us back to his place, and they were talking me to death, and I was chewing on this piece of chewing gum, like this, I couldn't care less what was happening. The other girl was crying, and I was just chewing, and he says 'You're really cocky you are, aren't you?' So I just chews and then I said 'Fucking hell, your house stinks, it does, there's all dog shit everywhere'. He says 'Dog shit? I'll show you fucking dog shit,' and then he lets this big rottweiler in and I thought 'Oh my God' and, 'Strip!' they said 'Strip!', and I thought 'Me life's going to end in a minute' because they kept on saying 'This dog's going to do something to you' . . . So then the dog went for me, and it got my hair all caught, and they were trying to get it off me, and I don't know what they done to it, but it died the next day. They threw it on the motorway. A big rottweiler, and they just threw it out of the car . . . One raped me. The others would have, but then they found out I was only fourteen and they tried to be ever so

nice to me after they found out I was only fourteen so I wouldn't go to the police. But I went to the police, but then later on I dropped my statement. I don't know why, I should have gone ahead with that, fucking rottweiler grabbing my hair ... I suppose they thought they was big time pimps ... I didn't see it as rape at the time. It was like, I'd been locked in a flat before with two Black men, rastas, about forty years of age and me fourteen. They raped me. I told me mum ... she took me down the clinic and I was all right, and it really upset me. I couldn't get to sleep or anything after. I had to sleep with me mum, because I thought 'What if they've give me AIDS? What if I can't live me life?' Stuff like that. But then after a few weeks I was all right.

Marlene describes her subsequent involvement in prostitution as an 'addiction', and certainly, if we compare her approach to prostitution with that taken by older and experienced prostitutes, it does seem to have the character of a very exaggerated form of self-harm:

It's like an addiction, like I'm on drugs or something. Because when you're skint and you've been a prostitute, you think 'I'm skint, I want to do something or get something'. You think 'I'll just do one, one won't hurt and that'll be it' and then you start and you do just one more and another and another and you can't stop. Because it's easy money and you've done it before, why not do it again? ... I don't know how to act like a normal girl, I don't even know what a normal girl acts like ... I don't know how a proper man treats you ... I really get scared sometimes, I think 'I hope I ain't doing this when I'm fifty', wearing an anorak ... But then if I stop, I do miss it ... I feel really on edge ... I met these two white guys that were quite nice looking. Beautiful big show house and that, I jumped on the bed and thought 'Here we go, Pretty Woman, and all that, hit the jackpot here'. Then they started on about [drugs and money]. I thought I'd hit the jackpot, did I fuck? They used to drive me round on the beat, they had to have a fix before they could drive. They must've been spending £50 a day on heroin ...

[When I work the streets] I'll be saying to the punter 'Oh come on, for fuck's sake' and then they say I put them off. 'Come on, hurry up!', or I used to go [makes snoring noise]. I never get regulars, I'd fuck them off that much they won't come back will they? ... I don't give a fuck. I need the money, that's it, 'Hurry up'. Or just get them in the car, get the £20 off them, then say 'Oh, this drink, I'm dying to go to the toilet. If you'd just take your trousers down and put this durex on, I'll be back in a minute.' Then I used to ... fuck off. I'll do anything ... I remember one time, it fucking killed ... I let this guy at me with the cane, £5 a stroke. He give me £50 ... He got this cane and I didn't think it was going to hurt me. Whack, whack, whack. I had great stripes across me arse ... Some girls really take [prostitution] seriously, don't they, like 'That's me job, that's the way I earn me money'. But it ain't a life really. People say it's a job, but at the end of the day, I think they've got to have some guilt about them...

I couldn't cope with doing [prostitution] without the drink ... all I look forward to is night time, when I can drink ... No matter what happens, it's like you couldn't give a fuck, honestly ... Someone would rape me and I would just get up, go to the clinic, and I couldn't care less ... I could cope with it. I'd be back to normal within the hour ... I couldn't give a fuck once I'd had a few drinks. I couldn't care less. I'd go in the countryside with punters, let them drive me off anywhere and everything. Looking back that really worries me, because it could've been me that was on the news. My mum always says 'Somebody up there loves you, or you'd be dead'.

Marlene does not work regular hours or days, but either tries to get a shift at a massage parlour or goes out on the street when she runs out of money or when a boyfriend or her sister needs money, and, as the interview extracts above show, it would be an under-statement to say that she takes an unprofessional approach to pros-titution. In the opinion of another prostitute who knows her, Marlene is not a prostitute but 'a fuck up'. In one sense, this dis-tinction seems to me to be a valid one. Marlene's involvement in prostitution is very obviously linked to the trauma of the rapes and assaults she suffered at such a very young age, since when she has felt under a compulsion to return to the site of her harm, to expose herself not simply to abuse but also to the risk of violence and death. Marlene told me that she remembered wishing herself dead after her first experience of kidnap and rape. She also spoke at length about the murder of a friend of hers who worked in street prostitution. She remarked several times upon her 'luck' in having escaped the same fate, but also stated explicitly that she does not take any of the precautions which she knows other street prosti-tutes take to avoid attack.

However, there is also something problematic about suggesting that Marlene's compulsion for self-harm means that she is not *really* a prostitute. Though she is unprofessional in her approach, prostitution is her means of subsistence (until she was eighteen she was ineligible for welfare support; although she has sometimes signed on for welfare benefits over the past two years, she moves around the country so much that she does not receive regular payments). Moreover, Marlene is a woman from a working-class background, she did not attend school beyond the age of fourteen and has no educational qualifications at all. She says that she would like a 'good career', but goes on to observe that the only alternative for her would be low-paid, monotonous factory work. In Britain, as in other economically developed countries, the prostitution 'labour market' relies heavily on the two groups for whom welfare provision is either wholly inadequate or completely absent – women who are single-parent mothers and children of both sexes (see Edwards, 1987, McLeod, 1982, Gibson, 1995). Of this latter group, many enter prostitution when they are runaways and homeless or in local authority care, and many have also been victims of sexual or physical abuse within the home (O'Neill et al., 1995, Kelly et al., 1995). Homeless children aged between sixteen and seventeen who have a background of abuse and/or local authority care are probably the group most vulnerable to prostitution, for, although local authorities do have the powers to accommodate homeless people of this age if this would safeguard their welfare:

> the interpretation of 'in need' is entirely up to the discretion of the local authority, and usually the discretion of the individual social worker. A Centrepoint survey of London's Social Services found that three-quarters of departments said that they did not have enough accommodation to meet young homeless people's need: 37 per cent of the departments did not even have the housing provision needed for young people already in their care. (*Gibson*, 1995, p. 166)

It is hard for a homeless adult to find paid employment and all but impossible for a homeless youth to do so. To compound their problems, in the 1980s the Conservative government withdrew the entitlement of sixteen- and seventeen-year-olds to welfare benefits unless the individual was on a youth training scheme, despite the fact that places on such schemes are not guaranteed and virtually impossible for a homeless youth to secure. In effect, then, the government made prostitution the only source of subsistence available to such children, and the fact that, between 1989 and 1993, 3300 children under the age of eighteen were charged, cautioned or convicted on prostitution offences gives some indication as to the impact of government policies (Morris, 1996; see also Kelly et al., 1995).

Given that a significant number of those working in Britain's informal prostitution sector share a background similar to Marlene's, it seems highly probable that they take the same kind of approach as Marlene to prostitution, and are out of control within transactions with clients for the same kinds of reasons. The fact that their involvement in prostitution is so very visibly an extension of the abuse and neglect that these children and young people have suffered in other contexts does not change the fact that their prostitution is an economic necessity.

The economic, emotional and physical vulnerability of children in street prostitution means that they are easy targets for all manner of abusers and all manner of abuse. They are clearly more open to exploitation by the kind of street-hustling pimps described in the previous chapter than are older, experienced women or men prostitutes, and even when they manage to avoid systematic control by any one individual they are vulnerable to opportunistic attacks and extortion. A Bradford-based project found that, of forty girls and young women they worked with in 1995 and 1996, twenty-seven had been raped by their clients or pimps, for example (*Young People Now*, 1996). Gibson's (1995) collection of life stories of boys involved in street prostitution shows that biological maleness is no protection against abuse and exploitation. Children's vulnerability in prostitution is often further compounded by drug and substance abuse, something that helps to dull the misery of their existence, but which (as well as potentially causing long-term damage to their health) also makes them less able to control transactions with clients, either in terms of insisting on condom use or setting limits to the transaction.

Pilcher (1995, p. 35) observes that, in the contemporary Western world, childhood is socially constructed and legally regulated through reference to 'notions of children as "separate", as innocent, happy, apolitical, asexual, vulnerable, as in need of protection and dependent, and of childhood as lived out in family settings, educational settings, and through leisure and play.' The status of children who do not conform to such ideals (i.e., children who have been sexualized through abuse, who have run away or been cast out of family and schools, who have no one upon whom to depend for economic support or protection) is ambiguous, and they are in a very real sense denied full community inclusion and the protection and care afforded to 'real' children. Law-enforcement practice in Britain has therefore been to prosecute children for prostitution offences rather than their clients for child sexual abuse, and it is only now that, as a result of campaigns by children's charities, police and magistrates are beginning to shift the focus of legal control (Sparks, 1997).

Again, it is important to recognize the *multiple* oppressions involved in prostitution. To be sure, law and law-enforcement practice is iniquitous and hypocritical, and it constrains the freedoms within the transactions of informal-sector prostitutes. However, changing the legal regulation of prostitution will not, in and of itself, transform the power relations which shape prostitutes' experience. The unfreedoms associated with this type of prostitution arise not simply from unjust laws but also from deeper systemic forms of social and economic marginalization. Meanwhile, the capacity of individual prostitutes to deploy their subjective powers in ways which minimize the destructive effect of these forms of marginalization rest very much upon their age, their experience, and their personal psychobiography.

4

Independent Prostitution and Tourism

Since the 1970s, when terms of trade for most exports declined and the import substitution industries of many former colonies ran into difficulties, many poor countries – often encouraged by the World Bank – have looked to tourism as a means of obtaining urgently needed foreign exchange (Wyer and Towner, 1988). Tourism has not necessarily proved to be an economic panacea for these countries, however. Truong (1990, p. 115) notes that 'many developing countries have not been able to retain a very large proportion of the foreign exchange earned from tourism.' In addition, tourism is a low wage and highly gendered industry which carries high environmental and social costs (Enloe, 1989, Pattullo, 1996), and its negative impact is heightened in heavily indebted countries where governments have been encouraged by world financial organizations to pursue tourist development policies that are ridiculously skewed to the interests of Western-owned and multinational companies, and that divert money from the kind of projects and spending which might alleviate existing social and economic problems. In the Dominican Republic, for example, generous incentives, including a ten-year exemption on 'income, corporate and local tax, as well as duty free imports of goods not locally available', have been offered to foreign investors in tourism, and 'government spending on infrastructure ... has been aimed at tourist areas and facilities ... neglecting basic services such as water supply and access in poor rural and urban areas. As a result, tourist zones operate as enclaves within wider areas of deprivation' (Ferguson, 1992, p. 71).

Tourist development in poor countries has also often been directly or indirectly linked to prostitution. The term 'sex tourism' is widely associated with organized sex tours, often conjuring up images of groups of middle-aged businessmen being shepherded into state-sanctioned brothels in South Korea or go-go bars in the Philippines and Thailand. However, if 'sex tourism' is used as a broad term to describe the activities of individuals who, whether or not they set out with this intention, use their economic power to attain powers of sexual command over local women, men and/or children while travelling for leisure purposes, it refers to a much wider range of people, sexual practices and geographical locations. Sex tourism to Thailand, the Philippines, South Korea, Taiwan and Sri Lanka is fairly well documented (Mitter, 1986, Enloe, 1989, Truong, 1990, Lee, 1991, Sturdevant and Stoltzfus, 1992, Hall, 1994, Ireland, 1993, Chant and McIlwaine, 1995), but sex tourists also travel to a number of Latin American, Caribbean, African and Eastern European countries (see, for example, Pério and Thierry, 1996, ECPAT, 1995b, O'Connell Davidson and Sánchez Taylor, 1996a).

It is important to note that there are differences between these countries in terms of the structure of their 'sex industries' and the relationship between tourism and prostitution. Furthermore, even within any one country that receives sex tourists, prostitution is not a homogeneous phenomenon in terms of its social organization. In Thailand, for example, early tourist development in the 1960s and 1970s attempted to maximize profits by capitalizing on accommodation and 'entertainment' facilities which had been put in place to serve US military personnel on 'rest and recreation' (Truong, 1990), and this is characteristic of several South-East Asian countries where, as Hall notes, a period of 'economic colonialism and militarisation in which prostitution is a formalised mechanism of dominance' has been a key stage in the development of sex tourism:

> For example, the American presence in Taiwan from the Korean War through to the end of the Vietnam War provided a major stimulus for tourism prostitution centred on Shuang Cheng Street in Taipei. Similarly, until the closure of the bases, the 12,000 registered and 8,000 unregistered hostesses in Olongapo City provided the major source of sexual entertainment for the United States military personnel based at Subic Naval Base and Clark Air Force Base in the Philippines. (*Hall*, 1994, p. 151)

But sex tourism does not always or only involve the maintenance and development of existing large-scale, highly commoditized sex industries serving foreign military personnel. It has also emerged in locations where no such sex industry existed, for instance, the Gambia, Cuba and Brazil, and even in countries such as Thailand and the Philippines tourist development has been associated with the emergence of an informal prostitution sector *as well as* the reproduction of an existing, formally organized sector. This means that tourist-related prostitution is just as diverse a phenomenon as is prostitution in general. Sex tourists make use of brothels, bar brothels, massage parlours, hostess clubs, working flats, escort agencies, call girls and private brothels; they avail themselves of prostitutes who solicit in hotels, discos, regular tourist bars, beaches, parks and streets; they exploit prostitutes who are positioned on every rung of the prostitution hierarchy, from debt-bonded child through pimped street prostitute to independent adult entrepreneur.

As the condition of third-party controlled prostitutes and independent street prostitutes who arrange their transactions with clients as narrowly contractual exchanges has already been considered, I want to use this chapter to discuss the experience of independent prostitutes who work in informal tourist-related prostitution and enter into much looser and more diffuse exchanges with clients, and then conclude with some more general comments about tourism and prostitution.

Informal tourist-related prostitution

Though tourism generates jobs in hotels, bars, restaurants and other leisure areas, this employment creation does not necessarily benefit local people. Foreign-owned companies operating in economically underdeveloped countries frequently bring in managers and staff from Europe and North America; indeed, in many parts of Africa, Latin America, the Caribbean and Asia 'expatriates hold virtually every position of importance, from general manager of a resort to assistant pastry cook' (Burns and Holden, 1995, p. 133). As a result, the economic opportunities that tourism provides for local people are mainly in the informal sector – 'much of the earning associated with [tourism] happens – as it always has – outside the organized economy' (Black, 1995, p. 1). The informal economy includes women, men and children working as unregistered taxi drivers, guides, souvenir sellers, fruit sellers, shoe-shine boys, masseuses, manicurists, hair dressers and cleaners in private apartments – even small children who, for a few coins, wash the sand off tourist's feet as they lie sunning themselves on sun loungers. It also often includes prostitution.

While prostitution within the informal tourist economy is sometimes organized along the lines of street/hotel prostitution described in the previous chapter (x 'service' for x sum of money), and is sometimes arranged along the lines of a contract of indenture or employment (x time with the client for x sum of money), it can also take an extremely loose and diffuse contractual form. This is true whether the prostitute is controlled by a pimp or working independently. One of the problems associated with research on loosely specified, open ended prostitute–client transactions in the informal sector is that such exchanges often shade off into non-contractual sexual relationships between adults who do not self-identify as 'clients', but are extremely economically powerful in relation to their sexual partners, and individuals who do not self-identify as 'prostitutes', yet are economically powerless in relation to their sexual partners. Some such relationships are long term and may even end in marriage, and this complicates the task of both empirical description and theoretical analysis (Sánchez Taylor, 1997).

Here I will attempt to bypass such definitional problems by looking only at the experience of those individuals who do self-identify as prostitutes, who work independently and depend upon prostitution for their subsistence, yet enter into diffuse and ill-specified exchanges with their clients. Such prostitutes hustle for custom on beaches, in bars, discos and hotels, and often take a fairly subtle approach to soliciting. The interaction between prostitute and client tends to proceed as if it were a flirtation rather than a business negotiation. Prostitutes flatter tourists and affect a genuine interest in them; tourists buy the prostitutes drinks, ask them to dance, sometimes even invite them to dinner. This kind of soliciting is a long, drawn out process, and it also requires a certain amount of skill actually to 'bag' a client, especially where the supply of prostitutes outstrips the demand for them (which is usually the case in sites of sex tourism).

Even when the client has made their selection, and either invited the prostitute back to their hotel or apartment or accepted an invitation to spend the night with the prostitute at some other place, the prostitute will not necessarily seek to negotiate payment or limits to the powers she or he is willing to transfer. Nor does a client always specify their 'requirements'. Instead, the two parties often embark upon a fairly open-ended exchange, which may go on for one night, two nights, a week or a month, and which is based on only a very general, implicit understanding that some form of payment will be made. This may be in cash, meals, drinks, clothing and other gifts, to a sum which is not specified or agreed in advance, and the exchange seldom involves only the transfer of powers of *sexual* command over the prostitute's person. Prostitutes often act as companion, guide and interpreter to the sex tourist; they will shop, carry luggage, tidy and clean for him, massage and manicure him and run errands. The way in which one sex tourist describes his arrangement with a Thai prostitute illustrates how diffuse these exchanges can be:

> I started off going a bit crazy, but then I thought I'd just settle with this one girl. I liked her so I told her how much money I'd got left for me holiday and I said to her I could give her 350 Baht a day, and she could do all my shopping, sort out the hotels and laundry and that, and then any money I've got left over at the end of my stay, she can keep it. She was dead pleased with that, and she's really got some bargains, so I'll be able to leave her quite a bit extra.

Although prostitutes who work in this way do not negotiate con-tractual limits to their exchanges with clients in advance, it would be wrong to claim that the absence of a closely specified contract, in and of itself, makes them powerless over the terms of the exchange. Skilled and experienced adult prostitutes can often squeeze more money out of clients (in cash and kind) by adopting this loosely specified contractual form than they would be able to obtain by entering into a straightforward x amount of money for x amount of time/x 'service' arrangement (indeed, sex tourists often complain that a particular woman has ended up costing them a great deal of money, and some prostitutes choose to operate in this way rather than to work in the fashion of street prostitutes described above). Neither does the fact that the relationship is con-structed as a quasi-romantic encounter rather than as an explicitly commercial transaction automatically imply that clients are in a position to command whatever kinds of powers they desire over the prostitute's person. The fiction of consent based on genuine desire rather than economic need can actually operate as a con-straint upon the client. If he is busily pretending to himself that he is involved in a non-commercial sexual 'romance', he is hardly in a position to specify the exact 'service' he requires.

While the loosely specified contractual form adopted by many prostitutes working in the informal sector does not necessarily imply that the prostitute is powerless to control the terms of the exchange, there are a number of other factors which do impact upon the level of control independent adult prostitutes enjoy within transactions with sex tourists. To begin with, such prostitutes are often under very intense economic duress. On the whole, sex tourism flourishes in countries where a large percentage of the population lives in poverty, where there is high unemployment and no welfare system to support those who are excluded from the formal economy. In these countries the annexation of subsistence land and/or promotion of cash-crop farming is often having a devastating impact on rural economies and creating powerful pressure on young people, especially young women, to migrate to urban areas or tourist resorts in search of work (see, for example, Crummett, 1987, Ekachai, 1990, Chant and McIlwaine, 1995, Black, 1995). Those involved in tourist-related prostitution are thus very often migrants from rural areas or urban conurbations, and may be attempting to support several dependants as well as themselves through their prostitution. It would be wrong to claim that all those involved in prostitution in sex tourist destinations are working from a base of absolute poverty, and it is important to recognize that the economic rewards of tourist-related prostitution are very often far higher than those associated with unskilled work in factories or the hotel or catering industries or those associated with prostitution serving local demand. However, as is the case for street prostitutes discussed in the previous chapter, the greater the individual prostitute's economic desperation, the less she is in a position to dictate the terms of transactions or to turn down a client about whom she has a bad 'gut feeling'.

In this regard we should note that, though men are involved in tourist related prostitution, adult male prostitutes who cater to demand from female tourists are typically a great deal less vulnerable than women prostitutes who serve a male clientele. This is partly because their economic situation is, as a rule, less desperate than that of their female counterparts (it is women who usually shoulder financial responsibility for children, infirm parents, etc.), but they are also empowered by the fact that they 'are not forced/controlled by pimps or any third party ... They are not at risk of violence from their female "clients", and their status is not affected by their sexual behaviour in the same way that a female ... who enters into multiple sexual relationships with men is affected' (Sánchez Taylor, 1997, p. 38). For female prostitutes, the same exchanges are inherently dangerous. As is the case for street prostitutes discussed in the previous chapter, their freedom to retract from exchanges or to delimit the exchange, and their ability to extract a benefit in cash or kind from the client, is much curtailed by their physical vulnerability in relation to male clients. Once again, this vulnerability is exacerbated by both the absence of legal protection and the presence of laws which penalize prostitutes. In Cuba, the Dominican Republic, Venezuela and South Africa, for example, women who had been raped or cheated by clients told us that the last thing in the world they would do would be to go to the police. If they did so, they would run the risk of being raped by police officers, and would most likely find themselves charged with some prostitution-related offence.

Again it is also the case that an individual prostitute's psychobiography, the extent of their experience in prostitution, whether or not they are a drug user and, above all, their age impacts on the level of control exercised within transactions. Unpalatable as it is, we have to acknowledge the fact that prostitution is very often the best means of subsistence available to children as well as to adults. As Black notes:

> Among street children engaged in cash-for-sex, the returns from prostitution are much higher than those for alternative earning options, particularly for girls who are usually confined to begging and flower-selling. In Dakar, Senegal, street girls report that they can earn between US$7 and US$90 per day trading in sex; whereas those who beg earn between US$7 and US$17. Similarly, in the Philippines, the average earnings of a street child are US$1 or less a day: those who sell sex bring in US$5 to US$25. The potential income from prostitution undoubtedly acts as a draw for many Thai girls. (*Black*, 1995, p. 36)

Children, as much as adults, long for the dignity that poverty denies human beings as well as to possess the material things that confer worth in any given society. In social and economic contexts where prostitution represents the only or most likely means of attaining such ends, they are capable of making a decision to prostitute. We interviewed a fourteen-year-old child in Cuba, for example, who had migrated from a rural village to a tourist area because she so desperately wanted to own a pair of shoes and had heard it was possible to make money by 'going with' tourists. To describe such children as making a 'free choice' to prostitute would be quite meaningless, but it is equally dangerous to deny the fact that children, as well as adults, can be placed in situations where they *must* take an option that is not of their choosing.

Moreover, children in tourist-related prostitution are often attempting to support not just themselves but also their dependants (a UNICEF survey in the Dominican Republic found that, in one tourist resort, almost half of the female prostitutes aged between sixteen and eighteen had one or more children, Silvestre et al., 1994), and their economic desperation undermines their bargaining position in relation to clients. But children are also vulnerable for other reasons. Let me illustrate with the case of one fifteen-year-old girl we interviewed in the Dominican Republic.

'Catalina' started to prostitute at the age of fourteen to support herself and her unemployed, alcoholic father. She is slightly built and stands only four foot seven inches tall. In relation to her adult male clients, then, she is physically powerless. Like many child prostitutes around the world, Catalina drinks heavily while she solicits, and by 1 a.m. (when sex tourists in the resort where she works tend to 'pick up' girls and women) she is usually visibly drunk. 'I like to drink', she says, 'it helps me to forget everything.' As well as helping her to forget, however, to work in this condition leaves her even less in control of transactions with clients and even more vulnerable to violence than she otherwise would be.

Catalina does not have lodgings of her own but accompanies the tourists and expatriates who pick her up anywhere they choose to take her. She describes some of her clients as 'easy' – for example, an Austrian expatriate in his late fifties who buys her meals and then takes her back to his apartment where he ejaculates almost as soon as she takes off her clothes. Others are more demanding, and she has experienced violence at the hands of some clients. But perhaps most telling of her powerlessness is her inability to enforce condom use, despite her knowledge of AIDS and how it is contracted. Catalina has a nine-month-old child fathered by a sex tourist (who contributes nothing towards the baby's maintenance), as she never used condoms when she first started to prostitute. Catalina still sometimes acquiesces to clients' demands for unprotected vaginal penetration because 'they offer you a lot of money for sex without a condom.' The UNICEF survey mentioned above also suggests that condom use by child prostitutes in the Dominican Republic is erratic. Not only had up to 48 per cent of their sample in some areas fallen pregnant but, further, 20 per cent of girls interviewed in beach areas had contracted at least one form of venereal disease.

Children are more susceptible than adults to HIV infection, partly because their immune systems are not fully developed, partly because they are more likely to suffer ruptures of body tissues during penetrative intercourse so that transmission is more likely to occur. Because child prostitutes are inexperienced, because they often use alcohol, solvents and other drugs to dull the misery of their lives, because they are economically desperate, they are simultaneously the group within prostitution *most* vulnerable to infection and the group *least* able to protect themselves by insisting on condom use. Figures on rates of HIV infection around the world are not always broken down by age; still less are official statistics likely to provide reliable information about rates of infection among individuals involved in prostitution. What information there is from health statistics and surveys and more circumstantial forms of evidence, however, points to the conclusion that children involved in prostitution are at very high risk of contracting HIV and AIDS (Black, 1995, p. 50, Human Rights Watch/Asia, 1995).

Inexperience and physical vulnerability make it difficult for children to enforce other limits to their transactions with clients. We interviewed teenagers in Caribbean and Latin American tourist resorts who told us that they had gone with a client thinking that they would have sex with him alone, only to find that he wanted to 'party' with friends and/or to make them 'perform' with another girl, and, though they did not want to do this, they found it impossible to retract from the situation. Likewise, teenagers tell of men who promise 'to treat them well', have sex with them and then tell them to leave the hotel, giving them only a bar of soap, a cheap T-shirt or nothing at all. Finally, children in this form of prostitution are as vulnerable to attack, opportunistic exploitation and extortion by junkies, pimps, robbers and corrupt police officers as children involved in other forms of street prostitution.

Parasites' paradise

Sex tourists spend a great deal of money in order to indulge their taste for unequal and exploitative sexual encounters, but it is certainly not prostitutes who get their hands on the largest share of these funds, for the proceeds of sex tourism are dispersed among all manner of people, many of whom take no direct part in organizing the prostitution of local people. In countries favoured by sex tourists, the informal tourist economy tends to be just as gendered and as 'racialized' as the formal tourist economy (Sánchez Taylor, 1997), and certainly the economic opportunities open to men are typically more diverse and more lucrative than those open to women. In Latin American and Caribbean countries, for example, tourism generates a good deal of work for registered and unregistered taxi drivers, but it is rare to see a female taxi driver. It is also the case that taxi drivers play a role in the reproduction of prostitution. Taxi drivers are usually a reliable source of information for prostitute-using men arriving in unfamiliar cities about where to find street prostitutes, as well as the bars, discos and night-clubs in which prostitutes solicit. Many taxi drivers are willing to do more than simply provide information, and actively solicit custom for specific massage parlours, brothels, hostess clubs or entrepreneurial prostitutes in exchange for a 'finder's fee' and/or procure prostitutes on behalf of clients in exchange for a 'tip' (this is equally the case in Western countries; see, for example, Jarvinen, 1993, p. 131). In countries where prostitution is concentrated in brothel districts that are set apart from port and tourist areas (as is the case in parts of India, for instance), taxi drivers play an absolutely critical mediating role, ferrying clients to brothels and/or prostitutes to clients' hotels.

While taxi drivers of this type may not exercise any form of direct control over prostitute–client transactions, they nonetheless constitute another drain on the surplus generated by prostitutes, for the cut that is taken in the form of a 'fee' generally comes out of the prostitute's takings (whether it is paid directly by the prostitute or by her/his 'employer') rather than being directly levied from the customer. In this sense they act as a pressure on prostitutes to enter into more transactions than are necessary to the prostitutes' own subsistence.

In sex tourist resorts as well as cities and port towns in countries where brothel prostitution is illegal and/or closely regulated, there are also owners of bars, clubs and discos who are economically dependent upon prostitution and yet play no active role in organizing the details of prostitute–client transactions. Instead, they encourage prostitutes to solicit on their premises, since this guarantees them a steady flow of custom from sailors, visiting businessmen, tourists and affluent locals. Sometimes men are asked to pay an entrance fee (or an exit fee when they leave with a prostitute) as well as being charged high prices for drinks, but sometimes bar owners simply benefit from the large volume of custom which they attract by allowing prostitutes to solicit in the bar. In many countries (for instance, the Dominican Republic, Venezuela, Cuba) the bar owner needs to have come to an 'arrangement' with corrupt police officers in order to do so. In exchange for regular payments, police officers will not only effectively 'license' the bar for prostitution, but often help to ensure that prostitutes work from the establishment by 'moving on' street workers to those bars which co-operate with the scheme.

Such arrangements benefit clients, as well as bar owners and corrupt police officers. Large numbers of independent female prostitutes are brought together in one or two specific bars where they must jostle and compete for custom, giving clients the upper hand in negotiations. If a prostitute does not seem to be going all out to please him, the client can simply turn to one of five or six others who will be jockeying for his attention. This depresses prices, decreases the individual prostitute's ability to make advance negotiations over the limits of transactions, and heightens the risk of violence for prostitute women. In some of the bars we have visited in tourist areas, a hundred or more prostitute women and girls will arrive and leave during the course of a night. It is dark, crowded, anonymous. A client can take a girl out of the bar and back to his own private accommodation, knowing that no one has any idea where or with whom she is and that no one is expecting her to return at any particular time.

For obvious reasons, hotels are also good places for prostitutes to solicit custom from travelling businessmen and tourists, and hotel porters, clerks, managers and security guards are thus all well placed to take a 'cut' from prostitution, either by accepting bribes or by actively soliciting custom or procuring on behalf of customers. In sex tourist resorts the larger hotels (especially those used by all-inclusive package holiday operators) often state that guests cannot take local 'friends' into their rooms. However, since these same hotels pay their security guards and receptionists pathetically inadequate wages, sex tourists can generally circumvent the rules by paying a bribe to someone on the hotel staff. Alternatively, prostitutes can take sex tourists to a room elsewhere, and this means that owners of cheap hotels and boarding houses are able to get their 'cut' from prostitution.

The fact that hotel staff are parasitic on prostitution impacts on prostitutes in two main ways. First, it operates as a downward pressure on the prices they can charge, since clients generally try to deduct some or all of the bribe or fee paid to a third party from the total sum they are prepared to pay for a night or 'session' with a prostitute. Second, in sex tourist resorts, the clients' desire to avoid paying such bribes contributes to the growth of a market for 'apart hotels' and private rooms/apartments (also favoured by those who wish to exploit sexually very young children). The privacy of these latter types of accommodation greatly adds to the prostitute's vulnerability. We should also note the existence of 'love hotels', especially in Latin America, which capitalize on prostitution more directly, renting out rooms on an hourly basis. These are sometimes owned by individuals who also own escort agencies or take-out bar brothels, and encourage the prostitutes in their indirect employ to take clients to their particular 'love hotel' (see also Kosovski, 1993).

It has already been noted that many of the young women and girls, as well as some men and boys, who are involved in tourist related prostitution are migrants. In resort areas a good living can therefore be made from renting out substandard accommodation to migrants who are working in the informal tourist-related economy, and the extortionate rents charged often serve to push and/or lock them into prostitution as a means of survival. Rentiers thus constitute another group that is parasitic on prostitution.

There are, in short, many layers of parasites, all skimming a living from the sexual exploitation of women, children and men, and the fact that prostitutes have to support so many active and passive exploiters out of the proceeds of their prostitution means that they are forced to enter into more transactions with clients than they would otherwise require for their own survival. Though male prostitutes in sex tourist destinations are often subject to these same forms of exploitation, as a whole the prostitution economy is highly gendered. The vast majority of those who benefit financially from prostitution (either directly or indirectly) are male, while the vast majority of the prostitutes upon whom they are parasitic are female. As Davis (1993, p. 8) observes, discriminatory social practices which are upheld by laws have a significant impact on the prostitution 'labour market', so that 'prostitution is merely one part of the larger picture of systematic gender injustice.' This is particularly striking in the informal economic activity surrounding tourism in poor countries. Women and girls typically shoulder the financial responsibility for children and other dependants, and low-paid domestic work or prostitution are

pretty much the only means of earning available to them. Yet the
phenomenon of sex tourism simultaneously generates a wealth of
opportunities for local men to enrich themselves by actively or
passively colluding with local women and children's sexual
exploitation. Its economic benefits for national and international
capital are still more striking, however (see Truong, 1990, Lee,
1991). Indeed, the airlines which transport prostitute users half
way around the globe and the hotels (many of which are owned by
international conglomerates) in which they stay, as well as the
travel agents which arrange their flights and accommodation, are
probably the prime beneficiaries of sex tourism.

Consider, for example, the case of one habitual British sex
tourist I interviewed who goes to Pattaya (Thailand's 'premiere
beach resort') for a three-week holiday every year. His holiday is
organized by a respectable ABTA-bonded tour operator and
booked through an ordinary high-street travel agent, and he pays
just over £900 for his flights, transfer and accommodation. He
allows himself a budget of £300 for meals and drinks and £300 for
purposes of sexual exploitation during his trip, and, because he is a
seasoned sex tourist and knows how to get what he terms 'value
for money' (mainly by using young and inexperienced prostitutes
and visiting cheaper brothels outside the tourist centre), this sum
allows him to live handsomely and, as he puts it, to 'go through
about thirty or forty girls' on each trip. He uses bar-brothel prostitutes as well as independent prostitutes working in the informal
sector, so that some of the money he expends on getting 'girls'
goes to bar/brothel owners. A large proportion of the total cost of
his trip, then, goes to enrich Western-owned travel conglomerates,
while the multiples of women and children he exploits probably
retain less than 10 per cent between them.

Most travel companies and airlines would, of course, be quick to
distance themselves from sex tourism and to insist that it is beyond
their power to affect what individual tourists choose to do while
travelling abroad. Yet tour operators typically promote travel to
known sex tourist destinations by emphasizing the pleasures of the
'nightlife' which exists in them, and, whether these third-party
beneficiaries connive with sexual exploiters by drawing attention
to the 'opportunities' on offer or not, companies which facilitate
tourism to known sex tourist resorts play a very active role in the
daily reproduction of tourist-related prostitution and derive substantial profits from it.

The political economy of sex tourism is perhaps the subject of another entire book, but I will conclude this chapter by noting that many of the countries which are exploited by multinational tourism conglomerates are simultaneously being exploited as a source of cheap labour by other transnational corporations, and that it is possible to argue that sex tourism actually helps to preserve an artificially low-wage economy ideally suited to the interests of this latter group (for prostitution provides a means of subsistence for female workers whose labour is surplus to capital's requirements in economic downturns, and women's sexual labour often wholly or partly supports the households that furnish both national and international capital with a cheap, disposable workforce). As well as reflecting and reproducing wider systems of gender injustice, then, sex tourism has to be understood as one facet of the larger problem of North–South inequality and exploitation.

5

Power and Freedom at the Apex of the Prostitution Hierarchy

This book is concerned with issues of power, consent and compulsion within prostitution, and in this chapter I want to address questions about power relations at the apex of the prostitution hierarchy and consider their significance for political and theoretical analyses of prostitution. I will start by looking at the experience of an extremely financially successful, self-employed, 34-year-old white British prostitute, who will be referred to as 'Desiree', in order to show how, under certain circumstances, it is possible for the prostitute to exercise greater control than does the client within each individual prostitute–client transaction.

The entrepreneurial prostitute's business

In Britain it is possible legally to operate what amounts to a private brothel, providing that only one person prostitutes in it (another person may be employed in it as a receptionist or maid, but must not provide 'sexual services') and providing that this individual is self-employed and does not use the proceeds of prostitution to support financially any third party (including a spouse or partner). There are certain other conditions which need to be met. If the brothel is too visible or too rowdy it may attract complaints from neighbours, and this could lead to closure under public nuisance laws. It may also attract a visit from a local authority environmental health officer, and if it does not conform to various public health requirements it could, again, be closed down.

The private brothel sector in Britain is not entirely homogeneous. Some prostitutes (male as well as female; see West, 1992) use their own home as a private brothel, others rent or buy a separate property from which to work; some specialize exclusively in what are known as 'domination services', others provide a range of 'sexual services'; some see only a small number of regular clients on an as-and-when-necessary basis, others take an entrepreneurial approach to prostitution and run the private brothel along the lines of the commercial massage parlours described in Chapter 1. Desiree falls into this last category, but offers both 'straight' and domination 'services'. Since I have described her business at length elsewhere (O'Connell Davidson, 1995b, 1996b), I will provide only a brief outline of it here.

Desiree first started working as a prostitute when she was in her late twenties, and she did so from a flat which she herself owned. In fact, it was because she was experiencing problems meeting her mortgage repayments that she decided to use prostitution as a means of topping up her income from her regular employment (clerical work). It proved so lucrative financially that she was able to buy a house in a residential area of a midlands town from which to work full time.

Desiree advertises her business daily in a newspaper and monthly in contact magazines, and she employs a receptionist to deal with the telephone enquiries generated by these advertisements. The receptionist asks callers whether they are interested in 'straight', domination or TV (transvestite) services, and proceeds from there into a sales 'spiel'. Many callers have no intention of entering into a prostitution contract, but are using the phone call for masturbatory purposes. Unless it is absolutely clear that the caller is not a genuine client, however, the receptionist makes an appointment with him over the phone. The appointment system is, in truth, merely a cosmetic device to give an air of professionalism to the business, since Desiree knows from experience that around 90 per cent of callers will break the appointments they make. The receptionist therefore makes appointments with any number of men for the same time, on the basis that the chances of them all arriving simultaneously are low, and this holds true as a general rule. However, sometimes two or three men (more on occasion) do turn up during the same hour, and Desiree does not want to lose their custom. This underlines the importance of employing a receptionist. If Desiree is busy with a client, the receptionist can answer the door, invite the next customer in, reassure him that he will not have to wait long, offer him coffee and so on.

Because Desiree cannot legally expand her income by employing other prostitutes, it is not feasible for her to pursue a low-price, high-volume strategy. There are physical limits to the volume of demand she can hope to accommodate by herself (though these are more elastic than it might be assumed: domination clients are sometimes left chained while she services another client in a different room), and, since it is her own sexual labour rather than an employee's which is being exploited, she has an interest in supplying as little of it as possible for as much money as possible. Her pricing policy represents a method of controlling both the volume and the nature of demand. Where local street prostitutes charge between £15 and £25 for penetrative sex, and men using women employed by massage parlours will pay between £25 and £40 for the same service, Desiree's rate is £100. Prices charged by entrepreneurial prostitutes like Desiree for hand, breast and oral 'relief' are also significantly higher than those charged in other sectors. Two years ago Desiree made a conscious decision to specialize in servicing domination clients, partly because such men are willing to pay high prices and partly because she finds their demands upon her person less intrusive and unpleasant than those made by 'straight' clients. However, most masochistic clients want hand relief following domination, and some want penetrative sex as well as domination.

Without access to a randomly selected sample of the entire population of entrepreneurial British prostitutes, it is, of course, impossible to say whether or not Desiree's experience is representative, but journalistic accounts of prostitution in Britain which include interviews with entrepreneurial prostitutes (see, for example, Boyle, 1994, Silver, 1993) suggest that the way in which Desiree organizes her work is fairly typical, though I believe her approach may be unusually self-disciplined. She works regular and very long hours, across a six-day week, and in the four years I have known her she has taken only two holidays and a handful of long week-end breaks. Even when she is ill with a heavy cold or flu she will work the same hours.

Desiree regularly earns between £1,500 and £2,000 per week. She has already saved more than £150,000 and owns several thousand pounds' worth of jewellery as well as three (immaculately renovated) properties after only five years in the business. Her aim is to save £250,000 by the time she is thirty-six, at which point she intends to stop working as a prostitute. Her financial success distinguishes her not only from most other prostitutes, but also from the majority of wage workers in Britain. Furthermore, Desiree, unlike most prostitutes and most wage workers, has chosen, designed and owns the physical environment in which she works. She plans and controls all aspects of her business: where and how to advertise, whom to employ and what tasks to assign to them, the pricing system, what services are and are not on offer, the hours and days of business. Desiree also exercises a great deal of control over the details of each of her business transactions.

Power and control within transactions

Desiree's clients make a conscious choice to enter into transactions with her. Likewise, no powerful individual forces Desiree to sell powers of command over her person to these men. In this sense, both parties volunteer to enter into the contract, which implies a degree of power and control on both sides. So far as individual clients are concerned, the power to choose such an encounter is primarily economic (they have the financial wherewithal to pay for 'sexual services') and the control they exercise is essentially over which prostitute to use and what to ask her to do. For Desiree, however, power and control within each transaction is an infinitely more complex matter. To understand this, it is necessary to consider the details of the exchanges: how the contract is negotiated; the skills Desiree employs to execute it; each party's relative freedom to retract from it; and each party's relative control over the boundaries and limits of their interaction.

Contractual specification and negotiation

Desiree's brothel is based in a private house in a residential area, and does not, therefore, attract passing custom. Because clients have to book an appointment by phone before being given the address, they all receive the receptionist's sales spiel and so have an idea of her general price range. They arrive and knock at the front door, and, providing she is not already with a client, Desiree unchains and opens the door herself and shows him to the massage room. She then tells the client to take off or loosen his clothing and lie down on the couch, whereupon she gives him a very brief and spurious massage. As she does so, the more confident or experienced client will generally tell her the kind of 'services' he is interested in (although even this is often in a somewhat coded form). But, with the inexperienced client, it is Desiree who has to lead the conversation to discover whether he wants hand relief or penetrative sex, whether he wants her dressed as a French maid, schoolgirl or nurse, and so on.

For a transaction to take place between Desiree and a client, his desires must be communicated to her and a price agreed. For those clients who simply want a quick fuck or a blow job there are few problems of *ex ante* specification and, since Desiree's prices are fixed and she *never* countenances reductions, initial negotiations over such transactions are usually fairly straightforward. Domination clients generally wish to purchase something that is more difficult to specify. Some will provide very detailed written specifications, describing a scenario or even providing a full script for her to follow. Others merely hint at their desires and leave it to Desiree to improvise, hoping that she will somehow decipher their secret wishes. Depending upon the nature of their requirements, Desiree charges domination and bondage clients by the hour (£100) or by the service in which they are primarily interested (watersports, anal penetration, foot worship, etc.). A contractual arrangement is thus struck in the very early stages of the encounter which defines, either implicitly or explicitly, both party's expectations and obligations. Unless they are trusted regulars, Desiree insists that clients pay up front. The money they give her is then safely stowed away.

It is Desiree who dictates the terms upon which she transfers powers over her person to clients. It is also Desiree who sets the boundaries of that transfer. She does not sell clients an unlimited, absolute licence to do as they will with her for the duration of the encounter. She will not contract to perform acts that she believes endanger her own health, or acts that she believes could endanger the client's life or cause the kind of damage that would require medical treatment. She absolutely refuses to grant clients the power to perform acts of physical violence against her person, and she will not contract to perform/submit to acts which she finds particularly repulsive (like giving enemas or receiving anal penetration) or excessively intimate (like kissing or cunnilingus), nor will she contract to transfer to clients powers to perform acts upon her person which she views as especially hostile, like ejaculating in her face. In short, the individual client's freedom to satisfy his wants is constrained by the control Desiree exercises over the terms and limits of the contract.

Interpreting and executing the contract

Desiree also exercises a great deal of control over the interpretation and execution of contractual agreements. Having negotiated a deal, 'straight' clients are led from the massage room to another room which is equipped with a double bed. Tape recordings of sessions with nervous, inexperienced clients suggest that Desiree is very much in command of the situation, guiding the man through the various stages of the transaction (see O'Connell Davidson, 1996b, for an extract from one such tape). But even when dealing with clients who regularly visit prostitutes, who are confident and who know exactly what they want, Desiree's far greater sexual skill and knowledge allows her to exert control over how much of her time and energy she exchanges for a set fee. The contracts that she agrees with clients are rarely time based, and, despite the illusions fondly cherished by most such men about their indefatigable sexual energies, very few can sustain penetrative activity for longer than a few minutes without climaxing, especially if they are suitably aroused and/or anxious prior to coitus.

Since Desiree's primary goal is to minimize the duration of the encounter, she pays close attention to the kinds of detail which encourage clients to reach orgasm quickly. This involves making use of a range of skills that would more usually be associated with the work of sex therapists and actors, and it is, in large part, these skills which allow Desiree such a high degree of control over the execution of contracts. By focusing her attention on the unspoken, unspecified, perhaps unspecifiable elements of the clients' desires, as well as the demands they actually articulate, Desiree can, to a certain extent, control and limit the length of encounters. Obviously, there are some exceptions. One regular, for example, referred to by Desiree as 'Every Which Way', is a man with wearisome powers of self-control and a high boredom threshold. Desiree balances the tedium associated with servicing such clients against the value of regular custom. But there are also large numbers of premature ejaculators, who contract and pay for penetrative sex but reach orgasm the moment Desiree touches them.

The same kind of skills are used to control encounters with domination clients. These men can, however, be far more difficult and demanding. Often their sexual excitement hinges partly on keeping their own desires a secret from themselves. Many want to imagine themselves as 'surrendering' to Desiree's 'wishes', but need to maintain a sham of reluctance, fear or horror in order to derive pleasure from certain acts, especially those which they associate with homosexuality. This means that they engage in a form of double-speak, such as moaning, 'No, no, don't touch my bottom' when Desiree moves a vibrator around between their legs. This, Desiree assures me, is in fact code for, 'I want you to penetrate me anally with the vibrator now'. To be forced to articulate their wishes explicitly would detract from their pleasure, but, clearly, a business contract that requires the seller to decipher the fact that the buyer wants the precise opposite of that which he is specifying is an unusual business contract indeed. Other domination clients are more open about the nature of their desires and the content of their sexual fantasies, and it has already been noted that Desiree is frequently provided with written scripts. But contractual specification can never be complete, and even the most detailed scripts require interpretation. To minimize the length of time it takes to bring a client to orgasm and to increase the likelihood of his returning to her in future, Desiree must employ her thespian skills and intuition to enact the role allocated to her in the script successfully.

Enforcing and retracting from contracts

Even where individuals mutually and voluntarily enter into contracts, there can be power differentials in terms of each party's freedom to retract from an agreement. The greater one side's power to enforce a contract, the more the other side's freedom to retract from it is restricted. An extreme example of this imbalance of power can be found in systems of debt bondage where adult individuals sell themselves into a period of servitude. In an abstract sense at least, both parties volunteer to take part in the exchange, but, having once entered into such a contract, the debt bondee cannot freely retract from it. The power to enforce a contract may be enshrined in law or may derive from one party's ability to coerce or intimidate the other, but it is important to note that there is nothing in the prostitution contract *per se* which guarantees the client absolute power over the prostitute. I stress this because some feminists have insisted that the prostitution contract is distinguished from other contracts, such as the wage labour contract, by its unambiguous nature. Pateman, for example, holds that:

> the prostitute is always at a singular disadvantage in the 'exchange'. The client makes direct use of the prostitute's body

and there are no 'objective' criteria through which to judge whether the service has been satisfactorily performed ... Prostitutes ... can always be refused payment by men who claim (and who can gainsay their subjective assessment?) that their demands have not been met. (*Pateman*, 1988, p. 208)

This assertion is quite simply wrong. Prostitutes are not *always* at a disadvantage and cannot *always* be refused payment, and this is well illustrated by examining what happens when clients attempt to withdraw from or renegotiate contractual arrangements they have entered into with Desiree, or to refuse her payment.

It is actually quite rare for clients who have undressed and specified the service they require suddenly to change their minds and try to leave. However, it is not uncommon for men to do this more or less as soon as they have arrived. Indeed, a recurrent problem faced by sex workers is that of 'time wasters', or 'pilchards', who obtain sexual satisfaction from the mere sight of a real, live prostitute (this is a problem for male as well as female prostitutes; see West, 1992). In the past Desiree found that such men would arrive for an appointment, then either sneak into the toilet and masturbate, or simply be greeted by her at the door then leave to have a much enhanced masturbation session in their car without paying anything at all. To stop this happening Desiree instituted a system whereby the receptionist will give her address only when a client books a definite appointment, and she then charges a set fee of £20 for the appointment whether or not they actually receive a massage or sexual service. In other words, so far as Desiree is concerned, as soon as a man steps over her threshold he has implicitly contracted to pay her at least £20. This policy affords her some control over the problem of 'time wasters', but it is also one which invites conflict, since a majority of would-be masturbators will assert that they never made an appointment, that they called on the off chance, or that they have no money on them, and refuse to recognize the contractual commitment which Desiree holds they have taken on.

By this time, however, Desiree will have closed and chained the front door, and she responds by telling such men that they could not possibly know her address unless they had made a definite booking. If the man still insists he has no money on him, Desiree will remove some personal effect from him – his wristwatch, glasses or wedding ring – and tell him that she will return it only when he returns with the £20 appointment fee. Sometimes customers who arrive with a genuine intent to buy sexual access to her want to retract when they discover her prices. For example, a client recently arrived for a domination session, but had brought only £30 with him. He had been told over the phone that prices for domination started at £60, and had then asked how long sessions lasted. The receptionist had replied 'One hour', and so the client had assumed, that for £30, he could have a half-hour session. He explained this to Desiree, who told him that his assumption was mistaken. He then attempted to retract from the contract altogether, but Desiree demanded the £20 appointment fee. He gave her £5, but refused to pay more, and so Desiree and her receptionist took his spectacles from him. He argued, but finally left, and the following is an extract from a letter he then sent to her:

> Dearest Madame,
>
> Please can I have my glasses back undamaged – I've no intention of being a victim of blackmail and paying you £15 for them (I'm in a low paid job and that represents over 4 hrs work for me). You have had £5 for your time less than 10 minutes ... anyway my glasses are no use to you, can I have them back PLEASE ... I don't want anymore hassle over this ... I wouldn't complain to the police we both want and need discretion although I have phoned the publishers of [contact magazines] and they have assured me that if I tell them [your name] future adverts will be refused ... the Inland Revenue could be interested but NO! I don't want that, please, please can I have my glasses back without charge.

This client rang Desiree a few days later. She explained to him that she pays income tax on her earnings, said that the police would be disinterested in his complaint, and told him again that he could have his glasses back as soon as he paid her the £15 he owed. He brought the money round the following day.

There are instances when disgruntled customers turn nasty and try to use physical force to escape. These occasions are fewer than might be imagined, and Desiree and her receptionists are imposing women who, together, invariably get the better of such men. This is not to say that there are no risks to their persons, and clearly if a man arrived ready and/or armed for physical conflict there would be little likelihood of Desiree being able to enforce a contract through these means. But most men do not relish the prospect of a fight and are unused to dealing with women who are not physically intimidated by them. Sometimes they respond by telling Desiree they are going to call the police, a threat which she finds laughable. Desiree is on good terms with the local vice squad. Her business is not illegal, and clients who do not wish to pay the £20 appointment fee are essentially making a civil complaint of no concern or interest to the police. She therefore offers such men use of her telephone, telling them that they are most welcome to call the vice squad, a strategy which almost invariably floors them.[1]

In short, Desiree is able to exert considerable power over the client to enforce the contract, and, in the past three years, no man who has contracted with her has escaped without paying her, and only a handful of pilchards have managed to avoid parting with the appointment fee. The same cannot be said in relation to the client's power to make Desiree fulfil her side of the agreement. The things which empower her to enforce the contract also give her the freedom to retract from it if she so chooses. It has been noted that Desiree does not contract to spend a set period of time 'servicing' the client, but rather implicitly contracts to bring him to orgasm. However, if a client cannot attain orgasm within fifteen or twenty minutes, Desiree generally ends the transaction by breaking off whatever she is doing and saying 'We don't seem to be getting anywhere, do we? The shower's through there and there's plenty of hot water.' I assume that clients subjected to such treatment are often far from satisfied, and yet they have already paid Desiree and, unless they were armed and prepared to resort to extremes of violence, they would certainly find it impossible to get a refund.

Equally, although the appointment fee of £20 is supposed to entitle the client to a 'basic massage', men who, upon realizing that, come what may, they are going to have to pay the fee and ask for the massage are usually simply told they can whistle for it. Though rare, there are also times when Desiree retracts from contracts made with genuine clients. An especially memorable example of this involved an unknown domination client who arrived when Desiree was in an extremely bad mood. He told her that he wanted domination, but added that he had only £60 on him. This is the 'starter' price for domination services quoted over the telephone, and normally purchases the client a short burst of corporal punishment followed by a hand job. Desiree explained this to the client and took the money from him. He then expressed a desire for her to urinate and defecate on him as well, and Desiree angrily told him he had to be joking if he thought she would do all that for £60, working herself up into a such a pitch of fury that she

ended by telling him to 'fuck off'. He remained very mild man-
nered and meek throughout her outburst, and when it was over
asked 'Can I just have hand relief for £30, then?' Calming herself
down, and with no intention of refunding him the other £30,
Desiree agreed and instructed him to undress, leaving the room
while he did so. On her return, she found him standing by the
couch wearing stockings and suspenders. Desiree told him that she
charged extra for transvestites, at least £80, and told him to give
her stockings back. 'They're not yours, they're mine', said the man,
who had arrived wearing the garments beneath his trousers.
Desiree, by now quite irrationally irate, called him a 'fucking
pervert' and, when he begged for his money back, told him to 'get
lost'.

   In a last bid to negotiate some kind of service in exchange for his
£60, the client promised to remove the stockings if he could just
have the spanking and hand job she had initially agreed to
provide. So Desiree went to fetch a clothes brush with which to
beat him while he changed his clothes, calling loudly to the receptionist, 'Some people are really fucking stupid. Winds me up, then
asks for a spanking. How stupid can you get?' She returned to the
client and set about beating him with great ferocity while he
screamed, 'Please stop, not like that, please stop', in tones which
the receptionist described as conveying genuine distress. Desiree
finally stopped. She did not give him a hand job, but simply told
him to leave, following him out hurling insults after him.

   This incident highlights not only Desiree's power in relation to
her individual clients but also the extraordinary nature of the
prostitute–client contract as a business arrangement. There is a
sense in which many business transactions involve the buyer
putting him or herself at risk of being attacked, robbed or cheated.
However, most of us assume that, if we take a seat in an empty
hairdresser's shop, the hairdresser is not going to slit our throats,
feed our bodies through a grinder and use our remains to fill meat
pies; we assume that shop assistants are not going to rob us at
knife point; that, if we give a milk-round person a £20 note, he or
she is not going to refuse to give us our change. This trust reflects a
generalized and necessary assumption that the world is not full of
psychopaths and that the vast majority of people are relatively
honest and harmless, but it also reflects assumptions that are
central to the ideological justification of a 'free market' economy.
We are told that it is in business people's rational self-interest to
behave well – a fiction that is maintained by ignoring the existence

of multinational industries which profit through the sale of cancer-inducing substances, dried baby milk to mothers who have no supply of clean water with which to prepare it and so on, and by focusing instead on the dependence of very small businesses on customer 'good will'.

It is true that, up to a point, Desiree is dependent on, and so must try to cultivate, the good will of her customers, for 'regulars' are important to her business. It is also the case that, if she took to slicing clients' penises off or robbing them at knife point, she would probably end up in court. But prostitution really is 'a funny old game', and the kind of constraints that encourage honesty and fair trading in other small businesses do not always operate on prostitutes like Desiree. For a start, they know that only a certain percentage of men will ever provide repeat custom because many 'straight' clients attach sexual value to completely anonymous sexual encounters, and many domination clients cannot bear to return to someone who knows their 'terrible secret'. Desiree obviously cannot know with certainty whether or not a client is a one-off, but it is not difficult to see why, on some occasions, she treats clients as though they were. The illegality of soliciting also encourages certain forms of sharp practice. Since prostitutes are forbidden by law from advertising their prices, they are in a position to adjust their tariffs at will. The secrecy of their prostitute use, something in which clients typically take enormous pleasure, further means that customers are unlikely to write complaints to local papers or consumer watchdogs about bad experiences with particular prostitutes.

It would be overstating the case to say that all this is unique to prostitution. Most of us have experience of other small business people (builders and plumbers spring to mind as especially good examples) who behave in the same opportunistic ways. But there are things which do make prostitution distinctive. When self-employed individuals provide services on a one-off basis to a series of different customers, the concept of personal honour, notions of professionalism and some general sense of respect for the customer usually play a part in encouraging them to fulfil their contractual obligations, even when they think it unlikely that the particular firm or person will provide repeat business. In the context of dominant Western discourses about sexuality and prostitution, however, it is extremely difficult for prostitutes to affirm a sense of personal honour through the execution of prostitution contracts. Furthermore, the extraordinary nature of the demand for prostitution means that the wants of some clients are actually satisfied even when they are cheated or abused. Since some men derive sexual excitement primarily from the idea of their own transgression and/or from any form of contact with a 'publicly available' woman, even being 'clipped' (cheated) by a prostitute can be a pleasurable experience for them. For domination clients, meanwhile, being maltreated in any way at all can also sometimes be experienced as sexually satisfying, and there is no necessary link between the effort expended on 'customer care' and the degree of pleasure domination clients derive from a visit to a dominatrix. Desiree once bound, gagged and blindfolded a domination client and left him in the dungeon while she attended to another client, intending to return to him in half an hour. However, three more clients arrived, and, because she did not wish to lose their custom, Desiree serviced them consecutively before returning, hours later, to the first man. When she took the gag off, he asked in a rather dazed voice, 'What time is it? I've got an appointment at two o'clock.' If a hairdresser left a customer under a dryer for two and a half hours in order to attend to four other people, thereby making them miss a business appointment, the customer would probably be more than a little annoyed. This client, on the contrary, was delighted with the 'service' he had received, and has returned for domination sessions since.

The sources of control

The difference between Desiree's experience of prostitution and that of prostitutes who have been discussed in previous chapters could not be more marked. Indeed, if we compare it against that of the enslaved brothel prostitute, it almost seems that we are speaking of wholly incommensurate phenomena. The question of what exactly it is that empowers Desiree is therefore of no small importance to theoretical and political debates on prostitution. We might begin to answer this question by looking at issues of contract. Desiree sets out to forge narrowly contractual, closed-ended relationships with clients, and, in so doing, she imposes limits on the degree of unfreedom associated with her own prostitution. By organizing the transfer of powers over her person in this way, she is able to draw clear boundaries around the client's freedoms and so constrain him in certain ways, and this, it seems to me, represents a huge advance upon those forms of prostitution in which the client's freedoms are contractually bounded only by a time limit. However, as the discussion of street prostitution in Chapter 3 showed, arranging the prostitute–client transaction as if it were a narrowly contractual commodity exchange does not, in and of itself, empower the prostitute. She must also be in a position to ensure that the contract is executed on her terms. I would argue that Desiree's power to do so rests on three main factors. The first is economic.

Desiree did not enter prostitution from a base of absolute poverty. She owned her own home, she had no economic dependants and she had a job. To be sure, this job held out little prospect of ever making her wealthy, but it still made her situation very different from that of, say, a lone mother living in a council property and struggling to subsist on welfare payments, or a child who has run away from an abusive parent and who lives on the streets without any source of income. Desiree was thus able to save her earnings from prostitution and amount sufficient capital to invest in a property, equipment, advertising, three phone lines, etc., all of which made it possible for her to develop a business catering to a 'niche market' of clients who will pay more than those who use street and parlour prostitutes. Her relative economic advantage allowed her to prostitute herself more profitably and also to prostitute herself legally. Meanwhile, the fact that she works from a house in a residential area and employs a receptionist means that she is at far less risk of physical assault than are street working prostitutes (West, 1992, found that male street workers were also more likely to report having suffered assault than were self-employed male masseurs in private brothels).

In terms of the risk of sexually transmitted disease, Desiree is probably less vulnerable than either street workers or employed sex workers, and certainly less vulnerable than most women who are sexually active non-commercially. She refuses to receive anal penetration with or without a condom, she refuses to fellate or to allow vaginal penetration unless the man wears a condom, she keeps a cap in permanently, she wears protective gloves to perform anal stimulation. Her relative security is associated with her ability to enforce limits upon contracts and with her relatively advantaged financial position. Some clients offer Desiree large sums of money for unprotected sex. Unlike many other prostitutes around the world, she earns enough to make it easy to turn down such offers.

The legality of her prostitution is a second factor which

contributes to Desiree's relative power and control within trans-actions. In Britain the criminal law 'has always concerned itself with the nuisance that may arise from prostitution, rather than the activity itself' (Home Office spokesperson, cited in Boyle, 1994, p. 181). Police response to 'off-street' prostitution is regionally varied (Bindman, 1997) and some forces do not actively police the legal infractions that might be occurring in private brothels (overt forms of solicitation, receptionists/maids supplying 'sexual ser-vices', third-party control, 'immoral earnings' being used to support spouses/lovers, etc.). The entrepreneurial prostitute's ability to enforce the terms and limits of transactions with clients is greatly enhanced where she is not subject to police harassment and may even be provided with a degree of support and protection by the police.

The third factor which I believe contributes to Desiree's power within transactions is her own character and 'career' history. Desiree had a great deal more emotional and life experience when she started to prostitute than have those individuals who, for various reasons, find themselves involved in prostitution in their early teens. It is also the case that Desiree is an extremely intelli-gent, well read, perceptive, assertive, charming and socially skilled individual, and these qualities contribute enormously to her ability to deploy her subjective powers to positive effect within prostitu-tion – that is, to negotiate and enforce contracts on terms which suit her, and yet still maintain a stream of repeat custom.

I am not trying to paint a picture of entrepreneurial prostitution as an idyllically autonomous existence. Desiree may exercise a high level of control within each transaction, but this merely enables her to limit the degree of unfreedom it entails, not to pursue any end of her own. The essence of each transaction for Desiree, just as for any other prostitute, is that she surrenders certain freedoms over her person. Furthermore, though her rela-tive financial advantage means that she can turn down clients who are drunk, abusive or threatening, she cannot begin to use her own desire as a criterion for entering into transactions, or her income would instantly plummet to next to nothing. Meanwhile, though Desiree is less vulnerable to assault by clients than are many pros-titutes, she is just as horribly open to premeditated attack by the kind of misogynist psychopath who dreads and hates prostitutes as is any other prostitute woman. Finally, the emotional, psycho-logical and physical toll of her work is immense and, since the support networks available to those who work in prostitution are far more restricted than they are for non-prostitute women and men (Bindman, 1997), opportunities for Desiree to offload any of this stress are limited. However, the control that Desiree exercises within each individual transaction does highlight broader questions about power and prostitution, which are considered below.

Choice and power

The aim of this chapter has been to show that successful entrepreneurial prostitutes can set limits on the degree of unfreedom they experience within the prostitute–client transaction, that they have certain powers to enforce contracts and a certain freedom to retract from individual contracts, and, further, that it is possible for them to make very large sums of money from prostitution. Does this mean that Desiree, and prostitutes like her, can be said to exercise 'free choice', at least inasmuch as any social actor makes a 'free' choice to do anything? Can they be said to elect voluntarily to endure the unfreedoms, stigma and risks associated with prostitution on the basis of rational calculations? Let me first consider the issue of choice.

Desiree is in a position to decide for herself whether £250,000 is enough to compensate for the personal costs of her work and to secure her the freedom she desires. She could, in fact, decide to give up prostitution tomorrow and set herself up in some other form of entrepreneurial activity and probably live quite comfortably. This distinguishes her not only from the vast majority of prostitutes, but also from the vast majority of wage workers, myself included. Now, given that Desiree takes no personal pleasure in her work, has nothing but contempt for the men who exploit her, and has enough money to invest in an alternative business, it is reasonable to ask why she does not simply stop prostituting herself and do something else instead. The answer to this question has to do partly with the fact that the returns on any other business venture she might set up would almost certainly be lower than those she currently secures, and Desiree wants very much to be wealthy. Her desire for financial security can, in large part, be explained through reference to broader structural factors, such as class and gender. She has never wanted to end up in the situation that so many women of her childhood and adult acquaintance were/are in, that is, economically dependent on a man, and, since she has neither the benefit of inherited wealth nor a higher education, entrepreneurial prostitution represented and still does represent the best of the economic options available to her.

But another part of the answer is actually very much along the lines that might be predicted by feminist theorists such as Kathleen Barry (1995) who view prostitution through the lens of a theoretical preoccupation with patriarchal domination. There is a sense in which, for Desiree, as for many prostitutes, prostitution is also about returning to the site of abuse and sexual victimization. However, I think it would be wrong to conclude that Desiree's psychobiography renders her choiceless in the matter of whether or not to continue working in prostitution. Some studies suggest that the experience of rape and/or childhood sexual abuse can be a contributory factor in prostitution (for example, Silbert and Pines, 1981, 1982), and logic suggests that, when people have been brutally and unequivocally sexualized in the ways implied by sexual abuse and rape, they are likely to have a strong sense of themselves as nothing more than sexual beings for others, and so to view prostitution as one of the 'options', or the only 'option', available to them. But it is important to recognize three things about this. First, not all prostitutes have been sexualized in these ways. Several of the women we interviewed who were involved in informal tourist-related prostitution in economically underdeveloped countries, for example, had no prior history of sexual victimization. Economic desperation is enough, on its own, to drive people into prostitution. Second, the experience of sexual victimization clearly does not and could not on its own *cause* people to enter into prostitution or to continue prostituting once involved in it. There are people who have suffered such violence and yet do not work as prostitutes, as well as individuals who have been raped and/or abused who have worked as prostitutes and then exited from prostitution. Third, it is far fetched (and dangerous) to attribute the complex set of choices people make within the constraints that operate on them to a single, determining event or psychological factor. Barry bravely acknowledges the fact that she herself was raped (1995, p. 252), for example, but I doubt that she would take kindly to someone interpreting the fact that she has spent two decades researching and writing on prostitution as a form of sexual violence as a reflection of nothing more than her own personal attempt to come to terms with that event. It would be as easy to interpret Barry's work in this way as it would be to interpret Desiree's decision to remain in prostitution as a direct result of certain events in her life, but I think that in both cases such an interpretation would be wrong.

In short, though one might personally disagree with Desiree's calculations as regards the risks and benefits of her chosen course of action, it makes no sense to describe a woman who is intelligent and articulate, has no children, is under no pressure from any third-party pimp or employer, owns three properties and thousands of pounds' worth of jewellery and has over £100,000 in savings as having *no* choice about her continued prostitution. Desiree is no more blindly driven to keep working as a prostitute than Kathleen Barry or any other academic is blindly driven to undertake research on prostitution. A psychotherapist might view the choices Desiree makes as indicative of various unresolved issues around dependency and intimacy, but it is almost certainly the case that, if I were to go into therapy, the therapist would find my choice to spend years of my life interviewing child prostitutes and their abusers equally suggestive of neurosis. This may tell us something about psychoanalysis, but it does not resolve questions about the relationship between structure and agency.

I do not claim to be able to settle such questions either. I merely take refuge in Marx's observation that people make history, but not in circumstances of their own choosing, and in the Weberian notion that individuals consciously choose a course of action on the basis of an evaluation of the possibilities open to them, the meanings they attach to actions, events and institutions and so on. These insights allow us to speak of people being in a position to exercise more or less choice over the details of their life, and to claim that, at the apex of the prostitution hierarchy, prostitutes' circumstances not only allow them to exercise a great deal more choice than can be exercised by people at the base of that hierarchy, but also as much choice as many wage workers exercise.

Of course this does not mean that an entrepreneurial prostitute in Desiree's position is an unbounded, free and wholly rational agent, unencumbered by either her own past or broader structural processes, still less does it constitute a defence of prostitution as an institution. Women like Desiree are still oppressed in Young's (1990) sense of the term, and recognizing the fact that a small minority of individuals can make good money from prostituting themselves and exercise a good deal of control over the degree of unfreedom implied by prostitution does not require us to celebrate prostitution as a positive 'career' choice. But I think there would be something faintly ridiculous about my lamenting Desiree's prostitution on the grounds that she is deprived of choice when in fact she is far better placed to change her occupation than I myself am, as well as something politically dangerous about refusing to recognize that the degree of unfreedom individuals suffer, and the forms of domination to which they are subject, matters. Feminist abolitionists would do better to focus on the fact that only a tiny minority of prostitutes enjoy the degree of control within prostitution enjoyed by those at the apex of the hierarchy than by insisting that women like Desiree are 'in denial' or are the victims of false consciousness, or by asserting that theorists who 'make distinctions between "forced" and "free", between adult and child, between East and West' are necessarily reinforcing 'the idea that there can be a good and reasonable form of men's abuse of women in prostitution' (Jeffreys, 1997, p. 348).

PART II

PROSTITUTION AND THE EROTICIZATION OF SOCIAL DEATH

NORTHBROOK COLLEGE LIBRARY

Introduction

> I am an invisible man ... I am a man of substance, of flesh and
> bone, fibre and liquids – and I might even be said to possess a
> mind. I am invisible, understand, simply because people refuse
> to see me. Like the bodiless heads you see sometimes in circus
> sideshows, it is as though I have been surrounded by mirrors of
> hard, distorting glass. When they approach me they see only my
> surroundings, themselves, or figments of their imagination –
> indeed, everything and anything except me. (*Ellison*, 1965, p. 7)

Desiree once remarked to me that there is only one plausible line
in the entire script of the popular Hollywood film *Pretty Woman*,
and that is when Richard Gere, playing a client, asks Julia Roberts,
playing a prostitute, what her name is. She replies, 'Anything you
want it to be.' This line captured Desiree's sense of the prostitute's
invisibility for clients – as she put it, 'I'm just a role, a fantasy ... I
don't exist for them as a person.' Desiree recently attended a conference in London on prostitution and violence at which she
experienced, once again, her own invisibility. This time she told
me it was feminist academics and activists who could not see her
(or other prostitute women like her), but only her surroundings,
themselves and figments of their imagination. The women who
had organized the conference wanted to talk about prostitution as
a form of male violence against women. The audience saw
paraded on the stage a visibly traumatized young woman who
had been forced into prostitution and had subsequently killed her
abusive pimp, they heard testimony from the mother of a young
prostitute woman who had been murdered, and they gave raptur-

ous applause to a 'survivor' who challenged those who treat prostitution as a form of work to tell her what other job there is for which child abuse is the necessary apprenticeship. Prostitute women who wanted to say that they had boyfriends who were not pimps or that they had not been forced into prostitution but had chosen it for rational economic reasons felt themselves refused and silenced just as surely as their counterparts at the US feminist conference on prostitution attended by Kate Millett more than twenty-five years earlier had felt excluded and denied by feminists who wanted to call them 'slaves' (Millett, 1975).

In the first part of this book I tried to show that the unfreedoms experienced by prostitutes vary and that this has implications for political and theoretical analyses of prostitution. Though many prostitutes are subjected to violence by third parties and/or clients, this is not the only, nor even a necessary, dimension of prostitutes' oppression. Questions about power and prostitution cannot be reduced to simple arguments about male violence against women, but require us instead to think about prostitutes as active subjects who are under differing types and degrees of compulsion to prostitute, either independently or for one or more third-party beneficiaries. In this second part of the book I want to tackle questions about prostitution, power and freedom from a slightly different angle. My aim is to explore the meanings that are attached to prostitution by a range of social actors, but most particularly by prostitute users themselves, and consider their theoretical and political significance.

The postmodern approach to such questions is to argue that 'the referent, the flesh-and-blood female body engaged in some form of sexual interaction in exchange for some kind of payment, has no inherent meaning and is signified differently in different discourses' (Bell, 1994, pp. 1–2). In pursuit of this ambition, Shannon Bell takes us on a tour of ancient Greece, nineteenth-century Europe, US feminists and prostitute rights groups in the 1980s, and recent US prostitute 'performance art' to reveal 'the prostitute body' as a blank sheet upon which cultures, groups and individuals 'write' and 'rewrite' meanings. Bell is right, I think, to follow Foucault (1979) in noting that, because prostitute women were one focus of late nineteenth- early twentieth-century campaigns around moral and 'race' hygiene, because they were interrogated and categorized within sexology's broader undertaking to classify and codify sexual aberrance, because they were medicalized and pathologized, they became subject to new forms of social control and exclusion (see also Walkowitz, 1980). Indeed, the way in which science and medicine became a site of power is graphically illustrated by even the most cursory glance at the legal regulation of prostitution in Europe at the turn of the century.[1]

However, Bell wants to do more than simply observe that 'scientific' discourses were constitutive of new mechanisms for *controlling* the prostitute. She claims that, in its 'reading' and 'writing' of prostitution, late nineteenth-century and twentieth-century Western research and theory *produced* the modern prostitute body 'as a negative identity ... an *empty symbol* filled from the outside with the debris of the modern body/body politic, a sign to women to sublimate their libidinal body in their reproductive body' (Bell, 1994, p. 72, emphasis added). Bell needs to stress the idea that 'scientific' discourses actually created 'the prostitute' as such an identity, for this allows her to argue that recent prostitute performance artists in the US have, through their novel discourses, 'produced a new social identity – the prostitute as sexual healer, goddess, teacher, political activist, and feminist' (p. 184). But the idea that nineteenth- and twentieth-century sexologists and reformers '*produced* the prostitute as a negative identity' is questionable, to say the least. Given that prostitutes had been vilified in Judaeo-Christian culture for centuries, they were hardly working upon an 'empty symbol', and it seems quite extraordinary to present the notion that women should 'sublimate their libidinal body in their reproductive body' as a *modern*, bourgeois idea.

Weeks (1985, p. 178) has observed that, when nineteenth- and twentieth-century sexologists constructed categories defining appropriate sexual behaviour ('normal'/'abnormal'), they were not embarking upon a 'neutral, scientific discovery of what was already there'. Certainly, the way in which men such as William Acton, Havelock Ellis and Sigmund Freud 'mapped the prostitute body' was neither neutral nor particularly scientific, and, certainly, the categories used to identify and pathologize prostitute women arose from the social and not the natural world. In this sense, then, they did not discover what was already there. But there is another sense in which sexologists and social scientific researchers did discover, or at least rearticulate, what was already there. Compare, for example, the portrait of a 'whore' spoken by a character in Webster's play *The White Devil*, written in 1612, and the portrait provided by William Acton in 1870 on the basis of his 'scientific observation and analysis':

Shall I expound whore to you? sure I shall;
I'll give you their perfect character. They are first,
Sweet-meats which rot the eater: in man's nostril
Poison'd perfumes. They are coz'ning alchemy . . .
What's a whore?
She's like the guilty counterfeited coin
Which whosoe'er first stamps it brings in trouble
All that receive it . . .
They are the true material fire of hell.
(*Webster*, 1965, p. 183)

What is a prostitute? . . . She is a woman with half the woman
gone, and that half containing all that elevates her nature, leaving
her a mere instrument of impurity, degraded and fallen she
extracts from the sin of others the means of living, corrupt . . . a
social pest, carrying contamination and foulness to every quarter.
(*Acton*, 1870, *cited in Bell*, 1994, p. 55).

Foucault was no doubt right to argue that the production and pro-
liferation of discourses on sexuality in the nineteenth century led
to the emergence of new sexual subjects, such as 'the hysterical
woman', 'the masturbating child', 'the perverse adult', but I do not
think we can say that the 'scientific mapping' of the prostitute
body constructed 'the prostitute' in quite the same way. There is a
difference between medicalizing practices or conditions which
have never previously been viewed as aberrant or problematic and
pathologizing those which have long been subject to moral
scrutiny and censure.

Robert Miles's comments on scientific discourses on 'race' are
perhaps equally pertinent to those on prostitution. While recognizing the significance of 'the transformation entailed in the gradual
epistemological shift from religion to science as the criterion by
which to measure and evaluate the nature of the social and material world', Miles draws attention to the existence of representations
of the Other which long predate European colonization and
pseudo-scientific notions of 'race':

the development of the discourse of 'race', and its subsequent
incorporation into the discourse of science did not entail a complete break with earlier representations of the Other and therefore the creation of completely new means of representational
inclusion and exclusion. . . . Because the emergence of science did
not displace these earlier hierarchies of inferiority . . . analyses of
the representations of the Other which focus exclusively on the

career of the discourse of 'race' arbitrarily detach that history from its roots. (*Miles*, 1989, p. 40)

Bell's thoroughly postmodern aim to show that there is no 'inherent meaning' in prostitution disturbs me not simply because it legitimates, even celebrates, a kind of 'take your pick' attitude towards empirical evidence that has seriously hampered theory development on prostitution but also because it implies a form of judgmental relativism which I believe is always and necessarily politically dangerous. She presents the discourse about prostitution promoted by a handful of relatively privileged white American women as though it carries a weight equal to any other discourse, whether based upon systematic research with a more typical sample of prostitutes or not. If 'the prostitute body' is an 'empty symbol', and anything that anyone inscribes upon it is neither true nor false but merely one among many discourses, what grounds are there for challenging the sexologists' claims about prostitutes, or even for challenging the discourses about prostitute women of the Yorkshire Ripper and other prostitute murderers?

This also highlights a problem with analyses that make uncritical use of accounts of prostitution written by prostitutes and former prostitutes and/or oral history projects involving prostitute women and/or materials produced by prostitutes' rights groups (see Barry, 1995, as well as Bell). Though a reliance on such data fits well with a methodological approach championed by some feminist methodologists, namely that of 'giving voice' and developing conceptual and theoretical categories on the basis of women's spoken experience (see Stanley and Wise, 1993), the limitations of this kind of 'experiential' data so far as theory development is concerned are well illustrated by feminist debates on prostitution. The argument between feminists who hold that we should campaign against prostitution as a human rights violation and those who maintain that we should push for the destigmatization and decriminalization of prostitution as a form of work can no more be resolved through an appeal to experiential data than they can by calling upon more conventional research data. It is not hard to find 'sex workers' who are prepared to 'voice' the view that they freely elected prostitution as a form of work, even to argue that prostitution allows them a greater degree of control over their own sexuality than that enjoyed by non-prostitute women (see, for example, Roberts, 1992, Nagel, 1997), and equally there is no shortage of former prostitutes who are prepared to 'voice' the view that their experience of prostitution was akin to that of rape or sexual abuse (see Barry, 1995, Wynter, 1988). Since prostitutes do not speak with one voice on the subject, it is very easy for theorists to 'cherry pick' in order to support their own preconceptions about prostitution.

I find myself in sympathy with Jeffreys' (1994, p. 524) comment that 'feminists cannot hide from using their political intelligence behind the argument that only prostitutes can speak about their experience when such very diametrically opposite views are all posing as the truth of prostitution', and yet I am reluctant to endorse the idea that feminists can rely solely upon their 'political intelligence' to determine the proper conceptual categories to be used in research and theory. Again, it is useful to look at the parallels between the problems facing theorists of 'race' and those confronting theorists of prostitution.

Those involved in the sociology of 'race' are investigating something which does not actually exist as a fixed, biological reality and yet remains 'a primary organising feature of social relations' (Small, 1994), and likewise we can say that, while the line demarcating prostitute and non-prostitute women (implicit in cultural representations of the prostitute as Other and sexologists' attempts to mark prostitutes off as emotionally and psychologically 'abnormal') does not exist in actuality, it is nonetheless used to structure and legitimate social relations and has huge significance for the way in which people view themselves. Equally, the idea that prostitution is something other than an economic institution may be an ideological fiction, but it is a fiction which informs the political and legal control of prostitution; it also serves to organize both prostitutes' experience of prostitution and non-prostitutes' attitudes towards it.

Solomos and Back (1994, p. 156) note that 'the question of how to conceptualise racism is not purely an academic matter', and the same point needs to be made in relation to prostitution. Social theorists cannot simply side-step dominant discourses about prostitutes as Other by deciding to conceptualize prostitution as a contractual commodity exchange like any other (Ericcson, 1980) or by deciding to treat it as a form of slavery or rape (Barry, 1979, 1995), but nor can they decide to treat these discourses as though they are identical with reality, as though social practices are constituted by the structures through which people talk about them, as though postmodern individuals can, by inscribing new meanings on prostitution, somehow miraculously transform it. And it is no use attempting to draw our conceptual categories from prostitutes' experience, not just because this experience can differ enormously, but also because, since prostitutes inhabit exactly the same symbolic universe as do other members of their society, their experience is itself informed by the exact same basic political fictions about human freedom and unfreedom, about consent, contract and community, which make prostitution such a difficult issue for social theorists.

E. P. Thompson's remarks about the historian's relationship with empirical experience are, I think, equally valid for sociological enquiry and of particular relevance for those who seek to describe, explain and mobilize politically around prostitution. He notes that 'historians . . . are concerned, every day, in their practice, with the formation of, and with the tensions within, social consciousness', and that it is these tensions which give rise to:

> experience – a category which, however imperfect it may be, is indispensable to the historian, since it comprises the mental and emotional response, whether of an individual or of a social group, to many inter-related events or to many repetitions of the same kind of event . . . experience is valid and effective but within determined limits: the farmer "knows" his seasons, the sailor "knows" his seas, but both may remain mystified about kingship and cosmology. (*Thompson*, 1978, p. 199)

The tensions which exist between the idea of prostitution as work and prostitution as sex, between ideas of consent and force, contract and rape, rational choice and victimization, arise from social consciousness, not from individual experience or any individual's moral, political or theoretical stance. This existent social consciousness does not determine action (human beings are purposive agents, and as such can 'make history'), but it is part of the 'circumstances directly encountered, given and transmitted from the past' (Marx, 1975, p. 104) within which social actors (in this case, those involved in prostitution and political struggles around it) must make history. The tensions and ambiguities which surround prostitution, and the experience to which they give rise, must therefore be the object of enquiry, and, with this in mind, I want to use Part II of this book to examine the social meanings that are attached to prostitution, the erotic significance those meanings hold (and do not hold) for clients, and the problems which these tensions create for those involved in the political and/or theoretical analysis of prostitution.

6

Narratives of Power and Exclusion

> There is a familiar myth that is sometimes, and wrongly, used to explain the origins of human sexual arrangements. This is the myth of the primal horde, the primal crime, in which the patriarch keeps all the women to himself and forces his sons to work for him; finally the sons rebel, kill and eat him, fuck the women, and then, guilt-ridden, promise to be good boys. (*Dimen*, 1989, p. 34)

Missing in this myth, Dimen continues, are women and their subordination. Related points are made by Carole Pateman, who observes that 'telling stories of all kinds is the major way that human beings have endeavoured to make sense of themselves and their social world' (1988, p. 1), and goes on to examine the way in which social contract theorists have told a story about once rampaging and now fearful sons promising to be good boys and abide by the rules of the social contract. Classical political theory starts from the proposition that human beings are naturally competitive and self-interested, and for this reason need safeguarding from each other. Hobbes (1968), for instance, holds that, in a state of nature, each man would use all means available to him to possess, use, and enjoy all that he would, or could, get. By agreeing (on condition that all men do the same) to a social contract which creates a political society or state, and transferring rights of law making and enforcement to that state, individuals can, it is argued, simultaneously retain powers of sovereignty over themselves and be restrained from invading and destroying others. The legitimacy of the liberal democratic state hinges upon its role as enactor of laws which preserve and protect the 'natural rights' of its citizens, 'rights', which include possessing property, disposing of their own labour and exercising sovereignty over themselves, their own minds and bodies. The powers exercised by the state are thus viewed as a condensation of the wills of a mass of individuals, each of whom has an equal interest in the construction of a legal juridical framework which safeguards life, liberty and estate.

According to this story, contractually organized commodity exchange is central to the preservation and protection of sovereign rights. No individual or group holds the power to snatch or commandeer goods or resources from another; instead individuals must voluntarily contract to alienate property in peaceable and mutually advantageous exchanges. This logic extends to the wage-labour contract, for, according to liberals, a person's labour is a commodity which can be freely alienated like any other. The abstract, sovereign individuals of capitalism cannot be invaded by another's will, even when they are denied access to any means of subsistence other than wage labour. Sovereign individuals are free because no monarch, lord or state apparatchik can command their labour, person or property – each juridical subject is safeguarded against threats to self-sovereignty by the contracts which regulate social interaction. In these ways, then, social contract theorists have told a story about 'how a new civil society and a new form of political right is created through an original contract. An explanation for the binding authority of the state and civil law, and for the legitimacy of modern civil government is to be found by treating our society as if it had originated in a contract' (Pateman, 1988, p. 1). Yet the original contract in which this sovereignty is embedded, Pateman argues, was a sexual as well as a social pact and, while the story of the social contract may be a tale of freedom, the sexual contract 'is a story of subjection':

> Civil freedom is not universal. Civil freedom is a masculine attribute and depends upon patriarchal right. The sons overturn paternal rule not merely to gain their liberty but to secure women for themselves. Their success in this endeavour is chronicled in the story of the sexual contract. The original pact is a sexual as well as a social contract: it is sexual in the sense of patriarchal – that is, the contract establishes men's political right over women – and also sexual in the sense of establishing orderly access by men to women's bodies. (*Pateman*, 1988, p. 2)

This is a pact which regulates men's competitive struggles over women as well as over other resources, then. As Andrea Dworkin puts it:

> many sexual laws ... serve ... to uphold male supremacy by keeping peace among men ... Women are property; adultery, rape, and some forms of incest hurt the rightful owners of women by damaging the value of the goods or by violating the man's integrity through violating his legal and deeply felt personal right of private, exclusive sexual access. Following the rules lets men have sexual access to subjugated women while moderating male–male conflict over that access. Rights of ownership are delineated because inside the community of men itself relations are ordered precisely by the laws that regulate women as property. (*Dworkin*, 1987, p. 161)

These authors draw our attention to the fact that the primal myth is commonly invoked to explain both sexual and political arrangements. In the West we are brought up to believe that, without the state and the rule of law, men's 'natural' competitive and sexual urges would engulf us all in a chaotic mayhem of rape and pillage, and that we all of us have an interest, therefore, in the existing contractual regulation of our sexual, social and economic relations. The fact that the same stories are used to make sense of human sexual and political governance should, Pateman rightly argues, alert us to the fact that these sexual arrangements are political and vice versa. But, and this becomes hugely significant in relation to the analysis of prostitution, it is important to remember that the primal myth is exactly that – a myth.

Patriarchy, rape and the prostitution contract

Feminists who make use of the concept of patriarchy are by no means a homogeneous group of theorists; indeed the origins, nature and theoretical significance of patriarchy are much debated within feminism(s). It is possible to identify a school of thought within one brand of feminism, however, which tends to forget the fact that the primal myth is a *story* employed to justify and explain a given political order and to treat it instead as a historically factual account of women's political subordination. Susan Brownmiller, for example, starts her book *Against our Will* by explaining that, where sexual behaviour in the animal kingdom is controlled 'by the female oestrus cycle', for humans there is no 'biologically determined mating season', and a human male's sexual interest does not depend on the female's 'biologic readiness or receptivity':

> What it all boils down to is that the human male can rape. Man's structural capacity to rape and woman's corresponding structural vulnerability are as basic to the physiology of both our sexes as the primal act of sex itself. (*Brownmiller*, 1975, pp. 13–14)

She goes on to argue that, at some point in the mists of time, men discovered that they could rape and women discovered that they *could not retaliate in kind*' (p. 14, emphasis original). After this,

> rape became not only a male prerogative, but man's basic weapon of force against woman, the principal agent of his will and her fear ... Man's discovery that his genitalia could serve as a weapon to generate fear must rank as one of the most important discoveries of prehistoric times. (p. 14)

From here, Brownmiller moves on to assert that 'it seems eminently sensible to hypothesize that man's violent capture and rape of the female led first to the establishment of a rudimentary mate-protectorate and then sometime later to the full-blown male solidification of power, the patriarchy' (p. 17). In other words, Brownmiller is saying that political and economic inequalities between men and women are historically rooted in physiological sex difference, and other feminists who accept this basic premise have gone on 'to analyse all forms of male sexuality in terms of a continuum of violence' (Segal, 1994, p. 57) and to conflate gender power with specific sexual acts. MacKinnon (1989, p. 118), for example, holds that gender is constructed by the social requirements of heterosexuality which 'institutionalizes male sexual dominance and female sexual submission', and other radical feminists have also insisted that penile penetration is, in and of itself, a cornerstone of male domination. The Leeds Revolutionary Feminist Group tells us that 'only in the system of oppression that is male supremacy does the oppressor actually invade and colonise the interior of the body of the oppressed' (cited in Kitzinger, 1994, p. 198), while Dworkin (1987, p. 133) states that, 'physically, the woman in intercourse is a space inhabited, a literal territory occupied literally: occupied even if there has been no resistance, no force; even if the occupied person said yes please, yes hurry, yes more.'

The idea that particular sexual acts can be divorced from the power relations which surround them and the meanings that are attached to them by social actors and adjudged *essentially* 'dominant' or 'submissive' on the basis of mere physiological fact is simplistic, and I can think of endless objections to Dworkin's formulation. If the woman saying 'Yes please, yes hurry, yes more' is a slave owner, and the man she is so instructing is her chattel slave, or if she is an affluent, adult, white Western tourist and the male she is urging on is a fifteen-year-old Black boy who has no means of supporting himself other than prostitution, is Dworkin suggesting that her 'literal occupation' means the same as it would mean if *she* was enslaved and the man penetrating her was her 'master' or if *she* was the child prostitute and the man penetrating her was the adult tourist? And if we are to abandon all concern for the material situation and subjective beliefs of individual actors and look only at the 'invasive' qualities of particular physical acts (as Dworkin does when she insists that women's bodies are *necessarily* 'violated' during heterosexual intercourse), then why draw the line at 'intercourse'? After all, it makes as much sense to say that the mouth is a 'literal territory literally occupied' during kissing as it does to say that the vagina is a territory 'occupied' during penetrative sex, so that a woman sticking her tongue into another woman's mouth is, by this logic, equally intruding upon the 'privacy' of that mouth, committing an act of 'colonization', and so on.

The reason why feminists like Dworkin view heterosexual intercourse as territorial violation is, I would argue, because they have mistaken the primal myth for historical fact, and so confused a 'discourse' with a reality. When Brownmiller (1975, p. 14) conjures with a vision of the original rape perpetrated in a 'violent landscape inhabited by primitive woman and man', she constructs a 'territorial' model of the self just as surely as Hobbes does with his vision of nasty and brutish men and women invading each other in 'a state of nature' (see Brace, 1997), and this forces her to work with a flimsy and shallow model of power.

If women's bodies are imagined as *territory* invaded during heterosexual intercourse, then there is no room for subtlety in the analysis of male power. Male heterosexuality must always and necessarily be a form of domination. This one-dimensional view of male sexuality is hugely problematic when applied to the issue of prostitution, for it completely obscures the specificity of prostitution as a form of oppression. Prostitute use becomes a straightforward expression of patriarchal domination (it is variously described as an act of aggression, of violence, and of rape), and, as Hart (1994, p. 53) has noted, we are encouraged to view 'either all men as prostitutes' clients or prostitutes' clients as somehow standing for/being symbolic of men in general'.

Although I am firmly of the opinion that prostitute use is an oppressive act, I am troubled by analyses in which clients and other heterosexual men are melded together as one homogeneous class of penis-wielding colonizers and in which distinctions between prostitute use and acts of male violence against women, such as rape or wife beating, are blurred. Such analyses, it seems to me, display an almost staggering disregard for the details of men and women's interactions and the meanings that are attached to these details. Men do not arrive home drunk and ask their wives whether they would mind submitting to a kicking in exchange for a twenty pound note, for example, and rapists do not negotiate limits to the powers they will exercise over their victims. Prostitution, however, is most usually organized as if it involved a mutual and voluntary exchange, and the various formalities which surround the prostitute–client transaction (such as payment and contractual specification, or 'flirting', and the making of sexual 'invitations' employed in more informally organized prostitution) make it possible for the client to read his sexual contact with the prostitute as consensual. Even where a client has negotiated with and made payment to a third party, rather than to the prostitute, he can tell himself that the woman concerned has agreed to work in this way. This veneer of consent makes prostitute use appear to be something quite other than rape or battery, and it is precisely because the contractual form is taken to imply consent that, when men set out to rape prostitutes, as they not infrequently do, they do *not* engage in any of these formalities.

Kathleen Barry holds such details to be irrelevant, and states that 'the issue of consent and the concept of force have falsely separated prostitution from rape, legally and socially' (1995, p. 90). For the actual participants in prostitution, however, the notion of contractual consent, and the formal and tacit rules which surround and produce it, does separate prostitution and rape at the level of subjective experience. When formally 'free' prostitute women say that they have been raped by a client, they rarely mean that he has simply failed to pay them.[1]

I am not arguing that the contractual elements of the prostitute–client transaction make it into something genuinely mutual. On the contrary, I believe that the façade of voluntarism makes prostitution all the more insidiously damaging to many of the women, children and men who work as prostitutes. What I *am* arguing is that, if you overlook the way in which a fiction of consent is constructed, if you dismiss the fact that, as a rule, both parties to the 'exchange' buy into this fiction, and ignore the tacit rules which govern this kind of interaction, you end up telling a story about prostitution which is unrecognizable to most of the people who actually participate in it, and thus cannot hope to explain *why* they do so. I would also add that, for political and moral reasons, it is dangerous to insist that tricks and rapes are one and the same thing. If prostitution is rape, then it is logical to define prostitutes as women who are publicly available to be raped, and this is precisely the position taken by many police officers, judges and jurists around the world who refuse to accept that a woman who works as a prostitute can ever be raped.

Carole Pateman's (1988) treatment of prostitution in her seminal work *The Sexual Contract* is interesting in this regard. The book is essentially a critique of orthodox political theory. It sets out to expose the political subjection of women implicit in political theorists' *stories* about 'the original contract' and about civil freedom in liberal democracies rather than to provide a detailed and empirically informed account of women's actual condition in the contemporary world, and there is a sense in which it is misplaced to criticize the details of Pateman's account of specific contracts (such as the prostitution contract), since she does not really claim to offer anything but a highly abstracted treatment of them. But I think it is nonetheless useful to engage with her discussion of the prostitution contract as though it were an attempt to describe actual prostitute–client encounters, for pinpointing what is wrong with this account of prostitution *as a description of clients' lived experience* helps to identify the limitations of analyses which focus on domination rather than power.

One of Pateman's aims is to explore 'contract as a principle of social association and one of the most important means of creating social relationships' (1988, p. 5), and it seems to me that her groundbreaking theoretical contribution is not so much to have noted how contract serves to conceal relations of domination and subordination behind a fiction of individual freedom and political right (this point has long been appreciated by Marxist theorists), but to show how a profoundly gendered political order 'is continuously renewed and reaffirmed through actual contracts in everyday life' (p. 114). It is this latter point which has been so completely overlooked by liberal and Marxist theorists alike, and, in gendering the notion of contract and the concept of civic individuality and freedom, Pateman makes a huge theoretical leap forward. When she turns her attention to prostitution, however, Pateman is concerned not only to show how contract serves to *mystify* highly gendered relations of domination and subordination, but also to identify the prostitution contract as 'another example of an *actual* "original" sexual contract' (p. 199, emphasis added) – that is, a contract which allows for 'orderly access' to women's bodies, and so publicly 'affirms the law of male sex-right' (p. 208). It is this latter ambition, I think, which makes it impossible for Pateman to explore the specificity of prostitute use as a form of social action and leads her to reduce prostitute use to a straightforward subset of some ubiquitous 'masculine sexuality'.

For Pateman, the 'original' sexual contract is the foundation of women's subordination and men's political supremacy, 'the sex act' is synonymous with patriarchal power and mastery, and 'masculinity' is displayed and affirmed by engaging in 'the sex act'. Viewed through this lens, prostitution becomes an institution which 'ensures that men can buy "the sex act" and so exercise their patriarchal right' (p. 199). In other words, Pateman recognizes the prostitution contract as a principle of social association only to insist that it creates a social relationship identical to those created by all other contracts to which women are party. There is nothing in her discussion of prostitution which would allow us to see how clients might be distinguished from some general category of 'men' or how prostitute use might be subjectively experienced as different from engaging in 'the sex act' with a wife. Meanwhile, her treatment of prostitution as an example of an actual original patriarchal contract forces her to define prostitution through reference to the particular sexual acts which are contracted, rather than through reference to the *contracting* of sexual acts. Thus Pateman ends up having to dismiss the demand for commercial domination as part of 'the wider sex industry', and to insist that 'the activities that, above all else, can appropriately be called prostitution are "the sex act", and associated activities such as "hand relief" and oral sex (fellatio)' (p. 199).

Quite apart from the fact that a distinction between the demand for domination 'services' and for 'the sex act' does not always hold good in the real world (domination clients often demand hand relief or penetrative sex as well as bondage and discipline 'services'), Pateman herself has noted that 'prostitution is the use of a woman's body by a man for his own satisfaction' (p. 198). Now whether a man's satisfaction lies in acting out a rape fantasy upon the woman or commanding her to act out a rape fantasy upon him, it seems to me that, as a prostitute user, he is always using his economic power to attain 'unilateral use of a woman's body' for a sexual encounter in which there is 'no desire or satisfaction on the part of the prostitute' (Pateman, 1988, p. 198). It is this power of command, not the particular ends to which it is exercised, which must surely represent the central problem in theoretical analyses of prostitution.

Prostitute use is not a simple matter of patriarchal domination. First, prostitution differs from rape in that it is an institution which allows men to *contract* for sexual use of bodies, rather than taking those bodies by force, and social relations which are imagined and organized as (either implicit or explicit) contractual *exchanges* are sustained by and reproduce more complex forms of power than are implied by the term 'domination'. Second, the mastery clients attain within prostitution is not conferred by the performance of any particular sex act, but by the fact that they can contract for powers of sexual command over the prostitute. Neither the client who pays a dominatrix to urinate upon him as he masturbates himself nor the client who pays prepubertal child prostitutes to submit to being cuddled and having their genitals 'fondled' by him are re-enacting 'the original rape' and neither of them invades the physical boundaries of a territorially defined self, yet through their prostitute use both are exercising almost unbelievable powers over another human being. These powers do not reside in a penis weapon that can prize open and dominate 'permeable' flesh (to use Dworkin's rhetoric). Nancy Fraser's commentary on Pateman's work is useful here:

> Pateman follows a long line of feminist thinkers, stretching from Mary Wollstonecraft and John Stuart Mill to Catherine MacKinnon, who construe dominance and subordination on the model of mastery and subjection. In this tradition, women's subordination is understood first and foremost as the condition of being subject to the direct command of an individual man. Male dominance, accordingly, is a dyadic power relation in which a male superordinate commands a female subordinate. It is a master/subject relation. (*Fraser*, 1997, p. 225)

Fraser goes on to argue that this dyadic master/subject model does not provide the best framework for theorizing gendered relations of power in the contemporary Western world. We need to hold on to Pateman's insights about the ways in which social relationships are created and power relations are mystified by contract, but add to this a more nuanced vision of the possible relationships between gender, sexuality, political community and prostitute use and, above all, a more relational view of power (see Layder, 1997). This, it seems to me, requires us to address the specificity of prostitutes' political subordination rather than focusing on similarities between prostitute and non-prostitute women's condition, a project which in turn makes it necessary to look more closely at the imaginary communities to which both men and non-prostitute women belong.

Imaginary communities

> Like power relations, relations structured by *eros* involve the establishment of relations with others. They, like exercises of power over others, or like the objectification of being Marx foresaw in unalienated production, represent the creation of community. This community may be fragile and instrumental or deep-going and intrinsically valuable to its members. The form of the community depends fundamentally on the shape of the human nature and human sociality it expresses, and thus on the mode of interaction or practice of power within it. (*Hartsock*, 1985, p. 155)

In all societies, human sexual behaviour is both regulated and given meaning by a complex web of rules and conventions concerning matters such as who can have sex with whom, and in what manner, and when, and where, and how often. Whether these rules are framed and justified through reference to traditional, religious or scientific beliefs, or some combination of the three, it seems that they almost invariably reflect and reproduce ideas about the proper boundaries of gender, status/class and 'race'/ethnicity. Hartsock's (1985) discussion of the relationship between erotic life and questions of 'fusion and community' draws attention to this political dimension of sexuality, and, in his analysis of institutionalized homosexuality and social control in Melanesia, Creed makes similar points:

> In order to grasp the broader political and social importance of sexuality we must reject the old public/private dichotomy, and

> realize that the private is political . . . if we assume that every sex
> act contains an element of domination and subordination, then
> by controlling the occurrence of sex – by structuring who can
> have sex with whom and how – the inherent individual qualities
> of dominance and subordination can be generalized and assigned
> to particular groups of a population. (*Creed*, 1994, p. 67)

Because sexual regulations correspond so closely with the creation and maintenance of community and hierarchies within that
community, the legitimacy of particular kinds of sexual relations
often rests critically upon questions of the social identity of the
participants (their gender, their 'racialized' identity, their age, their
social status, etc.). To give but a few examples, in most contemporary Western societies sexual relations between men and women
are encouraged and sanctioned in a variety of ways while same-
sex sexual relations are not legitimized; in South Africa, under the
apartheid regime, sexual relations between men and women of differently 'racialized' identities as well as all same-sex relationships
were illegal; in ancient Rome it was deemed acceptable for a free-
born man to have penetrative intercourse with a male slave but not
with another free-born man (Veyne, 1985; see also Daniel, 1994,
p. 62, who observes that, from the tenth century, certain Islamic
theologians began to accommodate some forms of homosexuality,
authorizing in particular 'sexual intercourse with non-Muslim
males and with slaves'). Meanwhile questions of social identity
may in turn hinge partly on the establishment (or refusal) of
particular sexual relations. Engaging in same-sex sexual relations
often leads to a person's gender identity being called into question,
and in racist societies a person's 'racialized' identity/privilege is
often compromised by sexual contact with an 'inferiorized' Other.
The more general point is well made by Francine Twine, who
observes that the regulation of heterosexual romance has played,
and continues to play, a significant role 'in the establishment of
racial identities and in the maintenance of the racial order', and
quotes a Creole proverb which reads, 'Tell me whom you love, and
I'll tell you who you are' (Twine, 1996, p. 292).

Since human beings are conscious, purposive actors and not
mere bearers of structural roles or puppets controlled by external
forces, it is of course possible for them to disregard the conventions, rules and laws which structure sexuality in their society. Yet
those who choose to transgress sexually (by having sex with
someone of the 'wrong' gender, 'racialized' or ethnic identity, age,

class or caste, or by having sex in the 'wrong' way or place, for example) often do so at the risk of suffering very real material consequences. When people break social strictures surrounding sexuality, they violate the boundaries of community and, to a greater or lesser degree, become exiles or aliens from that community. Depending on the society, on the particular nature of the transgression and on the social identity and social power of the transgressor, the consequences range from mild social disapproval and/or exclusion from the rituals and benefits enjoyed by 'full' citizens, through imprisonment and/or corporal punishments, to violent death at the hands of the state or outraged fellow citizens.[2] All of this is central to understanding the meanings that are attached to prostitution.

Imagining the prostitute as Other

At the heart of popular discourses about prostitution is an obsessive preoccupation with the 'double standard' which most societies apply to male and female sexual behaviour, and so a concern with the relations that individual members of dominant and subordinate groups in society may and may not form with each other (that is, a concern with what Hartsock, 1985, terms issues of 'fusion and community'). As McIntosh (1978, p. 63) notes, 'unchastity is much more evil in a woman than in a man. For a man, it is simply giving in to his sexual urge; for a woman, it is a betrayal of her husband or father and of her whole home and family life.' A man who uses prostitutes is often considered to be acting in a fashion consistent with the attributes associated with his gender (he is active and sexually predatory, impersonal and instrumental), and his sexual transgression is thus a minor infraction, since it does not compromise his gender identity and membership of the imaginary sexual community. By contrast, a woman who works as a prostitute is viewed as acting in a way wholly inconsistent with her gender identity. Thus we find that prostitution and, by default, prostitutes have been, and still are, vilified by religious zealots as 'unnatural' (for example, according to a Muslim activist campaigning against street prostitution in Bradford in 1987, prostitution is 'an immoral act involving extra-marital sex in a most debased form ... [prostitution] is ... venal and promiscuous in character, devoid of emotional commitment', Siddique, 1993, p. 123). A statement made to the House of Commons by the Reverend Ian Paisley during a debate on a Private Members' Bill to reform the laws on soliciting in 1979 captures the essence of the way in which prostitute women are seen both to degender themselves and to place themselves outside the imagined sexual community of 'good' and 'decent' men and women:

> I rise to oppose the bringing in of this Bill. I do so because I believe in the sanctity of our women folk ... In all parts of this House and in all sections of the community there is concern that the standards that have made this nation and protected its women folk in the past are in serious jeopardy ... The person who has been caught up in prostitution ... has lost the greatest thing in life – the purpose for which she came into the world. All of us here today remember our own mothers ... We all remember the sanctity of the family and joy and peace that flows from family life ... This is only the beginning of a scheme to undermine what lies at the very heart of our society. (*cited in Smart*, 1995, p. 55)

It is not just religious enthusiasts who construct prostitute women as somehow not *really* women. Psychoanalysts have described prostitute women as suffering from 'sexual frigidity' caused by '*unconscious homosexuality* and *unconscious antagonism to the male*' (Glover, 1957, p. 11, emphasis original). This idea of prostitute women as suffering from a gender disorder is also to be found in more recent works (see, for example, Welldon, 1988, p. 128, who states that what the prostitute really feels is 'contempt for herself and her gender, and it is then that she identifies with her male client'). Paradoxically, then, the more that men's prostitute use is justified and socially sanctioned through reference to the fiction of biologically determined gender roles and sexuality, the greater the contradiction implicit in prostitution. In order to satisfy their 'natural' urges, men must make use of 'unnatural' women.

The fact that prostitute women are viewed as somehow 'degendered' and 'unnatural' in itself places them outside the boundaries of the imaginary community of 'normal' gendered folk (and of course male prostitutes who accept male clients are outsiders by virtue of the 'unnatural' and 'unmanly' sexual acts they perform). But there is more to prostitutes' exclusion than this. Both male and female prostitutes are typically considered to be dishonoured by their transgression of codes and conventions pertaining to money-making as well as sexuality (and the concept of dishonour is relevant to modern as well as traditional societies, for modern societies remain honorific in many senses – see Miller, 1993). There are some things which people cannot honourably sell to the highest bidder. Thus people who sell their children, their military capabilities or their friendship have traditionally been viewed as people who are willing to betray ties of community and kinship for personal gain and so as people without honour, and the prostitute is censured for attaching a monetary value to something which, like a man's capacity to bear arms in defence of his king and country, is somehow constitutive of honour. Even in contemporary Western societies non-prostitute men and women often speak with intense bitterness of prostitutes wanting and obtaining 'easy money', and I have watched a number of recent television talk shows on prostitution in which prostitutes were berated by hostile audiences on grounds that they had 'chosen the easy way out'. Carol Smart's (1995, p. 58) interview work with British magistrates in 1981 revealed that some magistrates also buy into this idea that prostitutes make 'easy' (as opposed to 'difficult'?) money.

Because they break strictures around gender and sexuality and because they trade in something which cannot honourably be traded, prostitutes are almost universally constructed as moral and sexual 'outsiders'. As was seen in Part I of this book, the status of prostitutes (women in particular) as Other is often enshrined in law, and they have historically been and still are frequently subject to controls which would not be imposed upon full, juridical citizens (required to register with the police, forced to undergo medical tests and examinations, their freedom of movement restricted) as well as refused the protection accorded to full citizens (Smart, 1995, Edwards, 1987, Walkowitz, 1980, Alexander, 1991). To say that there is a sharp and significant dividing line between prostitute and non-prostitute women may sound like a statement of the blindingly obvious, and yet this truism often gets buried in those feminist analyses which emphasize the commonalty of women's oppression under patriarchy. For this reason I want briefly to look at how, where and why the line between 'madonnas' and 'whores' is drawn, and who polices this boundary.

Sex, objectification and exclusion

Sexuality promises oblivion, pleasure beyond endurance ... Sexuality has many layers, masks, disguises, rituals, but momentary dissolution is always sought; dissolution of the 'I' into the 'we' ... The dissolution of the frail, singular, mortal into the timeless

> moment where life goes on for ever ... Oblivion is the motive of
> sexuality. It is its purpose. Love can be its obstacle or its catalyst,
> even its vehicle, but the *petit mort* is sexuality's reason. (*Milligan*,
> 1993, p. 1)

It is not necessary to be a Freudian to recognize that human beings
often, at some level, make an association between sex and death. In
sexual relations, after all, our physicality is unavoidably a focus of
attention, and our physicality reminds us, among other things, of
our own mortality. Thus, as Simone de Beauvoir points out, from
the most ancient myths through to modern literature, we find love
and death conjoined and, more particularly, an 'alliance between
Woman and Death' – 'born of the flesh, the man in love finds fulfilment as flesh, and the flesh is destined to the tomb' (1972, p. 197).
Many cultures also make associations between sex and dirt,
between women and dirt, between women, sex, dirt and death,
and construct elaborate rituals to regulate the contamination that
women's sex and/or sexual contact with women threatens. These
rituals can be thought of as ways of separating the woman as a
social being from her physical sex (for example, injunctures for
women to withdraw from certain activities when menstruating
mean that, when they *do* participate in those activities, they do so
as 'clean' and so social beings). Many cultures have also been and
still often are obsessively fearful of the supposed power of
women's physical sex over men:

> Woman is the siren whose song lures sailors upon the rocks; she
> is Circe, who changes her lovers into beasts, the undine who
> draws fishermen into the depths of pools. The man captivated by
> her charms no longer has will-power, enterprise, future; he is no
> longer a citizen, but mere flesh enslaved to its desires, cut off
> from the community, bound to the moment, tossed passively
> back and forth between torture and pleasure. (*de Beauvoir*, 1972,
> p. 197)

The 'sex' of girls and women must therefore be concealed from
men. They must be locked away in convents or seminary schools,
or they must shroud those parts of the body which might ignite the
flame of men's passion, whether that be their breasts, their legs,
their hair, or in the case of the *Hejab*, their entire body (the civil
code currently practised in Iran, for instance, includes Ayatollah
Khomeini's command that 'no part of a woman's body may be
seen except her face and the part of her hand between the wrist to

the tip of her fingers'; Tohidi, 1991, p. 253). The boundary of community inclusion and exclusion which marks prostitute women off from their 'good' sisters can be understood, at one level, as a line drawn through reference to these fears – hence the symbolic association between prostitutes and death, decay, the fear that, unregulated, prostitution will spread disease and lead to the decomposition of community (see Ian Paisley's remarks, quoted above; also O'Neill, 1997).

The fears which underpin these sexual boundaries are fears about woman as sex, woman as object; consequently, whether it is willingly embraced or forced upon her, a woman's sexual objectification places her community membership in jeopardy. For females, community inclusion is predicated upon a 'refusal' to be a sexual object (except perhaps for her husband or partner), just as the prostitute's exclusion is predicated upon her 'acceptance' of herself as no more than her physical sex. Thus we find literary examples of women who have been cast out of their community not because they themselves have transgressed any sexual code, but merely because they have become the *object* of the sexual desire of a man who is not their husband (for instance, Webster, 1965). Even today there are societies in which rape victims are stigmatized within or expelled from their community (Kannabiran, 1996). Again this seems to me to reflect a sense that it is impossible for a woman to return to the community once having been sexually objectified and reduced to nothing more than her sex. It is often either explicitly or implicitly expected that rape victims will enter into prostitution following the assault.

In modern Western societies, women who present in ways which are interpreted as 'inviting' sexual objectification or taking pleasure in it (for example, by dressing in clothes which call attention to breasts or buttocks or legs, by expressing a preference for casual and uncommitted sexual relationships, and so on) are widely considered to be 'proto-prostitutes'. They are 'slags', 'sluts' and 'tarts', and they are 'asking' to be sexually harassed and even raped. Mere possession of physical attributes that are associated with woman as sex, such as large breasts, can jeopardize a woman's status in the community. I have a friend whose body developed in such a way that, while still in primary school, she needed to wear a bra sized 36B. The terror that this visible mark of her biological sex inspired in her parents was such that they felt it incumbent upon them to beat their nine-year-old daughter and call her 'little slut' and a 'whore' should she dare to do as other nine-year-olds did, by, for example, wearing a T-shirt or a bikini top. In Turkey, formal and informal processes of social exclusion on these grounds are more explicit. Turkish women who transgress social codes on appropriate gender and sexual behaviour are effectively forced into prostitution: accusations against women who commit 'immoral acts' can lead to their compulsory registration as prostitutes, after which they must work in a state-regulated *genelev* (Willey, 1993). Meanwhile, journalists report that the responses of 'respectable' local women's groups' to the growing number of economically desperate Russian and Georgian women prostituting themselves in Turkish Black Sea ports and towns has been to turn to Islamic fundamentalism, and to mount protests including the burning down of one hotel from which migrant prostitutes work (Eurofile, BBC Radio 4, 27 June 1997).

The boundaries of sexual communities are policed in many ways, some of which are subtle, some of which are crude and brutal, and in affluent, industrialized Western societies, as well as those that are more traditional and religious, people grow up with a clear, even if often tacit, understanding of those boundaries. Whether they have been exposed to the notion of exclusion on grounds of 'whoredom' only through film and fiction, or more directly threatened with the spectre of expulsion by parents and other authority figures, there can be few women who have not, at some point in their lives, been made conscious of the precarious and conditional nature of their status within the sexual community. Even though sexual mores change over time, so that what 'good' girls are allowed to do and still remain 'good' changes, a boundary persists and is vigorously policed both within the family and in more public arenas. I was forcibly struck by the role that women play in policing each other when the eighteen-year-old daughter of an (ex-)friend of mine told me that, upon finding her in a bed with a new boyfriend, her mother, who professes to be a feminist, told the boyfriend to 'get out', called her a 'slut' and then screamed, 'Do you make them pay or do you just give it away?' This, I think, draws attention to another of the weaknesses of those feminist analyses which play down the dissimilarities between the condition of prostitute and non-prostitute women on grounds that we are all alike oppressed by patriarchy.

'Good' women are often among the most vociferous defenders of the existing sexual status quo, and the most unforgiving of those who transgress gendered and 'racialized' sexual codes, and, while some might wish to argue that such women are victims of false consciousness, it seems to me there are equally strong grounds for arguing that they are voicing a real difference in political interests. Though denied full subjecthood, 'good' women are nonetheless *included* as members of the imaginary community. The rules and conventions which govern sexual life in that community may be patriarchal, constructed by and for men's 'benefit', but they do also afford women a limited degree of control over men's sexual access to their persons. If men generously agree not to rape women, for instance, the corollary is that women are accorded the right not be raped and so a degree of protection from rapists. The story of the sexual contract which Pateman (1988) discusses thus implies the existence of a community which incorporates women. The women in this community cannot exercise sovereign rights over their own bodies and selves in the same way that men can, but they are nonetheless entitled to protection from those forms of invasion that are outlawed by the sexual contract which men have agreed, and it is their *right* to this protection which they assert when they denounce prostitute women. What is the significance of the prostitute's symbolic exclusion for analyses of prostitution and prostitute use?

Prostitution as social death

Slavery is, as Orlando Patterson (1982, p. 38) has observed, 'a highly symbolized domain of human experience', and the same is true of prostitution. In their non-commercial sexual encounters people are constrained by a web of formal and tacit rules and conventions. They are expected to observe the confines of their gender and social status and the restrictions that go along with their 'racialized' identity; they find themselves checked by the social meanings attached to their age and physical form and restrained in terms of the desires that can be enacted. Of equal significance, entering into a sexual relationship with another person often means taking on certain obligations and duties towards them, acknowledging their emotional and material existence, being connected to them in some way and also being *seen* to be connected to them. Commercial sexual relations are another matter. As a client, the social constraints on sexual interaction are removed because the prostitute, who is symbolically excluded from the sexual community, does not have to be acknowledged as a full human subject. All obligations are discharged through the simple act of payment in cash or kind.

The corollary of this is that the prostitute is constructed as an object, not a subject, within the exchange. No matter how much control the prostitute exercises over the details of each exchange, the essence of the transaction is that the client pays the prostitute to be a person who is not a person. Clients thus get to have sex with a real live, flesh and blood human being, and yet to evade all of the obligations, dependencies and responsibilities which are implied by sexual 'fusion' in non-commercial contexts. They get to have sex with a person who is physically alive but socially dead.

Patterson (1982) argues that a person who is socially dead is a person without power, natality or honour. The slave is not distinguished by the fact that others exercise property rights over him or her, for these rights are also exercised over people who are not enslaved (husbands, wives and children, for example) but by the fact she or he cannot exercise claims, rights and powers over things or other persons. Likewise, the prostitute, whether female or male, cannot be distinguished from other sexual partners by the fact that clients make claims over them or demands within the sexual encounter (people do this in non-commercial relationships as well) but only by the fact that they are not entitled to make reciprocal claims over or demands of the client. The prostitute is without natality in the sense that her real identity and personal history are invariably concealed from the client, who has no real interest in them, and she is without honour in the sense that the degraded status of the 'whore' dissolves any entitlement to the protection and respect accorded to non-prostitutes. Whether or not a prostitute is subject to relations of confinement, and regardless of the control she enjoys in the details of her working life, then, there is a sense in which prostitutes are socially dead within each transaction. In this symbolic sense, at least, their condition resembles that of the slave.[3]

Recognizing prostitutes' community exclusion and social death raises questions about the specificity of prostitute use as a sexual practice. What manner of desire is felt for a person who is constructed as a socially dead, sexual 'Other'?

Otherness, objectification and desire

There is, as Hartsock (1985, p. 157) observes, 'a surprising degree of consensus that hostility and domination, as opposed to intimacy and physical pleasure', are central to the social and historical

construction of sexuality in the West. It is writers in the psychoanalytic tradition who have had most to say about the inner dynamics
of a sexuality so based, and, in attempting to make sense of
Western heterosexual men's prostitute use, the works that I have
found most illuminating are those of feminists who draw on that
tradition, such as Chodorow (1978), Butler (1990), Hollway (1996)
and Hartsock (1985), as well as those of more traditional psychoanalysts such as Robert Stoller (1979, 1990). The kind of hostility with
which these writers are concerned is more than mere aggression. It
is, as Stoller (1986, p. 4) puts it, 'a state in which one wishes to
harm an object', and the harm wished upon objects of sexual desire
reflects a craving to strip them of their autonomy, control and separateness – that is, to dehumanize them. The 'love object' can be
divested of autonomy in a number of ways, but the fetishization of
body parts and the objectification of persons into nothing more
than body parts are probably among the most common strategies:

> The sexual object is to be stripped of its humanity; the focus is on
> breasts, buttocks, legs and penises, not on faces. Or an inanimate
> object, an animal, or a partial aspect of a human such as a breast
> or penis is given the personality taken from the object. (*Hartsock*,
> 1985, p. 157)

This kind of dehumanization and debasement is thought to represent a defence against anxieties around dependency, either in the
sense that it limits the degree of dependency transferred in the
sexual relationship (it is possible to rely on and emotionally need a
whole person, but not a 'piece of pussy', for example; see Hollway,
1996), and/or in the sense that it represents a form of vengeance
against those who have rejected or would reject one's emotional
neediness. Developing Freud's (1912) discussion of what he saw as
a universal tendency to debase the objects of sexual desire, Stoller
observes:

> To the extent that, in its earliest relationships to its parents, a
> child feels it is debased, it will, in creating its sexual excitement
> throughout life, reverse this process of debasement in fantasy so
> that the sexual objects are now – in disguised or open forms – its
> victims. (*Stoller*, 1979, p. 13)

Though we might wish to challenge Freud's notion of a *generalized*
tendency to debase the objects of sexual desire, an interest in
dehumanized sexual objects is certainly relevant to the analysis of

prostitute use. Indeed, one might almost say that the social construction of prostitutes as 'Other', which was discussed above, actually serves to provide clients with a ready-dehumanized and debased sexual object. There can be few men who have managed to grow up without ever coming into contact with this construction, and it therefore seems to me impossible for prostitute users to avoid some kind of engagement with the idea of prostitutes as a separate class of dehumanized and sexually objectified beings.

However, while notions of exclusion and Otherness are central to popular thinking on prostitution in just the same way that concepts of biologically based difference are central to popular thinking about gender, I want to argue that popular discourses still allow room for very different interpretations and representations of 'the prostitute'. (See Smart, 1995, for an interesting discussion of the different discourses used by British magistrates to explain prostitution and justify its legal control.) As a moral being, the prostitute can be imagined as utterly corrupted and corrupting (a knowing temptress) or as tragic 'fallen' creature and a candidate for redemption, while as a sexual 'outlaw' she can be romanticized, pitied or vilified. In film and fiction prostitutes are often used as the Other against which 'normal' society's moral values can be endorsed, measured or debated (Gilfoyle, 1992, provides a fascinating account of nineteenth-century American representations of prostitutes in popular fiction), and competing representations of prostitutes are often juxtaposed in such a way as to construct a division between the prostitute as sexual *victim* and the prostitute as sexual *predator*.

The different ways of imagining prostitutes reflect, I believe, the fact that individuals in any given society or culture can draw on a range of competing and contradictory discourses about gender, sexuality and morality in order to explain and give meaning to prostitution. Moore (1994, p. 55) has observed that 'cultures do not have a single model of gender or a single gender system, but rather a multiplicity of discourses on gender which can vary both contextually and biographically', and that 'individuals come to take up gendered subject positions through engagement with multiple discourses on gender' (see also Segal, 1990, Cornwall and Lindisfarne, 1994, Connell, 1995, Mac An Ghaill, 1996). It is equally the case that in contemporary Western culture there are multiple and competing 'discourses' on heterosexuality, so that it is possible to think in terms of a number of different subjective heterosexuali*ties* even as we recognize the institutional power of heterosexuals as a group (Smart, 1996).

To be sure, heterosexual intercourse is represented in a great deal of pornography as well as in popular slang as a simple act of male power, and celebrated as such, but this is not the only message about heterosexuality to which men and women are exposed. In the contemporary Western world there is an immense amount of literature and air time devoted to telling us that there is an association between sex and romantic love, and we are also exposed to images and representations which implicitly communicate that heterosexual union not only should be but *is* consensual and fulfilling for both parties. Rich (1980) and Connell (1995) have commented on the fact that social pressures make heterosexuality something which is, in effect, compulsory rather than chosen, but heterosexuality is not 'sold' to us on the basis that it is men and women's inescapable destiny to meet and live together as brutalizer and brutalized, rapist and rape victim, master and slave. Quite the reverse. We are socialized to believe that heterosexuality is a form of symbiosis and that a lifetime commitment to a person with whom we have absolutely nothing in common is made necessary and desirable by our different, yet sexually and reproductively 'compatible', genitalia.

Meanwhile, moral conservatism remains a powerful force, so that people are further exposed to a message telling them that sex in general (or certain kinds of sex) is sinful, dirty and disgusting. The legacy of Judaeo-Christian 'hierarchies of sin' lives on in Western attitudes towards sexuality. Furthermore, sexual acts can be and are morally condemned without necessarily being viewed as 'perverted'. Many people consider male promiscuity to be 'natural' and male celibacy 'unnatural', and yet hold unfaithful husbands to be immoral and monks to be moral, for example. All of this has implications for the ways in which prostitute use is, or is not, eroticized. As the following chapter will show, depending upon personal biography and the way in which clients position themselves in relation to these various and contradictory discourses on gender, sexuality, morality and prostitution, different forms of prostitute use will hold different meanings for them.

7

Eroticizing Prostitute Use

Robert Stoller's (1979) account of the dynamics of sexual excitement starts with Freud's observations on the tendency to debase the objects of sexual desire, and then moves on to argue that sexual fantasies perform a similar function in adulthood to that performed by daydreams in childhood – namely that they provide a script within which the self can be avenged and preserved. In particular, erotic scripts offer the opportunity to re-enact childhood experiences of humiliation, rejection, cruelty, and so on, but with crucial differences. This time the fantasist is in control, and can direct the scenario towards an ultimately satisfying outcome – orgasm. The traumas of childhood can be 'undone'. Sexual excitement is, for Stoller, a defence against threats to the sense of self, particularly 'one's sense of maleness or femaleness': 'to dissolve that threat, one calls forth the mechanisms of hostility ... such as dehumanizing others, and then decks the scripts out with mystery, illusion, and safety factors' (1979, p. 21). Because of this desire for vengeance and control, Stoller identifies hostility as the basis for most people's sexual excitement, and goes on to distinguish the key components of a sexual arousal so based as secrecy, mystery and risk. Secrecy is an important element because 'others would not appreciate the selfishness, the ruthlessness with which they are treated in our daydreams and our consciences must also be fooled. Secrets, from others and from ourselves, do that job' (p. 14). The secrecy attached to sexual fantasies adds to arousal in a number of ways, especially when the secret is carried 'beyond one's mind and into the real world, where the risk of the secret being discovered can heighten the excitement immensely' (p. 15). While secrets belong to the fantasist, mystery must be a quality possessed by the object of desire, something he or she is unwilling to surrender:

> The excitement, then, depends on a belief that one is forcibly uncovering what is not rightfully one's own (stealing secrets). Should the gestalt shift from mysterious to familiar, the purpose of one's hostility is lost; when a view of flesh is freely given, it cannot then be stolen ... there can be a dynamic of pseudo-risk (controlled surprise) that drives the process to the level sensed as excitement ... the oscillation making up excitement in mystery is between knowing and not knowing, seeing and not seeing, safety and danger. The secret here is the one that must be hidden from oneself yet – paradoxically – still be conscious: the knowledge that the story is contrived, the daydream manufactured, the pornography a myth, the prostitute a paid actress, the spouse or lover a player in one's theatre. (*Stoller*, 1979, pp. 17–18)

To be in control, the author must be aware at one level that she or he *is* author of the script, while, to be excited by it, she or he must be able momentarily to suspend disbelief. The script further needs to incorporate an element of risk and danger in order to excite. If Stoller is right to suggest that childhood traumas are re-enacted and repaired through sexual fantasy, then the fantasist obviously has to make the threat seem real in some way if she or he is to obtain a sense of triumph from mastering it. Without the imagined *obstacle*, the danger, the risk of failure, the script would lose its resonance. Yet the obstacle must be surmountable in reality in order that the fantasist can direct the script towards the desired outcome. When constructing erotic daydreams 'the problem ... is how to maintain a sense of risk in the story – the delicious shudder – while at the same time minimizing true risk' (Stoller, 1979, p. 19).

Although Stoller's focus on elements of hostility, control, triumph, rage, revenge, fear, anxiety and risk in sexual fantasies captures the essence of many of the different scripts that Western heterosexual male clients make use of in their encounters with prostitutes, his analysis of sexuality is seriously limited by its refusal to address the broader power structures within which individuals live out their sexualities, and I shall return to this point later on. For the moment, however, I want to use Stoller's theoretical framework to investigate the different ways in which clients construct prostitutes as objects of erotic interest.

This chapter draws upon empirical data from a non-random

sample of European and North American male heterosexual prostitute users, most of whom are white. The analysis offered here is therefore an attempt to explore Western heterosexual males' prostitute use, rather than to produce a universal or general account of the demand for prostitution. My aim is to show that clients make very different sexual demands and eroticize their own prostitute use in a number of different ways, and that these variations reflect differences in terms of how the individual prostitute user positions himself in relation to competing discourses about gender, sexuality and prostitution.

'Fucking dirty whores'

For some clients, the image of a 'dirty whore' is sexually exciting in a very immediate way, and such men explicitly eroticize both the idea of the prostitute's public availability and her instrumental, impersonal approach to sex. The dynamics which underpin their sexual excitement are, it seems to me, very obviously rooted in the kind of wish to harm with which Stoller is concerned, but interviews with such men, as well as the analysis of their written representations of their prostitute use, suggest that there may be several layers of hostility present in the eroticization of the 'dirty whore'. I will start by looking at those clients for whom the image of a 'dirty whore' superficially appears to serve as a form of liberation from guilt about their impulse to debase sexual objects. One white British client in his late twenties, 'Ian', talked to me about what he saw as his dilemma in the following terms. He said he had been 'brought up to believe that women were soft and nice, you know, that girls liked things like picking flowers, not dirty things like sex.' At the same time, he was also convinced that men are universally possessed of biologically determined sexual 'needs'. At the age of about twenty-two he had a girlfriend whom he described as disinterested in sex, Catholic and 'very straight laced'. One day Ian 'just saw' a prostitute's card in a telephone box, and it *'made him'* think about going to a prostitute. Eventually he phoned for details and went along to the address supplied. The woman was, in his opinion, 'rough', and he made a great point of mimicking her cockney accent as he described their conversation to me. He also emphasized the contrast between her age and experience and his youth and sexual inexperience. He described her as 'the one in control' of the situation, and said that he 'would not have insisted' on having sex with her if at any point she had told him to leave. But, he continued, to her it was 'just a business transaction'. Ian told me that he became increasingly sexually aroused by the idea of her sexual experience, and that, while he was actually penetrating her, he looked at her and thought to himself over and over again, 'You're a prostitute and I'm not', which brought him almost immediately to orgasm.

In telling his story, Ian marked the prostitute off from himself by stressing her mercenary approach to sexual relations – it was 'just' business to her (no mention of the fact it was 'just' a commodity to him). What the madonna/whore discourse allowed him to do, then, was to construct a story in which he transgressed yet remained a moral innocent. He was enticed, controlled and directed by a 'bad' woman, a woman who was already debased by her 'whoredom'. He did not himself dehumanize and objectify a 'nice' woman. The hostility he felt towards her as a 'bad' woman was of sexual value to him (the thought 'you're a prostitute and I'm not' brought him to orgasm), and it also freed him up to enjoy his own sexual excitement in a way he could not enjoy it with his 'nice' Catholic girlfriend.

Sexual hostility towards 'dirty whores' can also have distinctly homoerotic elements. Clients are often sexually excited not simply by the idea that the prostitute is debased and available to them personally, but also by the idea that she has been sexually used by numerous other men (hence the widespread phenomenon of men driving around red-light districts to look at street prostitutes – 'peeping' – which can serve either as a prelude to an eventual transaction or as a sexual pleasure in and of itself; see Høigård and Finstad, 1992). Receptionists in massage parlours report fairly frequent phone calls from men asking whether it is possible to purchase prostitutes' used knickers at the end of a busy working day, presumably because sniffing at the soiled underwear allows them better to fantasize about *other men* using a 'public woman'. The idea of the 'dirty whore' can thus be sexually arousing not simply because it represents a singularly hostile image of women, but also because it evokes exciting images of men – men's penises, men's semen, men's physical strength and toughness. The image of an objectified 'cunt' becomes all the more arousing when constructed and visualized in relation to other men's 'cocks', perhaps because these imaginings endorse a fetishized view of human sexuality as a simple meeting of disembodied sexual organs and so help to normalize the desire to harm others by reducing them to nothing but their sex.

The demand for personal command performances of live sex shows in which the client watches the prostitute have sex with another man, woman or child is also worth considering. Again, such requests are not uncommon (they were reported by prostitutes interviewed in Britain, Cuba, the Dominican Republic, Venezuela, Costa Rica and South Africa), and they reflect several strands of the 'dirty whore' fantasy. The fact that the client can command such a 'show' simultaneously affirms *his* economic power and *her* whoredom ('look what the dirty slag will do for money'). Where the show involves another man having sex with the prostitute, it is typically specified that this should be roughly done so that the client can watch the domination and humiliation of a 'filthy tart', and, where it involves lesbian sex, clients usually want to see an enthusiastic display of oral sex to affirm the sexual 'indiscriminacy' of the prostitutes concerned. In Latin America and the Caribbean, sex tourists want performances which resonate with their racisms and tend to ask for shows involving Black 'studs' and/or couples of differently 'racialized' identity (for racists, the spectacle of Black and white people having sex is taken as a mark of the white person's sexual 'indiscriminacy').

Unlike other subgroups of prostitute users, clients who are sexually excited by the idea of the 'dirty whore' are quite willing to see the prostitute–client exchange as narrowly instrumental and economic. 'It's just basically a cold kind of situation and that's it', 'David', a British Jewish client in his forties, told me. He happily acknowledged that he pays for a performance, observing that prostitutes 'have to be bloody good actors ... It's acting, and very few of them are any good, and that's why very few of them make a lot of money.' Indeed, David was clearly empowered by the idea that he has the wherewithal to command such performances. Because of his fascination and pleasure in his own powers of command, he complained bitterly about those prostitutes who do not put on a good 'show':

> I used to go with them, and they just lay there, like a dead fish on the slab. They just lay there. I don't know how you can get any satisfaction with a woman just lain there like that. You might as well go home and have a wank.

For a prostitute to simply spread her legs and wait for him to finish indicated to David a certain disrespect, a refusal to be completely 'bought'/controlled by his money/power. But this is only one way of conceptualizing power and control, and, considering the fact that I have interviewed prostitutes who say that they *do* just stand or lie noiseless and motionless while the client penetrates them (like Marlene, who even pretends to snore if a client takes too long), there must be some clients who take pleasure in this same corpse-like passivity – perhaps because they find an erotic charge in the idea of a woman or child submitting to sexual acts that they visibly do not want in exchange for money.

All the clients discussed thus far are clearly sexually hostile men, but they do *not* believe that it would be right or proper for men to go about raping 'innocent' and 'good' women. Indeed, it is precisely because, like functionalist sociologists, they believe that prostitution is *consensual* that they defend it on the grounds that it soaks up excess male sexual 'urges' which would otherwise lead to rape, marital breakdown and all manner of social disorder. The idea of powerful male sexual 'needs' enables clients of this type simultaneously to naturalize their own prostitute use and to construct the sexual licence alienated by the prostitute as a 'good' or 'commodity' which satisfies a perfectly reasonable demand on the part of the 'consumer'. Despite their intense sexual hostility towards 'dirty whores', then, there is a level at which clients of this type are willing, perhaps even prefer, to treat prostitution as a form of contractual 'commodity' exchange, with all that this implies in terms of negotiating details and limits to the sexual interaction. They want the prostitute's consent because, by voluntarily accepting money in exchange for her sexual use, she *demonstrates* herself to be a 'dirty whore' and so a dehumanized and debased object.

A sexual script used by one of Desiree's regular customers, 'Christian', a Black British client in his thirties, captures the essence of this desire. Christian had always displayed an intense sexual interest in the idea of Desiree as a 'dirty whore', asking her to dress up in 'sluttish' clothing and parade around the room in high heels, stockings and suspenders, and requesting detailed descriptions of her encounters with other clients. His preference was to perform penetrative sex from behind, with Desiree on all fours in front of a mirror so that he could watch himself sexually 'dominate' her. One day he arrived with a large bank roll – about £2000 in £20 notes. Again he wanted to position himself in front of the mirror, and this time he asked Desiree to kneel at his feet and fellate him while he held the wad of money out above her.

Stoller (1986, p. 4) makes a distinction between 'hostility' ('the wish to harm an object') and 'aggression' ('which often implies only forcefulness'), and, though I would want to insist that sexual force always implies a wish to harm, I think it is equally important to recognize that a wish to harm does not always imply a wish to use force. Men like Christian derive excitement from the idea of a woman (seemingly) consenting to her own sexual objectification, rather than (or perhaps as well as) from the idea of physically forcing a woman to submit to a rape. Fucking a 'whore' is erotic because, in these men's minds, by taking money in exchange for 'sex' she strips herself of her own humanity, and so 'legitimately' becomes nothing more than the embodiment of his masturbatory fantasy.

Disempowering 'dirty whores'

Although social representations of prostitutes as 'dirty whores' equip some clients with a ready-dehumanized sexual object to eroticize, there are other prostitute users for whom the image of a 'dirty whore' is synonymous with a powerful and almost degendered woman – that is, a woman who is active, unemotional, able to control and use sexuality for instrumental ends. The prospect of fucking such a woman holds no great sexual charge for many prostitute users. In the following chapter I will discuss the way in which some sex tourists manage to reconcile their prostitute use with this kind of non-eroticized disgust for/fear of prostitutes by conveniently overlooking the fact that the women they fuck are actually working as prostitutes. Here I am concerned with those men (very probably in a minority among prostitute users) who deal with their fear of being 'manipulated' and 'exploited' by 'dirty whores' by deliberately seeking out prostitutes who are very obviously vulnerable and powerless, and who eroticize this powerlessness.

Sometimes clients of this type want the pornographic fantasy of the 'dirty whore' to be embodied in the person of a woman whom they perceive as utterly degraded (street walkers tell of 'bag ladies' and tramps on their 'patches' who do brisk trade), or in street walkers who appear to be particularly vulnerable (visibly bruised, drug addicted or pregnant, for example). White clients' fantasies of 'dirty whores' are also often 'racialized' – I have interviewed procurers in South Africa, Latin America and the Caribbean who say that white American, German and British men ask them to find 'really dark, dark, Black women', often specifying that the women should not be successful, professional girls; in one case the client even explicitly asked for a 'dirty, unwashed, poor, very Black girl'. Clients like this also seek out child prostitutes. This segment of demand within prostitution is perhaps the most difficult and disturbing to countenance, but we nonetheless need to ask ourselves what could make a man want to buy powers of sexual command over the toothless alcoholic vagrant who will agree to unprotected anal penetration for a paltry sum of money, or over the barefoot and hungry teenage girl that a procurer brings along to be used in a hotel room, or over the frightened, drugged child who is confined in some small apartment and prostituted by a pimp. I think that some tentative answers are to be found in two examples of clients interviewed during the course of research for ECPAT, both of whom prefer to use child prostitutes not because they eroticize children *per se*, but because they eroticize the extreme powerlessness of child prostitutes.

'Cosmo' is an Italian-Canadian, an unmarried, semi-retired cabinet maker aged fifty-four who regularly practises sex tourism in Cuba, the Dominican Republic and Mexico. He openly admits to his prostitute use as well as to sexually exploiting children as young as twelve and thirteen years old. Cosmo is a man who is enormously ambivalent about gender. On the one hand, he believes in biologically based sex roles and that men and women are 'naturally' different. But, on the other, he furiously resents the way in which he was treated as a boy child. He says that he was neglected (his sister got all his mother's attention) and expected to be tough and deny his own emotional needs, and that all this has left him vulnerable to humiliation and rejection at women's hands: 'Men are like yo-yos, emotionally they're controlled by women. It's always women who hold the strings.'

Cosmo is quite ready to acknowledge that he himself is a prostitute user, but he despises prostitutes as 'dirty whores'. 'Who's to blame for prostitution?' he asks, and answers, 'It's the prostitutes isn't it? If they weren't there, there wouldn't be any prostitution. They create the situation, they make the opportunities, and opportunity makes the thief.' Prostitutes take advantage of men's biological weakness, and, for this, Cosmo says that he 'hates' them. He has used prostitutes all over the world, and he hates European and North American prostitutes in particular:

> It's all businesslike. It's by the hour, like a taxi service, like they've got the meter running ... There's no feeling. If I wanted to fuck a rubber doll, I could buy one and inflate it ... A

prostitute in Europe will never kiss you. In Canada, it's ridiculous. You know, if you go with a prostitute and you don't pay her, you know what? They call it rape. You can be in court on a rape charge.

There is no difference between child and adult prostitutes. Prostituted children also 'know exactly what they are doing', and the twelve-year-old 'Third World' girl as much as the adult Canadian prostitute consciously takes advantage of men's biological 'urge' for sex. However, unlike the adult Canadian prostitute, the 'Third World' child prostitute is powerless, and this has a particular sexual and psychological value for Cosmo. Where he feels controlled by experienced, adult professional prostitutes in the West, in the 'Third World' he is the one in control. 'Here . . . they're not professionals . . . they're affectionate . . . they're responsive. They even kiss you . . . Here, they don't even ask for the money. It's up to you.' In Cuba sometimes he gives the girl her taxi fare home and a cheap item of clothing rather than cash, and he enjoys the knowledge that, as he put it, 'if you don't pay a girl here, there's nothing she can do. She's not supposed to be with you anyway. It's just tough.'

'Hans' is a 62-year-old German who emigrated to Africa in 1961 and has lived in Rhodesia, Kenya and South Africa, and he too likes to use child prostitutes. Hans worked for mining companies in Rhodesia, but currently runs his own security company which specializes in investigating fraud and embezzlement. He is an unashamed white supremacist, but, though more extreme in this respect, his worldview was familiar to us from interviews with other child sex exploiters in other 'Third World' countries. He is obsessed by his own economic power (he constantly juxtaposed comments about other people's poverty with remarks about his own opulent lifestyle), obsessed by the idea of his own stealth, courage and *savoir faire* in this 'uncivilized', lawless and corrupt environment, and obsessed by issues surrounding authority and the law. Indeed, he had chosen a profession in which he *was* the law (tracking down white-collar criminals) and in which he saw himself as outwitting wrong-doers.

Hans also described a brutal and brutalizing experience of gender socialization in childhood, and has always had problems in his sexual relationships with adult women. Hans is not only wary of the power women exercise in non-commercial sexual relationships, but also hostile towards adult prostitutes who appear to him to exercise too much control over themselves. They are able to set limits upon what he can and cannot do to them and to 'use' him for their own instrumental ends. Adult prostitute women are 'out for everything they can get'; you go to see them and 'it's just business to them, you can do this, but not this, so much and no more. Strictly business.' Child prostitutes, conversely, are delightfully powerless:

> The little girls, ten or twelve years old, I wouldn't describe them as innocent, they're not innocent, but they're fresh. They don't have the attitude of the older whores. The older whores have gone down hill. They use foul language. They drink. They're hardened. The little girls, they're not experienced. They're not hardened, they want to please you, they don't know what to expect, you get a better service from them.

These men, as well as other child sex exploiters we interviewed, struck me as somehow fascinated and obsessed with issues of harm and of care – a fear of being harmed, a fear of being uncared for, a fear of their own and other people's need for care, and a desire to harm, especially those who are most in need of care. Though I have not interviewed a client who admitted to using vagrants or to deliberately selecting the most obviously vulnerable street prostitutes, it seems likely that such men would exhibit similar obsessions. The prostitutes they seek out are in no position to set limits upon the powers over their person that are transferred to the client, which is to say they are in no position to assert themselves as separate and autonomous persons. For the client who wishes to strip all mutuality of dependency out of their sexual relations, this utter powerlessness has sexual value. As utter powerlessness always and necessarily implies a need for care, it is logical to suppose that clients like Hans and Cosmo who fuck ten- and twelve-year-old children, as well as clients who use vagrant and drug-addicted women, also eroticize the *refusal* of care to those who most need it. Since child sex exploiters like those discussed here speak with great bitterness about how they themselves were refused care in childhood (they were physically abused by authoritarian fathers, told not to cry by mothers who wanted them to be 'little men' and so on), their abuse of the vulnerable can easily be fitted into Stoller's model of sexual excitement. They eroticize a particularly brutal reversal of their own childhood experiences of humiliation, rejection and cruelty.

Thus far, it has been shown that clients respond in different ways to the representation of the 'dirty whore'. Some are preoccupied by the 'whore's' sexual debasement and take direct sexual pleasure in the idea of the woman's 'willingness' to perform as a dehumanized sexual object. Others are preoccupied by the 'whore's' seeming power and seek out visibly disempowered prostitutes upon whom to wreak vengeance. For other clients, however, the fantasy of the prostitute woman's power is explicitly eroticized.

Eroticizing the prostitute as 'phallic woman'

Some men are aroused by the idea of sexual contact with a dominant and sexually powerful woman and, because the prostitute woman can be interpreted as somehow defeminized and empowered by her instrumental approach to sexual relations and her (imaginary) sexual agency, such desires can readily be projected onto the commercial dominatrix. Clients who pay prostitutes for domination are no more a unitary group than their straight counterparts, but rather display interest in a broad and diverse range of sexual acts. However, all the domination clients I have interviewed, whether their preference is to be hurt or humiliated, dressed as a woman or as a 'slave', anally penetrated or masturbated with deep heat cream, have something in common. They want to construct the prostitute as an immensely powerful, 'phallic' woman, for it is her (illusory) power to debase them as masculine and sexual beings which they find erotic. They are not interested in the idea of 'fucking dirty whores'. They typically insist that the prostitutes they use are not *really* prostitutes, but 'professional ladies'. They do not like cheap saunas but prefer to visit entrepreneurial prostitutes working from 'classier' set-ups. They state most emphatically that they never use street prostitutes, and this is because they strongly associate street prostitution with powerlessness and vulnerability on the prostitute's part. The fact that they hold a stereotype of street prostitutes as under age, diseased, drug addicted and/or being exploited by a pimp means that they could not act out their erotic fantasies or obtain sexual pleasure from a transaction with a street prostitute.

Like their 'straight' counterparts, domination clients are preoccupied by the relationship between their sexuality, their masculinity and their prostitute use. One of Desiree's regulars, a white British man in his early forties, 'Terry', provides a good illustration of this. The script that Terry wants Desiree to follow is well worked out. On his arrival she must tell him to undress and then padlock a leather strap tightly around his scrotum. He then becomes her 'slave' and begins to clean her house and perform any domestic tasks she sets him. It is he who brings himself to orgasm through masturbation (and cleans up after himself if told to do so), and his desire to touch Desiree is limited to performing foot worship and massage. The only physical contact he wants from her is the odd prod or lash with an implement, and, though he is actually demanding a very highly skilled performance from her, his sexual activities can hardly be described as an expression of male violence. They do, however, reflect his ambivalence and pre-occupation with his own subjective gender identity, and he uses Desiree as an objectified vehicle for addressing those concerns just as much as 'straight' punters do. Terry is obsessed by his masculinity and its relation to his biological maleness. His own reproductive organs fascinate him, as the following extract from a letter to Desiree demonstrates:

> I still tremble as I remember the evening that you took me into your service. My balls stir and my sperm production increases as I think of you and your exquisite beauty and total domination . . . I believe in the superiority of all women and that as a male, my only purpose is to serve them, and to provide sperm when demanded. Mostly of course, my sperm is required to be ejaculated as a tribute to their femininity, as it was with you, ordered to be spurted for your pleasure.

The symbolism of constricting and padlocking his genitalia before performing housework at the behest of a woman is not difficult to decipher, and, although in his role as 'slave' he praises women (their bodies are beautiful and hairless, they are by nature more elevated than men, etc.), the fact that he wants to construct himself as utterly debased, as 'slave', before touching Desiree suggests that he also enjoys a certain disgust for women. It is central to his fantasy that the woman shares the interest he has in his own locked and swollen genitals. Indeed, the story he tells himself is about a Mistress who is as fascinated and awed by his testicles and their semen-producing powers as he himself is. She commands the display, she gazes upon the almost literally disembodied symbol of maleness, she demands that he yields his sperm for her 'to drink or smear over her skin'.

The tension in his story thus centres around what the Mistress (for which read phallic woman, for which read woman who is sexually active, instrumental, and powerful, for which read prostitute woman) can and cannot get him to surrender. It is a sexual script in which he (displaced and objectified as sperm, the essence of his masculinity) is wanted very intensely. He suffers trials and tribulations, he undergoes the humiliation of being forced to perform 'women's' tasks, to worship a woman's body, yet ultimately triumphs as, in his imagination, the Mistress revels in the magnificent juice that she, a mere female, can never produce. More than this, it is only his semen and not his Self to which the Mistress commands access. She might force him to wait on her hand and foot, she might demand that he lick the toilet bowl or her own vagina, but she does not and cannot command his intimacy. He is simultaneously the focus of her gaze and invisible to her; simultaneously exhibiting and withholding himself (see Stoller's analysis of male transvestism, 1986, pp. 63–74).

Functionalist sociologists have claimed that, among other things, prostitution provides an 'outlet' for society's 'sexual perverts' (Davis, 1961), and it might be argued that men like Terry need the services of a prostitute because their sexual interests are too outlandish to be accommodated in a non-commercial relationship. But, in practice, there are women (and men) who have sexual interests which are perfectly compatible with the tastes of domination clients, and numerous non-commercial avenues exist for satisfying a penchant for sadomasochism, bondage and discipline, cross-dressing, etc. An interest in S/M does not make a person a prostitute user. Domination clients do not simply want a specific sexual experience. Like 'straight' clients, the sexual pleasure they find in their encounters with prostitutes is predicated on the notion of prostitutes as socially dead, sexual 'Others'. As one remarked, 'I go to Desiree for one thing – a professional service. I just want to relax. I don't want to know anything about her, that would ... spoil the fantasy.' In short, erotic value is attached to the fact that the prostitute *is* a prostitute/'professional lady'. Her 'professionalism' (that is, her 'whoredom') not only intensifies and corroborates the fantasy of a powerful, phallic woman, but also means that she does not have to be recognized as a full human subject. The domination client, as much as the 'straight' client, dehumanizes the prostitute, refusing to acknowledge her as anything more than her sex.

It is also the case that domination as well as 'straight' clients often draw upon sexualized racisms further to 'Otherize' the prostitutes they exploit. One such client I interviewed is 'Stephen', a white British man in his early fifties who was brought up in a working-class family in a small midlands town. He had no contact with Black people throughout his childhood or early adulthood, but plenty of contact with white racism. 'Looking back on it', he told me, 'I suppose everyone I knew was pretty racist. So there was an association there, Black people were associated with slavery and animals and everything, well, everything low.' Stephen travelled widely and worked in the Gulf States, the old South Africa and the USA. It was while he was in the USA that he discovered what he describes as his 'sexual masochism' and began to visit a white dominatrix who worked with a Black woman. Part of his 'humiliation' at the hands of the white dominatrix was to be 'forced' into performing cunnilingus upon the Black woman, while the white dominatrix heaped racist abuse upon the Black woman and taunted Stephen for demeaning himself in this way. This Stephen found most erotic. He has since regularly used prostitutes for domination 'services', and has a particular preference for 'Black ladies'. The pleasure he obtains from 'risking' his masculinity is heightened when it is a Black woman (associated with 'everything low') who reviles and 'controls' him, for ultimately to triumph over such a truly 'animalistic' woman (a Black phallus) is triumph indeed. Even in his encounters with white dominatrixes, the code word he uses to indicate that he has had enough is 'township', and this, from a white man who has lived in South Africa, seems to me further to evidence the highly 'racialized' nature of his struggle with 'phallic women'.

'Tarts with hearts' and 'sexual healers'

It was noted above that competing representations of prostitutes are often juxtaposed in such a way as to construct a division among prostitutes. One such juxtaposition is that between the calculating, hardened 'whore' and the 'tart with a heart', and again this represents a concern with the prostitute's power and gender identity. Hardened prostitutes are not 'proper' women since they use their sexuality in an instrumental way, but the prostitute with a 'heart of gold' is a feminine, caring, almost 'mumsie' figure. She listens to the client's woes, allows him to rest his weary head on her ample bosom, and then takes care of his bodily 'needs'. There is also a discourse about prostitution as a form of sexual therapy or

'healing', which some journalists and academics, even some prostitutes as well as clients, buy into. To represent the prostitute as a
kind-hearted 'comforter' or sexual 'healer' is also to construct a
permissive narrative. The client can tell himself that it is not simply
base lust which prompts him to visit prostitutes, but rather his
loneliness and/or *need* for care. But behind such narratives there
are generally sexual scripts which have as much to do with
vengeance and control as those enacted by any other client.

Take 'Guy', for example, a white British 62-year-old who
ardently defends what he terms his 'clienting'. He argues that
human sexuality is something 'natural and innocent' which has
been distorted by Victorian values and attitudes. Children are
taught to feel shame about their bodies and the pleasures associated with them, he explains, and this perverts and blights our
adult sexual and emotional lives. Like Ian and David, Guy talks
about his 'clienting' as a response to a 'need', but he does not
describe this 'need' as specifically male. Instead, he talks about a
generalized 'human' need for contact and closeness: 'None of the
discussions on prostitution ever gets close to looking at the causes
of universal (sexual) and other loneliness – in men and women. A
far worse affliction than unemployment which gets all the head-
lines.' This allows him to tell a story in which he visits prostitutes
only to relieve his physical loneliness, noting in one letter that 'I
would like to be able to go to some non-existent "comforter-
woman" for holding and comfort and breast fondling.' In another
letter he explained that:

> men (and women) may not want penetration so much as 'moth-
> ering', sucking breasts, holding and being stroked – yet this takes
> more time – so women would earn less per shift – so fucking is
> the best way for them to make money. If I could swop a quick
> fuck (15 mins) for an hour's close cuddling in bed, I would do it –
> in fact I'm suffering from a splitting up with a lovely woman at
> the moment and I realise that the best thing I'd like at the
> moment is good 'motherly' comforting; – a lack of this in early
> childhood is, I believe, a prime cause of my relationship 'failures'
> – I put too much (however much I try not to!) onto my women
> friends – I convert them into goddesses or 'the divine feminine'
> which I should try more to discover inside myself, so I'm told.

Though Guy insists that his 'clienting' has nothing to do with
issues of gender, the above paragraph demonstrates a singular pre-
occupation with *women's* power to grant and withhold access to

their bodies. He is lonely, he does not know the divine in himself, he is out of control and cannot help putting too much on women. But he has been *made* so by a series of women who have denied him; his mother, the lovely woman friend, the prostitutes who insist on quick fucking rather than leisurely cuddling. His own desires and demands are not problematic in this story, but simply presented as 'natural needs'. What *is* constructed as difficult is women's control and management of themselves as persons, which in turn 'prevents' him from satisfying psychic and physical longings. But while Guy justifies his prostitute use in these ways, a marked shift in emphasis occurs when it comes to describing what he finds erotic about his *actual* encounters with prostitutes. He states that he derives pleasure from the following 'aspects' of visiting a prostitute:

> arousal, deciding to do it, negotiation, viewing the choice of women, the thrill, the undressing, the lead-in, the chat, the prostitute disrobing, the condom, the touch, the fuck, the payment, the good-bye, the feeling afterwards (also <u>the importance of breasts</u> I should add, and gaze and sexual/seductive dress of the prostitutes). (original emphasis)

Guy went on to tell me that he had 'early paedophile tendencies for which I (partly) had five years' analysis with an eminent Freudian analyst' and that, when choosing prostitutes, 'my preference is for the normal male prejudice of slim, young, full <u>firm</u> breasts and large nipples. But especially young' (original emphasis).

It is not difficult to believe Guy's assertion that he is sexually and emotionally lonely. What is harder to accept is the idea that his 'clienting' is a response to this loneliness. Guy knows perfectly well that he is not going to get 'cuddles' or 'comfort' or friendship from the prostitutes he visits. Indeed, he openly admits this. Rather, visiting prostitutes is a distinctive pleasure in and of itself, a pleasure which is founded on the fact that his 'clienting' allows him to make his selection from a 'choice of women', then undress in front of the attractive, young, big-breasted prostitute in the sure and certain knowledge that she will not reject him. It is this control and safety which carries an erotic charge for Guy – his sexual pleasure is intensely focused on his own ability to *command* access to that which women normally have the power to withhold. For Guy, the prostitute as sexual 'comforter' is in fact a woman reduced to objectified (and so controllable) breasts and vagina, and his sexual excitement hinges on the hostility and vengeance involved in reducing a human being to those body parts. Again, prostitution is valued because it strips women of the autonomy and separateness which clients find so very threatening.

Secrets and lies

No matter whether the prostitute is imagined as 'dirty whore', 'tart with heart' or 'phallic woman', to pay for powers of sexual command over her is a transgressive act, and often carries with it certain real or imaginary risks (such as discovery, robbery, disease), risks which are frequently eroticized by clients. As one married man put it, 'the risk and the danger are part of the thrill. It is a high, very real and exciting, as is the possibility of getting caught.' To do something dangerous and get away with it, to transgress and then return to 'normal' life unscathed, with no one who matters (wife, parents, colleagues, neighbours) any the wiser, can be experienced as exhilarating and contribute to a feeling of personal power, and, whether married or single, clients often state that the risk of discovery heightens their sexual pleasure. In this sense, the kind of prostitute use with which I am concerned in this chapter appears to be similar to a number of other quintessentially 'masculine' pursuits which are experienced as both exciting and affirmative because they involve pitting oneself against an intense anxiety about the extent and limits of personal control and conquering it.

Clearly, clients vary in terms of how much of their excitement derives from this kind of risk taking, perhaps also in terms of how much their risk taking is entwined with a form of exhibitionism. The married client mentioned above stated that the risk and secrecy attached to 'cheating' on his wife by doing something 'so dirty' were important elements of his excitement. However, since he does not use street prostitutes but finds them through the very discrete medium of contact magazines, the risk of discovery by his wife (or anybody else) is, in reality, entirely within his own control. Providing he does not deliberately leave 'clues' for his wife, she will remain ignorant of his activities. Other clients seem to want to live much closer to the edge, and can excite themselves only by courting genuine catastrophes. Directors of public prosecution, world-famous movie stars, university vice-chancellors and other well-off, upright pillars of society, for example, do not need to crawl the kerbs of red-light districts in order to secure the services of a prostitute. A myriad more discrete options are available to them, and, as they know only too well, they stand to attract a good deal of press attention if caught. Likewise, the behaviour of Western men who have been exposed to extensive public health campaigns around AIDS and yet still offer to pay prostitutes extra for unprotected sex needs, I think, to be understood at least in part through reference to the eroticization of risk. For such men it is clearly not enough to play an internal game of risk with *fantasized* dangers. To experience excitement and a subsequent sense of triumph and mastery, these men need to pit themselves against real world dangers, against people and events that are truly outside their control.

All these points are equally valid in relation to 'domination' clients. Such men also use prostitutes to embody sexual fantasies that centre upon tensions surrounding gender identity, risk and personal control. Most domination clients are sexually excited by a story in which they completely surrender control to the woman, and the thrill attached to such scripts generally combines elements of both risk and exhibitionism. The control that they fantasize about relinquishing is control over themselves as sexual and engendered beings, and the tension (thus the excitement) in these scripts has to do largely with fears about throwing off all that is most powerfully associated with their masculine identity. As with 'straight' clients, the degree to which domination clients wish to run *true* risks varies. Some visit the same prostitute a few times before working up a script in which they are physically powerless in relation to her, and/or negotiate the script carefully beforehand, specifying the limits of their desire for pain or humiliation. But there are other domination clients who clearly cannot suspend their disbelief or obtain a sense of mastery and triumph over their 'inner demons' unless they place themselves in situations which carry real risks.

To go to a complete stranger's house, and, with no idea who else may be in the building and with few preliminaries to establish the degree of domination that will follow, allow them to manacle, blindfold, gag and beat you, for example, is hardly the act of a cautious individual with a strong sense of self-preservation. Of course, the degree of actual risk involved in such activities is debatable. I have never yet read a newspaper report or even heard of an incident in which a prostitute has mutilated or murdered her bondage client (although cases of clients assaulting prostitutes are all too common). However, it is not difficult to see how the activity described above creates a powerful *illusion* of danger, nor how the act of surrendering control so completely to a stranger and coming out not only alive, but also having been brought to orgasm by the person who held such power over you, could be experienced as affirmative. It represents the mastery of a form of anxiety.

Interview work with clients suggests that, as well as seeking to prove to themselves that they can control their own anxiety, there is another kind of mastery to be obtained through prostitute use. A great many of the clients I have interviewed feel out of control in the sense of not being able to manage and direct other people's perceptions of them. They express great anxiety about what colleagues, parents, friends, lovers, wives and strangers think of them; indeed, they often verge on the paranoid and make transparently grandiose claims about themselves in an attempt to ensure that I, as interviewer, will see them through the lens of their own narcissism. (Many insist, for example, that they are, or have been in the past, fantastically successful entrepreneurs, millionaires even, and/or envied by other men for their sporting achievements, and/or praised by women for their sexual prowess, and/or greatly feared or respected by their subordinates/superiors at work.) The secret transgression involved in 'clienting' produces a sense of being able to control other people's perceptions. The client knows that he visits prostitutes, but other people are not privy to his little secret, and the pleasure that clients take in this seems to me to be underpinned by very similar dynamics to those which make the telling of lies pleasurable to children.

To make someone believe something that is untrue demonstrates, or at least creates an illusion of, a kind of power over others. To keep secrets and tell lies is to manipulate other people's perceptions, and can thus be a very effective medium of control. Clients describe experiencing a frisson of pleasure on arriving home to be greeted by a wife who is quite unaware of the fact that, but a few hours earlier, he was briskly 'fucking a dirty whore', or who knows nothing about the 'warm and caring relationship' he is having with a 'tart with a heart'. Equally, domination clients take pleasure in, for example, returning to the office after a long lunch break to colleagues who are oblivious to the fact that his buttocks are still smarting from the blows inflicted by a PVC-clad dominatrix. To men who, for various reasons, experience other people's knowledge and perceptions of them as a threat and a source of power over them, this creates a momentary sense of invincibility, triumph and mastery. The secret, and his ability to keep it, is a mark of the client's power, and can also be a source of exhibitionistic pleasure in itself. Alongside the thought 'I must and can keep my transgression secret' runs the thought 'What if I were discovered?' and the pleasantly arousing image of an audience thoroughly shocked by the sight of him dressed in the prostitute's lingerie, or 'fucking a whore', or performing demeaning tasks wearing nothing but a buckled strap around his testicles.

The transgression and risk taking involved in the kind of prostitute use I am discussing here is thus almost invariably entwined with vengeful impulses. Stoller has argued that perversion is essentially a gender disorder constructed out of a triad of hostility (*rage* at giving up one's earliest bliss and identification with the mother, *fear* of not succeeding in escaping out of her orbit, and a need for *revenge* for her putting one in this predicament – see Stoller, 1986), and this is, I think, helpful to understanding the kind of vengeance in which clients engage. The prostitute users I have interviewed mentally inhabit a ridiculously gendered world (whether this is a psychological 'disorder' or a perfectly normal adjustment to dominant Western ideas about gender is the subject of another entire book), but, while they typically regard men as physically and intellectually superior to women, there is another level at which the client understands his own masculinity not as a harbinger of power and dominance, but as something which has led to his emotional victimization, neglect and exclusion from care. Non-prostitute women are depicted as powerful, vindictive, careless. They are berated for their power to 'incite' sexual desire and then 'withhold' sexual access, for their power to refuse unconditional emotional support, for their ability to withdraw freely from intimate relationships. In short, they are perceived as hugely threatening simply because they are in a position to control *themselves*, that is to say, to exercise choice over whether or not to meet a man's sexual and emotional demands. For a woman to be in a position to exercise such choice is for her to assert her separateness and so to arouse these men's infantile rage.

As has been seen, prostitution is valued because it strips women of this kind of autonomy, and it is important to reiterate that the client's pleasurable sense of being in control of females has little to do with the nature of the sexual acts which are commandeered, or the way in which prostitutes are imagined. We should also recognize that this kind of vengeance can be multi-layered. It need revolve not only around the idea of being able to make prostitutes surrender what 'good' women withhold, but also on the idea of how unhappy a wife or partner, or even a mother, would be if she knew what her husband/partner/son was up to. One client observed that prostitute use is:

> something you want desperately, but you know it is 'morally wrong'. We, as children, are raised with the belief it's wrong to lust for someone on a purely physical level. By the simple act of booking an appointment, you are dominating your past, exerting your will over your parents (or other authority figures). And you will be rewarded by physical pleasure. It is a power play, yes, but a power play against yourself.

For men like this, prostitute use is exciting not simply because it involves sexual contact with a debased 'whore', but also because this contact represents an act of vengeance against 'good' women's demands for monogamy and sexual restraint. The client obtains a sense of mastery and power over the management of his own sexuality when he thwarts his wife's, or partner's or mother's attempts (real or imaginary) to restrict him. But there is more to his pleasure than this. The secrets and lies surrounding his transgression excite him. They not only affirm a sense of control over other peoples' perceptions of him, but also disempower and so harm those other people. Each secret kept from the hapless wife, each lie told to the unsuspecting partner is an act of revenge against her dependency on him and his dependency on her.

The contradictions of 'clienting'

One of the striking features of interview work with clients is just how many of them wish to construct some kind of fiction of mutuality around their encounters with prostitutes (see Plumridge et al., 1997, for an interesting discussion of this phenomenon among New Zealand prostitute users). Clients often want to believe that, although the prostitute is a paid actor, in *their* particular case she enjoys her work and derives sexual and/or emotional satisfaction from her encounter with them. Thus Guy, the client discussed above who is sixty-two years old and seeks out young, big-breasted prostitutes for 'comfort' and 'suckling', assured me that 30 per cent of the prostitutes he exploits take genuine pleasure in the sexual encounter to the point of attaining orgasm with him.

Likewise, those of Desiree's domination clients whom I have inter-viewed all assert that Desiree derives personal sexual satisfaction from the performances they command. Even clients who eroticize the idea of fucking 'dirty whores' will sometimes insist that they bring the prostitutes they use to orgasm. Thus David (quoted above) assures me, 'I can tell when they're acting and when they're trying to falsify an orgasm and when they're not ... it's just experience ... I can tell straight away, their eyes, their body move-ments, everything', and states that, when the prostitute he is with orgasms, he enjoys the experience of prostitute use more.

Stoller (1979, p. 18) has noted that sexual excitement often hinges on a paradox wherein the fantasist must simultaneously remain conscious of the fact that he or she controls and authors events and yet conceal this knowledge from him- or herself. As a paid actor, the prostitute can be controlled. Now, for those clients who specifically eroticize the idea of prostitutes as paid actors or objects (and there are some such clients), this is unproblematic. But those clients who pay the prostitute to act as something more or other than a paid prostitute (for instance, clients who want the prostitute to play out the role of 'tart with heart', or 'working girl who has never been fucked by a real man before' or 'dominatrix' or whatever) are to some extent dependent on the prostitute to help them suspend their disbelief – hence David's comment about how prostitutes 'have to be bloody good actresses', and hence also the fairly consistent research finding that some clients complain about the lack of warmth and affection displayed towards them by the women they exploit sexually (see Graaf et al., 1992, Høigård and Finstad, 1992, McLeod, 1982). When clients bemoan the 'cold-ness' of the 'professional' prostitute, what they are really com-plaining about, it seems to me, is the fact that few of the prostitutes they use are very good at acting out the particular part they wish her to play.

The importance of a fiction of mutuality for so many clients alerts us, I think, to some of the tensions and contradictions surrounding the idea of control within prostitute use. At one level it can be understood as a permissive and/or eroticizing narrative (the prostitute is really enjoying herself and so it is OK to use her sexually; the prostitute is willingly sexually objectified and so she *deserves* to be dehumanized). Thus, as Plumridge et al. (1997) found in their research on discourses of emotionality in com-mercial sex, clients 'cheerfully reject information that would subvert' their discourse of mutuality. But there is another level at which clients' interest in mutuality seems to me to reflect a wish truly to control the *person* of the prostitute, rather than simply to buy her 'services' as a paid actor. Erving Goffman's (1959) notion of 'back' and 'front' regions seems to me useful here. Many clients express a desire to get behind the professional, public face of the prostitute, and *really* 'get to know' – that is, really possess – her. Sometimes this ambition is pursued by asking prostitute women out for dinner and/or other attempts to become 'romantically' involved with them; in other cases clients attempt to insinuate themselves into the brothel or massage parlour as friend, handyman, protector or 'slave'. My own interview work with men like this suggests such behaviour is very much rooted in the kind of sexual hostility discussed by Stoller and other psychoanalytic authors, namely a desire to intrude upon, know/disarm and conquer the prostitute.

When clients express a wish for the prostitutes they use to achieve genuine orgasm, it seems to me that this too reflects a desire truly to possess the woman, rather than simply contract for her 'services'. Because they (wrongly) imagine that, if a prostitute orgasmed, it would be attributable to their own sexual performance, to evoke a genuine sexual response in a prostitute woman is seen as proof of having penetrated beyond the professional 'façade'. It is a victory over the prostitute woman because she is imagined to have lost control.

All this, I think, points up deeper contradictions in prostitute use. All the many and varied forms of prostitute use that have been discussed so far represent, at one level, an attempt to manage the tensions which inevitably surround competing and contradictory discourses on gender and sexuality. Certainly masculinity, or at least the dominant form of it in Western society, is a ludicrous and impossible ideal – it requires boy children to be socialized into the belief that their gender makes them only half human, for they are expected to relinquish the need for care and the capacity to give care. This, it seems to me, is both a brutal and a futile act, and that brutality and futility is reproduced in prostitute use.

Though clients make very different sexual demands and eroticize their own prostitute use in a number of different ways, their prostitute use can most readily be understood as a defence against anxieties around gender, subjectivity and selfhood. These are typically men who are hugely ambivalent about entering into close and dependent relationships with non-prostitute women because they fear that, in so doing, they risk being infantalized, engulfed, out of control, open to rejection and humiliation. Prostitution holds out the promise of control over the self and others as sexual beings. But there is a fly in the ointment. Prostitute women may be socially constructed as Others and *fantasized* as nothing more than objectified sexuality, but, in reality, of course, they are human beings. It is only if the prostitute is imagined as stripped of everything bar her sexuality that she can be *completely* controlled by the client's money/powers. But if she were dehumanized to this extent, she would cease to exist as a person. Now there are some clients who eroticize this total annihilation of the sexual object's autonomous existence (men like Cosmo and Hans), but they are in a minority. Most clients appear to pursue a contradiction, namely to control as an object that which cannot be objectified. Access to touch and sexually use objectified body parts is not enough for most clients, they want the prostitute *actually* to embody their masturbatory fantasies.

Another way of viewing all this is to use Benjamin's (1984) insights about the relational nature of subjectivity. Benjamin holds that the dynamics of subjectivity are based on recognition and that the need for recognition as a separate human being is constitutive of subjectivity (Hollway, 1996, p. 98). This reliance upon acknowledgement from others in order to develop and maintain a sense of self is again a form of dependency, and:

> The most obvious way to defend against the anxiety of dependency is to control the one on whom we depend. This is where Benjamin's analysis of erotic domination begins ... erotic domination is the result of an attempt to control dependency transferred into the sexual relation. However, to control is an inherently unstable solution. (*Hollway*, 1996, p. 98)

It is unstable because to control another person completely is to strip them of the autonomy, separateness and independence which makes them human, and they cease to exist as an other who can give the acknowledgement and recognition which is needed. Viewed in this way, the conundrum which faces the client is that, though the prostitute can be controlled as a paid actor, as such, she does not *really* recognize him – to her, he is just another client. If he tries to get behind this, and force her to acknowledge him as himself, he loses his ability to control the dependency transferred into the sexual relation.

Though I think it is important, for practical, political and theoretical reasons, to recognize the ultimate futility of prostitute use as a defence mechanism, I would not for a moment wish to imply that prostitute users are sad, misunderstood creatures who derive no real pleasure or satisfaction from their acts of sexual exploitation. Money cannot buy them the unconditional positive regard or the absolute control over another human being that they would like, but it can buy 'a bloody good substitute'. Though prostitute use is not a sexual practice which could in any way help genuinely to repair the psychological harm caused by childhood trauma, it does provide a sexual arena in which rage, vengeance and hostility can be very satisfactorily (from the client's viewpoint) expressed. And this, I think, draws attention to the limitations, as well as the value, of Robert Stoller's analysis of sexuality as a sphere within which childhood traumas can be re-enacted and repaired.

To treat sexual life as theatre and simply assume that it is played out on some private, inner stage, with each individual having equal power to direct and script what occurs thereupon, is to overlook the fact that the real world (replete with material, not psychic, injustices, cruelty and inequalities) intrudes upon both our lived sexual experiences and our inner lives. Stoller does not address questions about the impact of 'racialized', gendered and economic power on object choice and the scripts available for the dehumanization and degradation of those objects. While some men and women may be in a position to mark off and control their sexual life in the way Stoller describes (choosing sexual objects carefully, re-enacting childhood dramas in the safe and controlled environment of their choice, experiencing excitement and triumph), others are not so fortunate. If we are to accept that there is merit in the idea of sexuality as a sphere in which control over infantile emotions and childhood traumas is pursued, it is essential to add the proviso that the likelihood of any individual attaining this kind of control over their lived sexual experience is powerfully affected by his or her gender, class and age as well as his or her 'racialized' identity, and even more important to note that, when this kind of control is pursued through prostitute use, the client is exploiting precisely these same structural divisions. In short, I would argue that, while prostitute use can be usefully psychoanalysed as a defence mechanism, both the clients' desire and their freedom to use prostitution as a psychic defence rests upon economic and political inequalities structured along lines of class, gender and 'racialized' identity and upon the legal and ideological construction of prostitute women as sexual and social Others.

8

Through Western Eyes: Honour, Gender and Prostitute Use

Who uses prostitutes? What little evidence there is on the identity of prostitute users all suggests that they vary in terms of age, occupation, socio-economic and educational background, marital status and nationality (see, for example, Kinnell, 1989, Høigård and Finstad, 1992, Chetwynd and Plumridge, 1994, Hart, 1994, Benson and Matthews, 1995, McKeganey and Barnard, 1996). Though there are male prostitutes who cater to demand from homosexual men (West, 1992, Cornwall, 1994, Davies and Feldman, 1997) and some women who participate as prostitute users (Karch and Dann, 1981, Pruitt and LaFont, 1995, Momsen, 1994, Monet, 1997), the vast majority of clients are heterosexual men. Certain groups of men appear to be particularly prone to prostitute use. The military is a case in point. Local and foreign soldiers have long represented a substantial portion of the demand for prostitution around the globe, and there are brothel districts in many countries which were developed precisely in order to meet this kind of demand (see Enloe, 1993, pp. 142–60, for a detailed analysis of military prostitution). Links between the military and the development of sex tourism in Thailand, the Philippines, South Korea and Taiwan were noted in Chapter 4, and it is also the case that the Vietnam War led to a massive increase in prostitution in Vietnam itself (see Long, 1993, p. 334). More recently, the relationship between the military and prostitution has been demonstrated in Cambodia, where the presence of around 16,000 UN soldiers in the early 1990s is believed to have fuelled a phenomenal increase in the scale of prostitution, and in Mozambique in 1993, where UN peacekeeping troops are known to have paid for the sexual services of hundreds of orphaned, abandoned and displaced children as well as women forced into prostitution as a means of survival (Kirshenbaum, 1994, see also Kadjar-Hamouda, 1996).

Brothels and informal prostitution also develop in port towns to serve a clientele of merchant seamen, fishermen and naval personnel, and similarly exist in and around 'pit stops' for truckers. Sometimes men who have migrated from rural to urban areas in search of work are the main source of custom in city red-light areas, and brothels in isolated mining areas, such as those described by Sutton (1994), are almost exclusively dependent on the custom of migrant workers. Prostitute use by businessmen, especially those who travel locally and abroad, is also widespread. The provision of 'call girls' and/or visits to brothels can form part of the 'hospitality' provided by business associates. Some companies are reported to 'reward' loyal or efficient managerial employees with sex holidays abroad (Mitter, 1986), and in contemporary China and in Vietnam foreign businessmen represent a key source of demand for prostitution (Ren, 1993, Long, 1993). Our interview work with sex tourists and expatriates suggests that prostitute users sometimes establish business links in particular countries precisely because this facilitates frequent visits to places where they can easily obtain access to their preferred sexual 'objects'. Tourists, meanwhile, represent another group which supplies prostitute users and, again, demand from this group can impact upon the scale and organization of prostitution in a given location.

Soldiers, seamen, truckers, travelling businessmen, migrant workers and tourists are people who (albeit for very different reasons) are away from home either temporarily or on a long-term basis, and those who believe that prostitute use is a simple function of biologically based, sexual 'need' might be tempted to take demand from these 'displaced' groups as evidence that prostitute use can be explained through reference to a straightforward urge for sexual 'release'. However, there is also demand for prostitution from local men, many of whom are married or involved in non-commercial sexual relationships, and, furthermore, local and travelling clients are often one and the same people – I have interviewed businessmen, sailors, migrant workers, sex tourists and soldiers, for example, who are prostitute users both at home and abroad. In short, demand for prostitution comes overwhelmingly from men, but there is no reason to suppose that it comes predominantly from men who are 'deprived' of opportunities for non-commercial sexual relationships, for prostitute use and non-commercial sexual relationships are very different, and often non-substitutable, domains of sexual experience.

The previous chapter focused primarily on furtive forms of prostitute use which rest upon the eroticization of secrets and lies, risk taking and the mastery of anxieties about self and others as sexual beings. The psychological motivation for these forms of prostitute use arises largely from inner struggles with social representations of gender, 'race', age and sexuality. In this chapter I am concerned with more public forms of prostitute use and their linkages to the 'primary *social* emotions' (Scheff, 1990, cited in Layder, 1997, p. 58, emphasis added) – pride and shame.

Ritual reinscriptions

Prostitute use is not always a response to a personal erotic interest; sometimes it is enacted for the benefit of other men and/or in order to heighten a sense of group belonging. Certainly, Allison's (1994) account of forms of ritualized male dominance in Tokyo hostess clubs provides a compelling argument to the effect that the practice of corporation-sponsored visits to such clubs contributes to the construction and maintenance of a particular masculine identity. Though hostesses in 'up-market' Japanese clubs do not provide 'sexual services', they do service groups of men in ways that consolidate and confirm a highly sexualized masculine identity, and Allison argues that the particular kind of male bonding facilitated by hostess clubs serves the interests of the Japanese corporations which pay for their male employees to be so indulged. A similar case could be made in relation to the many Western firms whose 'hospitality' for senior employees, prospective buyers, etc., includes visits to hostess clubs, strip joints and even the direct provision of prostitutes. There are also male-only leisure organizations, such as rugby, football and kick-boxing clubs, that arrange group outings to brothels, live sex shows and strip joints, and it could likewise be argued that this type of organized, group sexual exploitation is valued because it promotes an *esprit de corps*. The not uncommon practice of hiring stripograms for, and/or arranging visits to strip shows or brothels as part of pre-nuptial 'stag parties' in the West is another instance of highly ritualized sexual exploitation which serves to cement the relationships between a group of men and publicly consolidate their masculine identity rather than to satisfy any particular personal desire or sexual 'urge'.

As well as being arranged on behalf of groups of men, prostitute use is sometimes something expected of individual men by a peer group. The army and the navy are perhaps the most obvious example of institutions within which individual men are subject to intense pressure to become prostitute users, but merchant seamen and migrant workers can be placed under similar duress by fellow sailors/workers. As one British oil-rig worker I interviewed put it:

> They all did it, you see. I'd never been to a prostitute, I can't say that I liked the idea of it really, but it was a case of 'Oh, come on', and you know, 'Are you a pansy or something?', type of thing . . . You're living with these blokes day in, day out. You don't want to be the odd man out, type of thing.

I have also interviewed a number of clients who state that their first visit to a prostitute was instigated and arranged by their own father, or another older male relative. (The age at which they report having been so 'initiated' varies between fifteen and eighteen, and it could therefore be considered to constitute a form of sexual abuse by the older male.) Although even the most reluctant client may go on to become sexually excited by the process of selecting and then exploiting a prostitute, it is important to note that participation in the forms of prostitute use I am discussing here is not generally *motivated* by any particular sexual interest or desire on the part of individual participants. Nor does it involve sexual abandon. Men who leer at striptease artists in mainstream strip and hostess clubs or at private stag parties letch within what appear to be tacitly understood limits. They ogle, they call out tired, predictable insults and invitations to the stripper. They do *not* frantically masturbate themselves to orgasm in public. Likewise, when prostitute use is organized by men for boys or other men as part of some 'rite of passage', the expectation is for the initiatee to perform, rather than to lose himself in unrestrained, sensuous wantonness.

This type of sexual exploitation is grounded in a social pressure to be demonstrated and accepted as 'a man' by other men, and, if we are to understand how these forms of collective, ritualized sexual exploitation might serve to affirm masculinity, I think it is useful to focus on the *absence* of personal sexual desire or erotic interest. This, after all, is what makes this kind of prostitute use so very bizarre. What, one wonders, would it be like to be taken to a total stranger by your friends or relatives and expected immediately to undress and engage in penetrative sex with this unknown person? What would it feel like to be expected publicly and anonymously to do that which you have been taught to believe is both private and intimate?

It seems to me that, in order to meet such expectations, one would need to exercise quite amazing powers of self-control. A man would need to control his own body's sexual responses to the point that an erection, if not orgasm, could be achieved on demand, regardless as to whether he felt inhibited by the circumstances in which he found himself and regardless as to whether he found the individual prostitute woman or child attractive. This in turn implies that he would need to control his *emotional* response to the woman or child as an individual, and see her as nothing but 'a prostitute', a function, an object, since to think about whether she was young or old, pretty or plain, cheerful or miserable and so on would be to think about whether she was attractive to him or not, perhaps even to wonder whether she found him attractive.

Seidler has talked about the way in which dominant forms of Western male sexuality are grounded in a Cartesian and Christian tradition which views the body as part of the physical world which must be controlled:

> Men could only assert their humanity by mastery over the physical world, and by learning to dominate their passions and desires. It is this inherited notion of self-control as *dominance* that has been so closely identified with modern forms of masculinity. (*Seidler*, 1987, p. 94, original emphasis)

Certainly the kind of prostitute use I am talking about here seems to express a masculinity in which manhood is equated with the capacity to displace sexual experience from emotion, feelings and desires, with the power to control one's own body and one's own sexual and emotional responses to others. Indeed, I would argue that this is why collective and ritualistic forms of sexual exploitation are promoted in settings in which it is important that men do learn to distance themselves from their own emotional and physical responses. The military provides the most extreme example, for, in order to kill, soldiers need to shut off from their own, as well as other people's, humanity,[1] but there are also other contexts in which men are required to deny their own emotional needs (for example, where they are separated from family and friends and/or expected to compete intensively). Prostitute use can thus be a ritual through which men acquire and demonstrate to each other their capacity to control themselves and so reinscribe a particular form of masculinity. Layder (1997, p. 58) follows Scheff (1990) in noting that informal emotional systems function as 'a very compelling form of social control because we experience the pleasure of the emotion of pride and fellow-feeling or the punishment of embarrassment, humiliation or shame', and the quote from the oil-rig worker shows very clearly how conformity to this form of masculinity is policed through emotions of pride and shame.

These rituals affirm a masculine identity, and they also reinscribe the boundaries of a particular sexual community. Soldiers, sailors, oil-rig workers and so on do not usually bring their mates home to watch blue movies and gang-bang their wives, mothers or daughters. Their powers of mastery and self-control are demonstrated upon 'whores'. This is an important point, and again draws attention to weaknesses in feminist accounts which either explicitly or implicitly treat men's prostitute use as a simple extension of the patriarchal power they exercise in relation to all women. The kind of sexuality expressed through ritualistic prostitute use is, as a general rule, very different to the kind of sexuality expressed with wives or girlfriends, and, if you talk to men like this about why they feel OK about treating a prostitute in ways that they would not treat their 'own' women, they are quite clear about the fact that it is because the prostitute woman is an Other. When they visit a brothel they are, of course, crossing the boundary of community, but, since there is no real fusion with the Other, no intimacy, no desire, this is not a transgression which threatens or undermines that boundary. In their ritual acts of sexual exploitation, men publicly mark the boundaries of community and their own proper place in it. This kind of prostitute use is not grounded in a private erotic or sexual interest (although men who are introduced to prostitute use in this way may go on privately to eroticize prostitute use and pursue it independently), for it is very much a public matter. The primary motivation here is a desire to be *seen* as a particular kind of sexual and engendered being by other men. I want to turn now to prostitute use which takes a very different form, and yet also reflects an obsessive concern on the part of prostitute users with the way in which they are seen by others and so with emotions of pride and shame.

The pursuit of honour

> Honour is the value of a person in his own eyes, but also in the eyes of his society. It is his estimation of his own worth, his *claim* to pride, but it is also the acknowledgement of that claim, his excellence recognized by society, his *right* to pride ... Honour, therefore, provides a nexus between the ideals of a society and their reproduction in the individual through his aspiration to personify them. (*Pitt-Rivers*, 1977, p. 1, emphasis original)

The concept of honour as defined by Pitt-Rivers can, I think, help us to understand certain aspects of prostitute use. Let me start with an extract from an interview with a 37-year-old white British sex tourist in Cuba which expresses – among other things – his sense that a man's capacity to secure powers of sexual command over women is a measure of his social status and worth:

> It's funny, but in England, the girls I fancy don't fancy me and the ones that do fancy me, I don't fancy. They tend to be sort of fatter and older, you know, thirty-five, but their faces, they look forty. But in Cuba, really beautiful girls fancy me. They're all over me. They treat me like a star. My girlfriend's jet black, she's beautiful. She's a ballerina. She's so fit it puts me to shame really. I don't get much exercise ... Women in England want too much nowadays ... I'm a market trader, but I've done quite well for myself. I bought a house on the Isle of Dogs before the property boom, and I made a lot of money on that. So I'm residing in Wimbledon now. But English girls, they want someone with a good job as well as money. They don't want someone like me. They want a lawyer or a doctor or something, they want to move up in the world, and I can't blame them ... Cuban girls don't expect so much. If you take a Cuban girl out for dinner, she's grateful, whereas an English girl, she's grateful but she wants more really.

It is fairly common for male prostitute users to speak of women as though they are units of currency in a competition among men, and their capacity to relate to women as such is underpinned by two more general beliefs. The first is that the human male has a natural, biologically based *need* for penetrative sex with females, and that women's bodies are thus a resource vital to men's well-being. The second is the belief that a 'value' therefore attaches to each woman, and that this value is determined in a straightforwardly Hobbesian way, i.e., it is 'measured by the Appetite of the

Contractors' (Hobbes, 1968, p. 115). The more that a woman is wanted, the greater her value, and it follows that the capacity to command valuable resources at will signifies power and success. Successful men get to fuck the pick of the crop, while losers must make do with the fat, ugly, old women that are spurned by successful men, or even do without all together. A white British sex tourist in Thailand told me: 'I'm forty-eight, I'm balding, I'm not as trim as I was. Would a charming, beautiful, young woman want me in England? No. I'd have to accept a big, fat, ugly woman. That's all I could get.' He went on to make explicit his feeling that an association with a 'big, fat, ugly woman' is a public, as well as a private, humiliation when he said: 'I know men who are that desperate, and you see them arrive at a function, we have quite a lot of works' functions in sales, and they arrive with these dreadful women, and I think, "No, I'd never be that desperate. I'd never accept that".'

For prostitute users like this, then, a man's worth – as well as a woman's 'value' – is a matter determined through the eyes of others, and, while men may consider themselves to be quite something, as Hobbes observed, 'their true Value is no more than it is esteemed by others' (1968, p. 152). Pitt-Rivers (1977, p. 2) draws attention to this same point when he notes that 'the claimant to honour must get himself accepted at his own evaluation, must be granted reputation, or his claim becomes mere vanity, an object of ridicule or contempt.' The linkages between honour and power are as real for these prostitute users as they were for Hobbes, who stated that 'to obey, is to Honour: because no man obeyes them, who they think have no power to help, or hurt them' (1968, p. 152), and held that the power of an individual, like a person's honour, varies according to perception and is inextricably linked to the value which people place upon themselves: 'The Value, or Worth of a man, is as of all other things, his Price; that is to say how much would be given for the use of his Power: and therefore is not absolute; but a thing dependant on the need and judgement of another' (1968, p. 152). Hobbes divided this power into the natural (the eminence of faculties of body or mind) and the 'instrumentall' (the means and instruments to acquire more power), and this too finds resonance with the worldview of many prostitute users (Brace and O'Connell Davidson, 1996).

Power is demonstrated through a man's ability to command resources/women, and this power of command can derive from his natural qualities (if a man is 'trim', youthful and has a full head of hair, he will be able to attract beautiful girls) or from possession of certain means and instruments (such as those possessed by 'lawyers and doctors'). Honour and power are conjoined, then, for the power to command the sexual attentions of a desirable (highly valued) woman affirms the man's value not only in his own eyes but also in the eyes of other men like himself. The 'charming, beautiful, young woman' at his side is a visible measure of his success, and confirms his estimation of his own worth in a way which *has* to be acknowledged and recognized by society. As a series of enchanting women wilt before him, or as he walks into the works' function with a gorgeous nymphet on his arm, he personifies an ideal of manly success.

I do not wish to suggest that *all* Western men subscribe to this ideal of manhood (as Pitt-Rivers, 1977, p. 2, points out, there is not always a uniform consensus around moral values and social ideals in any one society and, as a consequence, 'the individual's worth is not the same in the view of one group as in that of another, while the political authorities may view him in a different light again'), but simply to argue that sexuality is viewed by some as a medium through which honour is pursued and lost. How does this relate to the practice of sex tourism?

Sex tourism and the competition for honour

Notions of honour and shame are linked to basic ideas of community inclusion and exclusion, for, as Patterson observes:

> To belong to a community is to have a sense of one's position among one's fellow members, to feel the need to assert and defend that position, and to feel a sense of satisfaction if that claimed position is accepted by others and a sense of shame if it is rejected ... *those who do not compete for honor, or who are not expected to do so are in a real sense outside the social order. (Patterson,* 1982, p. 79, emphasis added)

Now if men imagine themselves part of a community within which honour is accorded to those who can sexually command female bodies of 'value' (i.e., bodies which are youthful and conform to very specific criteria of desirability), then the inability to be a serious competitor for such female bodies places a man, in this very real sense, outside the community of men he imagines. On the basis of observational work in sex tourist resorts, I would say that a sizeable portion of demand for sex tourism comes from men aged over forty, and there is also a smaller, but nonetheless visible, segment of demand from men who might be deemed physically disabled, disfigured or 'abnormal' (for instance, men who are mountainously obese). It is often the case that such men feel that their own ageing and/or disability and/or 'ugliness' excludes them from a competitive struggle among men, or else disadvantages them so substantially that they can only be dishonoured through their attempts to compete.

Sex tourism represents a means through which they can attain a sense of inclusion and so a sense of belonging to their imagined community of 'real men'. Look, for a moment, at how such men contrast their experiences at home against their experience in sex tourist resorts. A British man approaching forty told me: 'When I was in me twenties, like, I'd go down to the disco and that was that, really. I'd pick a girl up and at the end of the night, we'd have sex ... It's not like that now.' In Thailand, however, he is 'surrounded by girls'. A 52-year-old Canadian in Costa Rica said: 'In the Third World, a man has no age ... In Canada, a seventeen-year-old would spit in my face just for looking at her, but here thirteen-year-olds smile at me in a come-on way.' Another British sex tourist in Thailand who had a withered leg as a result of childhood polio spoke at length about how difficult it was for him to find a girlfriend in England – 'They don't look twice at me, not with this leg.' He then went on to say that all his Thai 'girlfriends' look like 'models' and that he returns to Thailand year after year because 'Out here I can take me pick. I really live like a playboy.' Social class can also be viewed as an impediment to the pursuit of masculine honour, as the comments (quoted above) of the sex tourist to Cuba show.

It is important to emphasize the fact that these men are not just lonely people looking for sexual affection or romance. Sex tourism and/or prostitute use more generally is almost never the only possible option for physical closeness available to such men, for the simple reason that the world is also full of single and lonely women, some of whom are also older, disabled, disfigured, obese or considered to be 'ugly', who also want to find romance and sexual affection. The real problem for the kind of sex tourists I am discussing here is not that they are unable to find sexual partners back home, but rather that, while they themselves may be disabled or obese or disfigured or ugly or old, they do not care to have sex with a woman who shares these qualities. It is only when they attempt to win powers of sexual command over young and 'beautiful' women that their own physical characteristics become a burden to them.[2]

These men's reluctance to form sexual relationships with women like themselves is, it seems to me, simultaneously understandable and extraordinary. I do not think it strange that they look upon 'beautiful' young women as objects of sexual desire. After all, men who are obese, or who are considered to be ugly, or disfigured, or disabled, as well as men whose advancing years have taken a physical toll, have been socialized in exactly the same way that their firm, fit, 'handsome', able-bodied, younger brethren have been socialized, and can therefore be expected to attach erotic value to female bodies which conform to cultural ideals of sexual beauty. What strikes me as odd about these sex tourists is, first, the extent to which they detach sexuality from personhood and so are able to rank and grade females through reference to their physical form alone, and, second, their exclusive and uncompromising interest in attaining powers of command over women as such objects. And it is not only old, fat and 'ugly' sex tourists who objectify women in this way and feel thwarted as a consequence. Even sex tourists who are perfectly normal-looking individuals (and the vast majority of sex tourists are just ordinary men), who are not actually old (and again, it is only a small minority of sex tourists who could be described as elderly or decrepit) and who do not find it difficult to establish sexual relationships with equally normal and ordinary women back home place enormous value on the idea of being able to command sexual access to an unending series of 'gorgeous' females.

This says something to me about the way in which they view their own sexuality, as well as how they view women. I have interviewed domestic prostitute users as well as sex tourists who draw parallels between owning a car and sexual experience (fucking a new woman is like driving a new car, visiting a prostitute is like taking your car to the garage for a service, having a beautiful girlfriend is like owning a Porsche, etc.), and it is the idea of a sexuality so utterly objectified and so completely alienated from self that I find bizarre. Given that these men view their own sexuality in such terms, however, their sex tourism can be understood, at one level, as a simple means of attaining the access to female bodies of 'value' which would otherwise be denied or restricted. They use their 'instrumental'/economic power to buy time with large quantities of women and/or girls who conform to socially constructed ideals of female sexual beauty. But I think there is more to it than this. It seems to me that through their sex tourism they also pursue a sense of inclusion and prestige in a masculine community which otherwise escapes them.

This would help to explain another of the observable and peculiar features of sex tourism. Like the ritualistic form of prostitute use discussed above, and unlike the furtive and secretive forms of prostitute use described in the previous chapter, sex tourism often has an almost collective character. For many men, the joy of sex tourism is not confined to bed or brothel, but also found in the company of other men. Some sex tourists travel in groups, but even those who travel alone quickly team up with men like themselves with whom they drink and share tales of glory. Indeed, many more hours are spent with other men in ludicrous drink-sodden posturing and boasting bravado than are actually spent interacting with their 'dream women', for the fact of the matter is that language barriers generally prevent communication with the prostitutes they exploit. Even when these barriers are removed, prostitute and sex tourist have little to say to each other, and, though sex tourists tend to think of themselves as insatiably virile studs ('I'm a walking sex machine', one told me), the amount of time they actually want to spend in sexual congress is limited.

Ambiguity, racism and esteem

When Pateman (1988, p. 199) argues that 'the exemplary display of masculinity is to engage in 'the sex act' ... The institution of prostitution ensures that men can buy 'the sex act' and so exercise their patriarchal right', she suggests that the relationship between exercising powers of sexual command over a woman's body and the affirmation of masculinity is a simple and direct one. A focus on the concept of honour helps us to appreciate the fact that the relationship between prostitute use and gender identity is rather more complex than this. Honour, as both Pitt-Rivers (1977) and Patterson (1982) have observed, is an elusive concept. It is not a quality which attaches to particular acts ('acting honourably is not the same thing as *being* honorable'; Patterson, 1982, p. 80), nor does the bestowal of honours upon a person necessarily imply that they are honourable. Medals won for sporting achievements or degrees awarded for academic performance are honours bestowed. If it transpires that the person so honoured cheated or paid for these tributes, they become worthless in honorific terms. Equally, for men who pursue honour by competing to command 'beautiful' women, the act of sexual 'mastery' is not enough, on its own, to demonstrate themselves men of honour. Rapists 'master' women's bodies, but they are rarely honoured by other men. Equally, to pay to succeed in a competition will increase a person's honour neither in their own eyes nor in the eyes of society.

Sex tourists are not a homogeneous group in terms of their social identities or their sexual interests, and here I want to focus on one particular subgroup of Western male sex tourists – those who wish to deny that their sexual encounters with local people take place on a purely commercial basis and to imagine themselves instead as chosen and sexually desired by the prostitutes they exploit. Consider, for example, a 'guidebook' written by a sex tourist, Bruce Cassirer. Like many of the Western male sex tourists I have interviewed in Thailand, Latin America and the Caribbean, Cassirer clearly thinks a very great deal of himself. He hands out folksy cautions ('remember, wherever you are, you are an ambassador', 1992, p. 78) and even takes it upon himself to write a section on 'Sexual disease, Aids and other hazards', in which he includes such gems as 'an observant male can notice a certain uneasiness of the infected female. Latent syphilis in the female can possibly be detected by unusual nervousness and a shaky and illegible handwriting' (1992, p. 215). But what is most striking about Cassirer is that he never once actually uses the term 'prostitution' or 'prostitute', despite providing detailed (though often inaccurate) information about formally organized and informal prostitution in six countries. His descriptions of his experiences in brothels are interwoven with talk of 'one night stands' and 'lusty ladies' who 'live for sex':

> [This travel book will tell you about] places where the women will chase and fight over you, and your biggest problem will not be *who* but *when*. These are places where being an American male is a pleasure, the beaches ... aren't polluted, the hotels are reasonable, the environment exciting, young women are appreciative, and you are a KING. (*Cassirer*, 1992, p. xiv, emphasis original)

Given that Cassirer's 'guidebook' merely communicates to us the fact that, when he offers to pay in cash or kind, women who are economically desperate will have sex with him, its nauseatingly self-congratulatory tone seems misplaced. But for him, like so many sex tourists, the beauty of the form of prostitution he has stumbled upon is that it lends a certain ambiguity to the prostitution contract. This ambiguity stems from the fact that prostitute–client transactions in most sex tourist destinations are loosely specified and diffuse exchanges within which prostitutes will often perform the kind of acts that in the West are taken to signify genuine affection (kissing, cuddling, sleeping in the bed with clients, providing physical care such as rubbing in sun-tan lotion, washing their hair or feet, and so on), and which an experienced Western prostitute would never perform. Furthermore, the existence of an informal prostitution sector means that sex tourists, expatriates and foreign businessmen do not have to go into a brothel, or even into a 'tacky' go-go bar, in order to pick up a prostitute, nor do they have to negotiate a 'deal' in advance (the two things which, to most Westerners, are viewed as integral to 'prostitution'). They can therefore interpret the process of 'picking up' as confirmation of a mutual attraction rather than as initiating a commercial sexual encounter, and, when the adult or child later confides their desperate need for cash, the client constructs the act of giving them money not as payment for services rendered, but as a gesture of compassion or generosity. All of this makes it possible for clients of this type to tell themselves that they are not *really* involved in prostitution, and so not really buying tributes, even as they pay a series of prostitutes for sex.

This also helps to explain the fact that men who do not and would not use prostitutes in the West can become prostitute users in sex tourist destinations. Take the case of a mature student, a white British man aged thirty-five, who came to see me following a lecture I had given on sex tourism. He wanted to tell me that he had been backpacking in Thailand, where he had entered into sexual relationships with two Thai women (one of whom was almost fifteen years younger than he), both of whom worked as prostitutes, but that he was not a sex tourist. I asked him whether he would let me interview him about his experiences and he agreed. In the interview he explained to me that one of these women worked in a bar brothel, and that he had paid a 'bar fine' to the bar owner for every night he had spent with her. He had also had sex with her. But, he insisted, the sexual relationship they had was based on mutual attraction. He had also paid money to the other woman, but he was not paying her for sex, of course, since she too was *genuinely* attracted to him:

Basically the thing was, she basically said to me, 'I'm going to have to go and sleep with somebody because I need the money.' So we were left in this awful situation where ... she was going to have to sleep with somebody unless I paid her money not to ... So we talked about it and we agreed, I would give her money so that she didn't go off and sleep with somebody.

Throughout the interview, the student protested that the women were not acting on an instrumental basis:

I suppose ... there had to be a power thing, because I was the Western guy that walked into the bar with money and she didn't have money. But I'm fairly certain that's not the reason she went off with me. I just don't believe it was. I'm a reasonable judge of character and I wouldn't have gone off with just an out and out girl that was going to be with me just for money. I think I'd have sussed her out.

So I asked him why he would not have gone off with a girl that was just going to be with him for money (that is, a prostitute). He replied as follows: 'Why? Because it wouldn't be a turn on. There would be no point to it, as attractive as they are ... If I ended up in bed with someone, I'd have to feel there was more to it than that.' In other words, he needed to believe in himself as genuinely chosen (so truly esteemed) in order to enjoy his fuck, and the ambiguous nature of the prostitution contract he entered into allowed room for this self-deception. However, he appears to have had something of a struggle to suspend his disbelief and convince himself that he was genuinely desired by the women he used:

I actually had this conversation with my friend. I said, 'Have you noticed that a lot of the guys walking with Thai girls are not attractive guys?' and that disillusioned me, because I'm thinking, 'I hope she's with me because of who I am.'

Few sex tourists are blind to the fact that 'lovely' girls in Thailand, or wherever they happen to be, appear to be completely indiscriminate about their sexual partners, and they often comment on the fact that you see 'really beautiful girls' with 'fat, old blokes'. Sex tourists thus need to find a way in which to view themselves as esteemed and successful in a competition with other men even in the face of the knowledge that the 'beautiful' girls they bed actually work as prostitutes. It is here that racism comes into play.

Highly sexualized forms of racism are espoused by sex tourists; indeed, sex tourism is perhaps *the* exemplar of the white West's 'romantic fantasy of the "primitive" and . . . concrete search for a real primitive paradise, whether that location be a country or a body, a dark continent or dark flesh' (hooks, 1992, p. 27).

When sex tourists visit South-East Asian countries they view local women as naturally subservient and eager to please them sexually. When they visit Caribbean and Latin American countries they view local women as animalistic and hypersexual. Without exception, the sex tourists we interviewed reproduced the classic racist opposition between the 'primitive', who exists in some 'state of nature', and the 'civilized', constrained by powerful legal and moral codes, in their (mis)understandings of their host cultures. Prostitutes are not prostitutes out of economic desperation, then, and there is nothing untoward about a fourteen-year-old girl going off to have sex with a man old enough to be her grandfather or a 'beautiful' girl going off with an ugly man. It does not mean they are like Western prostitutes (far less that they should be considered child prostitutes). They are just doing what comes 'naturally' to them.

On top of this, white Western sex tourists consider that their own whiteness, in and of itself, is enough to make them irresistibly sexually desirable to 'Third World' women and girls. They comment on the 'fact' that all women in the countries they visit want to marry a Western man. Since they want to be wanted for more than a 'green card' or its equivalent, they tell themselves that their white skin is 'valued' for other reasons, and that to be white skinned is to be socially constructed as sexually desirable in the countries they visit. There is an element of truth in this, inasmuch as they generally practice their sex tourism in places where one of the legacies of plantation slavery and/or colonialism is what James (1993) terms a 'pigmentocracy', within which white men have historically held out and still do hold out the promise of some kind of social mobility for women of colour and their children. As a consequence, certain phenotypical characteristics associated with whiteness (such as straight hair, blue or green eyes, light skin) may be sexually prized. But prizing certain characteristics is hardly the same as having an indiscriminate fetish for whiteness. When we talked to women and girls in Latin America and the Caribbean who did say that they found white men attractive about what that meant to them, it meant that they fantasized about having a boyfriend who looks like Leonardo DiCaprio or John Travolta, not one who looks like Benny Hill or Bernard Manning.

Sex tourists use racism to shore up the fantasy that they are genuinely sexually desired by the prostitutes they exploit, and they also use racism (and to a lesser extent nationalism) to attain a sense of being esteemed in other ways. Let me return to Bruce Cassirer:

> Bangkok is sexy, lusty, sleazy . . . It's sad to see these girls with no choice in life, waiting for their next customer. It's amazing that they seem to have fun and put a smile on their faces. Many Arabs and Europeans are known to abuse these girls. As an American you are the preferred customer . . . (I'm not saying that all Americans are gods when compared to other cultures, as I do know some very sadistic Americans, but in general we seem to fall in love more easily and treat our women as equals.) But in the Orient, women are second class citizens, often treated in dehumanizing ways. There's nothing you can do to change it, but you can still be one of the kind and generous ones who helps. (*Cassirer*, 1992, pp. 176–7)

This is vintage sex tourist twaddle, but it is fascinating to observe the way in which Cassirer, like many sex tourists I have interviewed, manages to construct himself as esteemed and honourable by contrasting himself favourably against other 'abusive' and ungentlemanly prostitute users. He continues his chapter on Thailand by explaining how to go about finding Bangkok brothels in which women and children are confined, observing that:

> These are village girls from Burma or China who are barefoot and who knows how old . . . If the service is good, tip; if extra special, tip more. These girls live here and are *owned* by the hotel. Your tip is their spending money, so let your conscience be your guide . . . One way to rationalize it is to say, if it's not me then it's the guy behind me, and who's more likely to be the gentler of the two? (*Cassirer*, 1992, pp. 180–1, original emphasis)

It has been noted elsewhere (Brace and O'Connell Davidson, 1996) that, for many men, sex tourism restores a sense of masculine honour because, in the poor countries that they visit, their privileged economic, gendered and 'racialized' position endows them with the power either to harm or to help the women and children they exploit. To exercise such a choice over the fate of another human being is momentarily to exercise an almost God-like power, and men like Bruce Cassirer, whose 'conscience' about sexually abusing enslaved children is salved by giving them a tip afterwards, can tell themselves that they have used this power well. They were gentler than the guy behind would have been. But it also seems to me that the idea of being chosen above other clients is important, and often spills over into a sense of beating Other men in a competitive struggle. The idea that men from the Gulf States are somehow more abusive than other prostitute users is quite widespread among white sex tourists to Thailand, for instance, who assert that Thai women hate 'the Arabs' and avoid 'going with them' (see O'Connell Davidson, 1995a). In Latin America and the Caribbean, meanwhile, white sex tourists often construct themselves as 'civilized', as 'gentlemen', even as non-sexists, through the denigration of local men. They insist that local men are physically abusive towards women and children, and that local women prefer white men because white men 'treat them with respect'.

These men's fantasy that it is their 'civilization', egalitarian nature and personal charm rather than their wallets which attract local women to them is a fiction which serves two ends. On the one hand, it allows them to feel truly esteemed by the women they fuck (and also makes that woman's status as 'whore' ambiguous). But being chosen over and above local men is also significant. The fact that he can take women away from such 'hypermasculine' 'natural/primitive' beings is visible validation of the sex tourist's most excellent powers (see Brace and O'Connell Davidson, 1996).

Thus far I have been focusing on the question of how the practice of a particular form of sex tourism can be linked to the construction and expression of a particular masculine identity, that which associates 'manhood' with success in a competitive struggle with other men for sexual access to 'valuable' female bodies. I now want to complicate matters by turning to the question of female sex tourism.

The case of female sex tourism

In the phenomenon of female sex tourism we find a form of prostitute use which self-evidently has absolutely nothing to do with the construction or maintenance of the prostitute user's masculinity. Some researchers differentiate between male and female sex tourism, referring to the latter as 'romance tourism' (for example, Pruitt and LaFont, 1995, Meisch, 1995), but, in practice, the behaviour of the female sex tourists they describe is in many ways similar to the subgroup of male sex tourists discussed above (those who seek to deny the economic basis of their sexual encounters with local women, men and children). Certainly in our interview and observational work in destinations which attract female sex tourists (Jamaica, Goa, Costa Rica's Caribbean coast, Venezuela, Cuba, the Dominican Republic), we found that Western women, like their male counterparts, used their greater economic power to initiate, control and terminate sexual relationships with the partner(s) of their choice, and used the same kind of exoticizing racisms to delude themselves that the men/boys concerned were genuinely sexually attracted to them and were not *really* prostitutes. The comments about male sex tourists who use their economic and 'racialized' power to secure sexual access to bodies 'of value' are equally applicable to female sex tourists, and white Western women are just as much concerned to construct their own whiteness (see Frankenberg, 1993) as sexually desirable as are white Western men. Thus one finds Western women of fifty and sixty years of age having sexual 'romances' with boys aged between fifteen and twenty, and obese and 'ugly' Western women with young men who conform to Western ideals of male physical beauty.

On the basis of observational work in seven countries and information from NGOs and campaigners based in other countries which are host to sex tourists, it is my view that heterosexual female sex tourism is, in numerical terms, a far, far smaller phenomenon than male sex tourism, and that it is unusual – though not unknown – for Western lesbians to practice sex tourism. Our own interview work with male prostitutes also suggests that female sex tourists are less likely than their male counterparts to seek out a large number of different sexual 'partners' (though there are exceptions, and some female sex tourists do appear to engage in 'notch scoring' sexual behaviour), and to require more convincing displays of *real* desire from prostitutes before they are willing to enter into sexual exchanges with them. Several male prostitutes observed that they found it easier to work with male homosexual sex tourists than female sex tourists, as male clients require little or no 'wooing' and are happy to pay in cash. With women, on the other hand, great energy has to be expended on concealing the commercial nature of the contract, ensuring that she buys 'gifts' which can readily be converted into cash, feigning delight at her 'generosity', and so on.

What is the relationship between the practice of sex tourism and

women's subjective gender identity? Some have suggested that
female sex tourists are rejecting or reversing traditional gender
roles, but, as Pruitt and LaFont observe on the basis of their
research on female sex tourism in Jamaica, this is an oversimplifi-
cation:

> In that gender identity is a relational construct, the Western
> women who seek to break from conventional roles require a dif-
> ferent kind of relationship with men in order to realize a new
> gender identity. Yet, these women who seek more control in
> defining their relationship are simultaneously drawn to conven-
> tional notions of masculinity. Ideas about masculine power are
> central to the women's attraction to local men, in particular the
> 'natural' Rasta. The women's own gender scripts include a sense
> of appropriateness of the dominant male from a dualistic concep-
> tion of man/woman constructed on hierarchical power relations.
> The farther the women push the boundary of feminine conduct
> to incorporate qualities conventionally defined as masculine, the
> more they confront internalized ideas about masculine power . . .
> The women are drawn to the strength, the potency of the mascu-
> line even as they experiment with the power they acquire
> through financial superiority. (*Pruitt and LaFont*, 1995, p. 437)

I would take this argument further. It seems to me that many
female sex tourists are not the least interested in realizing a new
gender identity but rather seek opportunities to act out very traditional gender scripts. There are multiple discourses around femininity as well as masculinity, and a 'real woman' is not always or
only signified by passivity, economic dependence and bovine
domesticity. Western women are also taught that 'femininity'
means being glamorous and beautiful, and, because female sex
tourists are flattered, charmed, wooed and indulged by local men
and boys, their sex tourism gives them the illusion that they are
esteemed as 'truly feminine'. Such women are not *challenging* the
traditional gender dichotomy or redefining what it is to be a
woman by using their economic power to affirm this kind of femininity any more than a rich woman who pays for plastic surgery to
make her body or face conform more closely to cultural ideals of
feminine beauty can be said to resist or challenge existing gender
ideologies. The Western female sex tourists we observed and interviewed did not want to stop playing the gender game any more
than their male counterparts did; in fact, I am not even certain that
they wanted to change the rules so very much. They just wanted to

win, and the massive inequalities in wealth and life chances between a Western tourist and a beach hustler in Jamaica, Cuba, Goa, or Costa Rica, for example, placed them in a position to do so.

There is a tendency to view male and female sex tourism in a different light. Momsen (1994) refers to female sex tourists in the Caribbean as 'lonely', and journalists and campaigners I have spoken to often either dismiss female sex tourism as a laughable phenomenon or else insist that the women are actually being exploited by the local men. This perhaps reflects an essentialist model of female sexuality within which women are 'naturally' passive, emotional and dependent, but I think it also reveals a misunderstanding of sex tourism. The point about informal tourist-related prostitution is that its ambiguities allow for self-deception, so that, even when women tell themselves that they can only have sex in the context of romantic intimacy, they are not disbarred from sexually exploiting local men and boys in the poor countries they visit. Since they do not have to enter into narrowly contractual cash exchanges they can tell themselves that this intimacy does exist – thus a young German woman in the Dominican Republic told us that in the first week of her holiday, she had had sexual relationships with three Dominican men, for whom she had bought meals, drinks and gifts. She described these relationships as 'holiday romances'. Likewise, a 62-year-old Canadian woman tourist who sexually exploited a Cuban boy of sixteen over a two-week period told him that she 'loved him passionately', and for some months after her return to Canada (presumably until her guilt wore off) wrote him love letters every week.

Emotions of honour and shame are, I would argue, just as relevant to the analysis of female sex tourism as they are to male sex tourism. To be considered sexually unattractive, to be 'left on the shelf', visibly unwanted, is quite as shaming for women as it is for men, and women can be just as fiercely competitive as men in pursuit of tributes to their power in the arena of sexuality, even if there are differences in terms of what is deemed to constitute a tribute (see Bartky's, 1990, discussion of shame and gender).

Contradictions and constraints

When Max Weber (1968) spoke of the unintentional consequences of purposive action and made a distinction between 'formal' and 'substantive' rationality, he drew attention to the fact that, while human beings are conscious agents who interpret and give meaning to their world, and act intentionally on the basis of those meanings and interpretations, it does not follow that they always act in ways which *actually* advance their own aims. Their actions can have unintended consequences, and furthermore, because people can make mistakes, they can rationally employ quite the wrong means in pursuit of a particular end. In interview work with sex tourists I have been struck by the fact that, while their prostitute use appears to be motivated by a coherent (if noxious) set of sexual, psychic and emotional ambitions (which is to say that their prostitute use appears to be a strategy rationally employed in pursuit of particular ends), it does not always seem to work. Certainly, habitual sex tourists and 'sexpatriates' do not usually present as happy, balanced individuals who have found an effective means of dealing with their sexual, gender and existential *Angst*. In fact, they more commonly communicate a sense of bewilderment, disappointment and/or anger about their lived experience of prostitution (see also Seabrook's, 1997, account of interviews with sex tourists).

Mistaking power for honour

Orlando Patterson has remarked upon the elusiveness of honour as a social concept. He points out that honour and social power are related but goes on to observe that while power is necessary to defend honour, 'it is one's sense of honor that often drives one to acquire the instruments of power in the first place' (1982, p. 80). Furthermore, honour is not *merely* a reflection of material power or social status. Persons of the same social rank or standing can be more or less honoured and so compete for prestige among themselves (Miller, 1993), for honour does not simply attach to the powers a person can or does exercise, but to the whole person, and 'because honor envelops "the whole man," it is seen as an intimate personal quality relating to both his physical and characterologic attributes' (Patterson, 1982, p. 80). Honour, I believe, is a slippery concept not just for those who seek to theorize it, but also for those who seek to possess it. It is possible for individual social actors to confuse power with honour, and so to make misjudgements and mistakes in their pursuit of honour. This is particularly true in relation to the kind of honour which habitual sex tourists seek to possess through their sexual relations.

Honour and esteem are very much to do with distinguishing

oneself from other people (Rousseau, 1991), and the competition for honour, like all true competitions, is therefore a zero-sum game. A competition which everyone wins is not a competition, and tributes paid to all alike are not honours – they do not mark one person off from another. Sex tourists think of sexual life as a competitive arena. To succeed is to command the desire of people with bodies of value, and vice versa. Those who win in this competition demonstrate to themselves and to others that they possess powers and/or qualities which others do not possess and yet would desire and envy. Thus the sex tourist envies the handsome playboy or the beautiful movie star surrounded by a myriad admirers, and seeks to personify this 'ideal'. No one who buys into this model of sexual competition as a signifier of gender honour is going to be particularly enamoured of those forms of prostitution that are organized as a straightforward commodity exchange. Simple possession of enough money to pay for a blow job or any other sexual 'service' does not distinguish one from the masses. But, through Western eyes, the kind of prostitution which takes place in sex tourist resorts superficially appears to be a different matter. A contributor to a guidebook for women travellers, for example, describes her trip to Negril, Jamaica, as follows:

> A human free-for-all (except everything has its price), Negril is home to one of Jamaica's most popular tourist souvenirs. This is where the walking, talking and frequently dancing male dolls, commonly known as 'rent-a-dreads' or 'rastitutes' make their living by patrolling the beach and "entertaining" unattached visiting females. From sixteen to sixty, female tourists are bombarded with lyrical sweet talk. This is something we were unprepared for and it took me several looks in the mirror to check that I hadn't turned into a Kim Basinger clone before I realised what was going on. (*Noakes*, 1995, p. 374)

I find this passage interesting partly because of the sense of hostility and resentment towards Black male prostitutes it communicates. They are simultaneously objectified (referred to as 'souvenirs' and 'dolls') and attributed with malign powers as agents (they *use* their blackness – their dreads and their 'rasta-ness' in an instrumental way, 'bombarding' unprepared female tourists and manipulating them with 'lyrical sweet talk'). Noakes also conveniently overlooks the fact that many of the female tourists, whether sixteen or sixty, have gone to Negril precisely because they *want* to be 'sweet talked' in this way. But the comment about having to check herself in the mirror is revealing as well. Before she 'realized what was going on', Noakes presumably found the experience of being 'sweet talked' seductive (indeed, the hostility expressed towards the prostitutes is, I would imagine, directly related to the disappointment she experienced when a long hard look in the mirror revealed that she had not turned into a Kim Basinger clone). In sex tourist resorts, the illusion of being genuinely desired can be a very potent one, and this helps to explain why sex tourists who are prostitute users back home state that sex tourism compares so very favourably to domestic prostitute use, as well as to illustrate how it is that people who would not dream of using prostitutes back home end up paying for sex in the 'Third World' holiday destinations they visit.

The illusion rests partly on the fact that the disparities of wealth between rich and poor countries are *so* obscene that people from the affluent world are often unable to imagine the living conditions endured by the mass of the people in the economically underdeveloped countries they visit nor, in many cases, to comprehend how the paltry 'benefits' they offer (a hot shower and bed with clean sheets in their hotel room, a three-course meal in a restaurant, unlimited drinks, an item of clothing or a pair of shoes, a few dollars) could be a sufficient inducement to make a person have sex with someone they do not actually desire. In other words, sex tourists do not always immediately recognize the full extent or significance of their own economic power in the countries they visit. As a consequence, and always providing they avoid looking in mirrors, they can mistake this power for honour. But, given that people who are interested in competing for gender honour are obsessed with questions as to how they are perceived by others, they cannot generally help but look in mirrors (whether metaphorical or literal) and so cannot help but realize that the honour they win in sex tourist resorts is a chimera – hence my mature student's sense of 'disillusion' when he noticed that 'a lot of Thai girls went out with unattractive Western guys'.

Habitual sex tourists understand this all too well. They frequently describe the resorts they visit as 'Disneyland', 'Fantasy Island', 'Every man's dream come true' and 'Paradise', and this is not simply because prostitute use is inexpensive in these places (indeed, in some sex tourist destinations many women charge prices comparable with those of Western prostitutes). They are 'a dream come true' because (through Western eyes) the uncertain status of both the prostitute and the client makes it possible for sex tourists to imagine themselves as esteemed even as they buy honours and win out over 'opponents' who are hamstrung by their relative economic disadvantage. The ambiguity of prostitution further allows the sex tourist to exercise powers of control over the prostitute as object (she or he can be discarded and replaced at whim, she or he is not in a position to make the kind of demands that a non-commercial sexual partner could make back home, but must, for economic reasons, comply with the sex tourist's wishes rather than pursue her/his own ends, etc.) and yet pretend that the prostitute is complying as a subject.

Such deceptions are made more plausible by the sex tourists' experience of power. They see their power as attached to them as individuals, rather than understanding themselves as bearers of a form of neo-colonial power. Their vision of themselves is thus detached from the structures and the valuations which render them both powerless at home and powerful in the 'Third World'. It is this detachment which allows them to (mis)take submission for honour, to see themselves as 'gentlemen' and more deserving of honour than 'Third World' men (Brace and O'Connell Davidson, 1996).

But there are contradictions at the heart of this kind of honorific sex tourism. To begin with, uncertainties of status simultaneously allow for and undermine a sense of honour. If prostitutes are not really prostitutes, then there is no clear way to distinguish in advance between 'nice girls' and 'hardened whores' and so no way in which the sex tourist can be certain whether his/her evaluation of his/her own worth is being accepted and recognized or ridiculed and 'exploited'. Thus many habitual sex tourists are ambivalent towards the prostitutes they exploit, lurching irrationally from paternalistic sympathy – 'They do it for their families' – to malevolent hostility – 'They're hard bitches really' – in the space of only a few minutes' conversation. The sex tourist's racism is also a dual-edged sword in the struggle for honour. On the one hand, it bolsters the kind of self-deception necessary to the illusion of being chosen above other sexual partners, but, on the other, it devalues the esteem accorded to the sex tourist. To be admired or envied by unworthy competitors ('uncivilized' or 'subservient' beings), by those who are despised and excluded from one's imaginary community, does not necessarily generate a sense of honour.

These contradictions perhaps help to explain the fact that habitual sex tourists and sexpatriates do not always appear to be happy even though they tell you they are in 'paradise', but instead often present as intensely bitter and morose alcoholics. Their affliction, it seems to me, results from their confusion of power with honour. Like characters from a Somerset Maugham short story who set out to the colonies to try to 'make good', they imagined that simply exercising the powers exercised by those they honour would be enough to make them honourable. When they looked in the mirror, they found that it was not.

Miles (1989, p. 10) has observed that, 'if racism brutalises and dehumanises its object, it also brutalises and dehumanises those who articulate it', and the same can be said of sex tourism. Yet the idea that racists or sex tourists are also dehumanized by their practices is rather too abstract to inform immediate struggles against either racism or sex tourism. As I write, hundreds of thousands of sex tourists from affluent countries are having what they subjectively experience as a whale of a time feeding on the economic misfortunes of local women, children and men in poor countries, and, though I have noted that many present as embittered alcoholics, I am not convinced that they would all change if we could only get them to understand that they too are dehumanized by their quest for absolute control over other human beings as sexual objects. It seems to me that, because sex tourists work with a model of power which is zero-sum and conflictual, because they actually believe in primal myths about political power, their response to such arguments would simply be to say that they would rather be dehumanized by brutalizing and dehumanizing others than by being directly brutalized and dehumanized themselves. As one sex tourist remarked in regard to power relations within marriage: 'In a democratic relationship, you have to compromise, and a compromise means that neither of you is happy. It's better to have a dictatorship. That way, at least the guy is happy.' This underlines the fact that sex tourism, as a social practice, is embedded in both structural inequalities and the broader ideologies used to justify them, so that identifying the emotional and psychological contradictions that sex tourism (and indeed prostitute use more generally) reflects and generates for *individual* participants does not mean that we have identified some tragic flaw that will ineluctably lead to its demise.

9

Diversity, Dialectics and Politics

Without the possibility of action, all knowledge comes to one labelled 'file and forget', and I can neither file nor forget. Nor will certain ideas forget me; they keep filing away at my lethargy, my complacency. Why should I be the one to dream this nightmare? Why should I be dedicated and set aside – yes, if not to at least *tell* a few people about it? . . . The very act of trying to put it all down has confused me and negated some of the anger and some of the bitterness. So it is now I denounce and defend, or feel prepared to defend . . . I denounce because though implicated and partially responsible, I have been hurt to the point of abysmal pain, hurt to the point of invisibility. And I defend because in spite of all I find that I love. In order to get some of it down I *have* to love. I sell you no phony forgiveness, I'm a desperate man – but too much of your life will be lost, its meaning lost, unless you approach it as much through love as through hate. So I approach it through division. So I denounce and I defend and I hate and I love. (*Ellison*, 1965, p. 467).

Knowledge about prostitution should not come to us labelled 'file and forget', but, though I am firmly convinced that change is possible, I have no faith in simple, single 'policy solutions' which abstract prostitution from the social and political relations in which it is embedded. This chapter looks at the constraints on collective political action around prostitution and the problems with various proposals to change the legal regulation of prostitution, and argues that, ultimately, the ills associated with prostitution can be addressed only through far broader political struggles to rid the world of poverty, racism, homophobia and sexism.

Collective political action

Prostitution, like both wage labour and slavery, is an institution through which certain powers of command over the person are transferred from one individual to another. It is not fully distinguished from either slavery or wage labour by the kind of variability discussed in Part I of this book, for the powers exercised over slaves has varied historically and contextually, and hierarchies (often gendered and 'racialized') have existed within slave systems (hooks, 1981, Patterson, 1982, Archer, 1988, Yavetz, 1988, Beckles, 1989, Potts, 1990, Morrissey, 1989), and the experience of wage workers has been and is equally diverse. It is also important to note that both wage labour and slavery, like prostitution, are institutions which involve more than just the *economic* oppression of human subjects. However, in terms of the possibilities for collective political action implicit in these institutions, it seems to me that prostitution *is* distinguished by the fact that the contradictions implicit in the relationship between prostitutes and clients, both as individuals and as collective groups, does not generate an immediate or straightforward dialectic for change. Let me elaborate this point.

Capitalist employers have an economic interest in the wage labour exchange, for it is only when they purchase living labour that it becomes possible to set in motion the labour process, that is, the process through which surplus value is produced and extracted in capitalist economies. Since the capitalist class is dependent upon that surplus, while the working class is dependent upon the wages they receive, the capital–labour relation is, as Marx noted, characterized by a mutual economic dependency as well as an antagonism of interests. Depending upon various political, ideological and economic factors, this contradiction is to a greater or lesser degree also present in relationships at the point of production. The extraction of surplus is enhanced where workers are brought together to work co-operatively on a labour process that is designed in such a way as to maximize the productivity of labour. But no matter how much control an employer exercises over the design of the labour process, no matter how much work is stripped down to a series of unskilled, repetitive tasks, the fact remains that workers are human beings, not automatons. As conscious, purposive actors, they can – either individually or collectively – put more or less effort into their work and they can mount various forms of resistance. Relationships at the point of production thus embody a contradiction – capital wishes to control labour in the same way that it controls other commodities, yet at the same time wishes to harness its active human co-operation (Cressey and MacInnes, 1980). These tensions open up political possibilities for labour as a collective group. It is often possible for workers to bargain with their employers over how much surplus value can be squeezed from them and/or how much of that surplus they will get to keep (for instance, trade unions can pursue short-run economic goals, negotiating x increase in productivity for x increase in wages).

Certainly clients are often just as much interested in exploiting willing and co-operative prostitutes as employers are in exploiting willing workers, and we can also say that clients are dependent on the existence of a class of prostitutes to maintain their own position in a gendered and 'racialized' status hierarchy. But clients have no direct *economic* interest in securing prostitutes' co-operation – it is not necessary for clients, as a collective group, to accumulate sexual value, or to socialize prostitution, or then to deal with prostitutes as a collective group. From the client's viewpoint the prostitution contract involves a relation of consumption, not production. Negotiations over the prices and terms of prostitution contracts are thus highly atomized. They represent an individualized form of haggling over an existing exchange value, not a struggle over how much sexual 'value' is collectively produced and retained by prostitutes, and this seriously limits the potential for collective resistance by prostitutes.

If prostitutes are directly employed, it is, of course, possible for them to combine to try to restrict the amount of surplus creamed off by their employer, and there are instances of prostitutes doing exactly this. But brothel owners are usually mindful to adopt the kind of indirect employment relations that hamper effective collective action, which is, in any case, only a viable option under certain circumstances. Where labour market conditions are slack and workers' rights are not legally protected, collective action is more likely to lead to lock-outs or mass dismissal than any meaningful improvement in wages or conditions. And if we further take into account the fact that large numbers of prostitutes are self-employed, and so directly faced by market relations with a mass of clients, not an employment relation, then we must recognize that, even in unity, there is little strength. Prostitutes' organizations therefore typically resemble pressure groups rather than trade unions, and they have to campaign without either the backing of a powerful and self-interested fraction of the class that exploits them or the possibility of damaging the national economy by withdrawing their labour (see Jaget 1980 for a description of the 1975 prostitutes' strike in France). Moreover, though prostitution is an economic institution which allows for the sale and purchase of powers of command over the person, and which, like wage labour, is predicated on a set of social relations that deny the prostitute a meaningful choice as to whether or not to enter into such contracts, it is *not* acknowledged as an institution that helps to reproduce an entire mode of production. This makes the relationship between the state and prostitutes, as a collective group, very different from the relationship between the state and organized labour.

Capitalist employers have an economic interest in securing workers' active co-operation, but they have historically used, and still do use, everything from brute force through the imposition of 'fines' to legal sanctions and the threat of dismissal as strategies for reducing worker resistance. However, their power to secure compliance by brute force and/or non-economic forms of compulsion is historically contingent, and it is here that the role of the state is so critical. Capitalism, as a mode of production, 'is based on the fact that the workman sells his labour-power as a commodity' (Marx, 1867, cited in Sayer, 1991, p. 34), and state power has been, and still is, 'integral to the construction, and regulation of', a 'free' market in this vitally important 'commodity' (Sayer, 1991). Political struggles over the apparatuses of the state which guarantee the relations of production, and reproduction, as well as struggles over relations within production, are thus hugely significant for workers' lived experience (Burawoy, 1985), for the state is not a political institution that manages the formal economy but rather, to quote Miles, an institutional complex (government, courts, army, administration, etc.)

> which organizes social relations within a social formation to ensure the reproduction of a particular mode, or articulation of modes, of production. It therefore organizes a particular ensemble of class relations ... it attempts ... to secure, by direct force and/or in law, the particular conditions considered necessary at any time ... to determine the relations between producers and non-producers and to determine that those relations are reproduced and/or reformed in particular ways ... [the state] is a relation of production in its own right. (*Miles*, 1987, p. 181)

As such an institutional complex, the state can also be said to organize relations between prostitutes and clients as well as between producers and non-producers. But since neither capitalism nor any other mode of production is *based* on the commodification of powers of sexual command over the person, state regulation of prostitution has typically had a very different character to the regulation of wage labour.

State apparatuses which are designed to regulate relations of reproduction (welfare systems, systems of family law, etc.) as well as particular economic policies (for example, shifting from import substitution strategies to using tourism as a foreign exchange earner, annexing subsistence land for cash crop production, etc.) have a critical impact upon the prostitution 'labour market'. The state also directly involves itself in the regulation of prostitution through the criminal law, and the truth of the matter is that governments – and indeed national and international capital – benefit from prostitution. It operates as a kind of alternative 'welfare' system in most countries of the world and so reduces the level of state expenditure necessary to ensure the reproduction of labour and also provides a means by which to supplement below-subsistence wages. In countries where brothel prostitution is legal there are also fiscal benefits for the state, as indeed there are financial benefits from 'taxes' levied by means of fining prostitutes. In tourist-related prostitution the benefits for national states and national and international capital are yet more obvious (see Truong, 1990). And yet governments are rarely willing to acknowledge an interest in ensuring the conditions under which clients can obtain access to prostitutes in the same way that they will acknowledge their concern to ensure conditions for capital accumulation (South Korean government ministers in the 1970s praising 'the sincerity of girls who have contributed to their fatherland's economic development' by 'servicing' Japanese sex tourists, quoted in Mitter, 1986, p. 64, provide an exception to this general rule).

Though states will intervene directly to mediate and regulate conflict between capital and labour, hypocrisy and denial of the ends served by prostitution mean that states do not openly mediate and regulate conflicts of interest between clients and prostitutes. Indeed, states rarely even guarantee prostitutes the kind of basic protection afforded to either entrepreneurs or private citizens as they go about their daily business. This leaves the prostitute at a double disadvantage at the point of contract with the client. The asymmetry of economic dependency in prostitution weakens her bargaining hand, and, because prostitution is generally treated as a problem of social control rather than as an economic institution, states do not seek to impose a regulatory framework which delimits the powers of clients as a class or to establish basic minimum rules for the treatment of prostitutes by clients and third parties. By the same token, states typically provide a juridical framework which strengthens the client's bargaining hand (that is, one which criminalizes prostitutes, indirectly assures a well-stocked prostitution 'labour market' through a range of gender-discriminatory policies and failure to guarantee adequate welfare support for women and children, and disempowers migrant prostitutes by denying them basic rights of citizenship).

Even if our point of comparison is between clients and slave holders, the same kind of problems arise. The institution of slavery is typically of economic significance for an entire mode of production, which is to say that slave holders as a class are often dependent upon a class of slaves for their own daily reproduction and for the reproduction of the society in which they live. Inasmuch as there is a degree of mutual dependency between two classes whose objective interests are fundamentally opposed, then, a mode of production which rests on slave labour, like that which rests on wage labour, hinges upon a contradiction. This contradiction is also manifest in the day-to-day relations between individual slave holders and individual slaves, and it makes an enormous difference to the ways in which power is exercised:

> As Georg Hegel realized, total personal power taken to its extreme contradicts itself by its very existence, for total domination can become a form of extreme dependence on the object of one's power, and total powerlessness can become the secret path to control of the subject that attempts to exercise such power. Even though such a sublation is usually only a potential, the possibility of its realization influences the normal course of the relation in profound ways. (*Patterson*, 1982, p. 2)

Though Hegel was concerned with a very theoretical existential predicament supposedly faced by masters who sought recognition and acknowledgement from their slaves, he nonetheless draws our attention to the inherent instability of all social institutions which rest on vastly unequal relations, an instability which derives from the fact that it is not actually possible to strip human beings of their subjectivity and free will (see Patterson, 1982, p. 100). Active and passive forms of collective resistance by enslaved persons are well documented, and slave owners have frequently found it necessary to adjust their methods and techniques of control to counteract and/or reduce such resistance. Thus Patterson argues that, while the notion that slavery created an existential impasse for the master is quite wrong (persons of slave-owning classes have generally been quite happy with the recognition and status accorded to them by other free persons, and have rarely depended upon their slaves for acknowledgement), slavery did inspire in the enslaved a unique understanding of the value of human dignity:

> Confronted with the master's outrageous effort to deny him all dignity, the slave even more than the master came to know and to desire passionately this very attribute ... What does the master make of the slave's yearning for dignity ... ? In all but a handful of slaveholding societies the master exploits this very yearning for his own benefit ... by manipulating it as the principal means of motivating the slave, who desires nothing more passionately than dignity, belonging, and release. (*Patterson*, 1982, pp. 100–1)

A dialectic thus emerged. Manumission – the negation of slavery – 'became an intrinsic part of the process of slavery' (Patterson, 1982, p. 340).

Problems of control and resistance are present in relations between prostitutes and their third-party exploiters, and, to the extent that clients want untrammelled powers of command over willing prostitutes, they are also present in relations between prostitutes and clients (thus clients complain about the 'cold' and 'businesslike' approach of Western prostitutes). But clients enter into only brief relationships with individual prostitutes, and they do so as consumers. Failure to resolve these problems of control satisfactorily does not threaten the client's daily livelihood, and, since clients are rarely dependent on prostitute use alone for their sense of gender and/or 'racialized' worth, nor does it completely undermine their status. The contradictions implicit in the prosti- tute–client relation are without doubt often a source of dissatisfac- tion to clients (who sometimes respond by seeking out 'fresher', 'less commercial' prostitutes), but they do not spark off a process of adjustment which negates prostitution as an institution.

Finally, I would argue that political opportunities for prostitutes are restricted by the fact that it is nigh on impossible for them to deal with clients as a collective group. The ideologies which sur- round sexuality and prostitute use make it unlikely that clients would ever openly organize for their interests as consumers, and therefore unlikely that they would seek to negotiate with prostitutes as a collective group. I cannot imagine a clients' collective emerging, negotiating agreements with prostitutes' collectives whereby experienced adult prostitutes promise to be warmer and less businesslike in exchange for clients agreeing not to use child prostitutes, for example, and then enforcing such agreements.

Policy debate and political strategies

Because there is no mutuality of economic dependency between prostitutes and clients, political struggle at the point of exchange is futile. Political activists therefore tend to focus their efforts upon campaigns to reform or transform the state apparatuses which are used to control and regulate prostitution, as well as more general campaigns to destigmatize prostitutes and/or prostitution (see O'Neill, 1997, for a clear review of the political issues). In the contemporary world, state intervention in prostitution is generally informed by one of three basic models: prohibition/abolition, regulation/registration, or deregulation. The law in England and Wales, with its emphasis on controlling public manifestations of prostitution and the restrictions it imposes on the lives of prostitute women, provides a fairly good example of what the prohibition model means in practice, and most feminists object to this approach, which criminalizes prostitutes and subjects them to the punitive power of the state, and does nothing to address the conditions which push women into prostitution.

The second model, regulation/registration, operates in several countries and regions, including Turkey, Germany and the state of Nevada in the USA, where prostitution is legalized but 'restricted to licensed brothels or particular neighbourhoods' (Zatz, 1997, p. 283, Willey, 1993). The civil-rights violation implied by requirements for prostitutes to register with the police and/or other authorities, have compulsory health checks, etc., are fairly obvious, and this model finds little favour with either prostitutes' rights feminists or feminist abolitionists: 'legalized brothels have increased police powers and institutionalized pimping by the state, making it harder for women to keep their earnings or bargain to determine their working conditions' (ECP, 1997, p. 91), and 'Regulation ... *enforces* prostitution' (Barry, 1995, p. 228, original emphasis). Deregulation is the policy favoured by many prostitutes' rights groups as well as libertarians on the grounds that prostitution is a form of work and that 'neither women nor men should be criminalized for consenting sex' (ECP, 1997, p. 91; see also COYOTE, 1988). In Britain the idea of introducing designated 'toleration zones' has recently received support from some local councillors in various cities as well as from certain police chief constables, and Davis (1993, p. 8) has noted that the deregulation model is actually being implemented, either explicitly or by default, by many states 'not for the humanitarian impulse that apparently fuelled the initial reform – but for other reasons: financial exigency, prosecutor indifference, court deadlocks, and resistance to the overreach of the criminal law among some social sectors.'

Deregulation is not without its critics. As Laurie Shrage (1994, p. 83) observes, in their eagerness to challenge the patriarchal laws which criminalize prostitution, many feminists as well as prostitutes' rights advocates have endorsed a decriminalization policy which proposes 'the sort of minimal regulation on industry that even Milton Friedman would approve', that is, one which provides no regulatory controls whatsoever over the degree of exploitation to which prostitutes are subject by third parties and clients. But Shrage's own solution to the dilemmas posed by regulation and deregulation is equally problematic. She argues for 'a new kind of regulatory apparatus, one that avoids some of the problems in systems built around publicly licensed private brothels, or in systems built on the public registration of prostitutes' (1994, p. 159), and proposes a system within which individual prostitutes, rather than brothels, are licensed, in rather the same way that 'other professionals and demi-professionals' are licensed to practice. The standards for licensing would be set by 'public boards or commissions made up of service providers, community leaders, educators, and legal and public health experts', and 'candidates' for a prostitute's license would have to 'complete some number of college-level courses on human sexuality' (p. 159). Shrage then goes on to suggest that clients should be:

> inspected for disease before they can visit a prostitute. And perhaps the easiest way to do this is to train prostitutes themselves to perform the necessary blood tests, etc., and to enforce the period of waiting for test results. Of course, it will also be of prime importance to keep sex workers drug- and alcohol-free. (*Shrage*, 1994, p. 161)

This form of social regulation might be all very well if we lived in cloud cuckoo land. In the real world, however, it is absurd to imagine that people like Catalina or Maria are going to complete a number of college-level courses before entering into prostitution (if they were in a position to attend college rather than work they would not be prostituting themselves in the first place), or that a woman like Marlene would go along to a licensing board to obtain a license before prostituting herself. Even if we consider the most professional and experienced of prostitutes (like Desiree), who might conceivably think it worthwhile to obtain such a license, the idea of them taking blood samples from prospective clients and asking them to come back for their appointment in three weeks when the results are through is almost as laughable as the idea that clients who want to 'fuck dirty whores' would subject themselves to such tests and deferred gratification when they could simply walk down the road and find themselves a Catalina or a Marlene to exploit on the spot.

Except for a small minority of people, prostitution is not a positive career choice like deciding to become a brain surgeon, or even an aromatherapist, but a condition either forced upon individuals by third parties or selected as the best of a bad bunch of economic options. Regulatory apparatuses designed to control *prostitutes* are therefore pointless, whether they involve orthodox patriarchal criminalization or progressive, feminist licensing *à la* Shrage. Should the focus of control be shifted to clients, then?

Action against clients?

There have been instances of direct action against clients – for example, that organized by Japanese feminist groups at airports, which involved ridiculing and insulting men arriving home from sex tours, and that proposed by the Filipino guerrilla group that adopted the slogan 'Kill a sex tourist a day' (Lee, 1991). Public humiliation has also been used as an instrument to control Taiwanese businessmen caught using prostitutes while in mainland China:

> Chinese authorities not only sent them to a poultry farm in the outskirts of Beijing for a short period of labor reform, but also sent letters to their employers in Taiwan to inform them of the 'repulsive deeds' committed by their employees in China. Hoping that public exposure will deter such behaviour, Chinese

authorities have also stamped the words 'patron of prostitution' on the travel documents of those men who have been found guilty of committing 'repulsive deeds'. (*Ren*, 1993, pp. 102–3)

I will confess that I find this latter idea rather satisfying and have spent many a happy moment daydreaming about which of the sex tourists I have interviewed I would most like to send for labour reform in a poultry farm in the outskirts of Beijing. But I am also conscious that these kinds of action are a luxury that few prostitutes can afford. They reflect a tendency to abstract prostitution from its systemic and structural roots and treat it merely as a question of individual morality. The same kind of problems arise in relation to legislation against kerb crawling (introduced in Britain in 1985) and the 'John schools', designed to re-educate prostitute users, which are being piloted in the USA and Britain (Mills, 1997). To the extent that such moves reflect a growing discomfort with the legal harassment of prostitutes and the hypocrisy and sexism implicit in traditional prostitution law and law-enforcement practice, they are to be welcomed. But, unless meaningful steps to address the structures which drive people into prostitution are simultaneously taken, legal and other measures aimed at preventing prostitute use will do little to improve the lot of those who are exploited by prostitute users. Indeed, kerb-crawling legislation (as well as direct action by local residents to drive street prostitutes from 'their' area) can actually make the most vulnerable prostitutes even more vulnerable. It increases the pressure on prostitutes to negotiate quickly, for example, or to get into clients' cars and so off the street before they have negotiated a deal, both of which reduce the prostitute's control over the situation.

Joining forces with other marginalized groups?

It is out of an appreciation of the economic exigencies behind prostitution that the English Collective of Prostitutes (ECP) locates its campaign for deregulation within the broader struggle for Wages for Housework, and for 'higher welfare benefits and wages, student grants and housing and other resources so that no woman, child or man is forced by poverty into sex with anyone' (ECP, 1997, p. 83). In so doing, it seeks to conjoin a political battle for prostitutes' and non-prostitute women's rights. The ECP defines prostitution as a form of sexual and emotional work, and argues that non-prostitute women perform identical work in non-commercial

contexts such as marriage and other heterosexual relationships –
prostitutes 'get paid for what all women are expected to do for
free' (p. 83). If women's unpaid reproductive labour in the home,
on the land and in the community were properly classified, that is,
recognized as work, then prostitution would be identifiable as a
subcategory of women's labour: 'Counting all women's work,
including sex work, is a strategy for crossing the divide between
sex workers and other women. It strengthens all women's case for
... the economic power to refuse prostitution' (p. 100).

Truong's comments on the problems associated with merging
prostitutes' rights campaigns with Wages for Housework campaigns are incisive:

> there is a confusion between housewives and housework, and
> between prostitutes and prostitution. Housework is not necessar-
> ily performed by housewives, and not all facets of prostitution
> can be associated with prostitutes. Wages for housework would
> also benefit housewives who already have domestic servants,
> and the abolition of prostitution laws would also benefit those
> who control prostitution as a business. Secondly, relations
> surrounding prostitutes' work and the work of housewives are
> not the same, and therefore the control over such work, the legal
> framework and rewards are different. The social conditions of a
> housewife and a prostitute cannot be homogenized, even though
> they are both engaged in reproductive tasks. (*Truong*, 1990,
> pp. 51–2)

Feminist activists who treat prostitution as the *sine qua non* of male
domination also often try to mobilize around the idea that *all*
women share a common set of interests – see, for example, Wynter
(1988, p. 268) and Barry (1995, p. 317), the latter of whom asserts
that 'prostitution makes all women vulnerable, exposed to danger,
open to attack', and more generally assumes that all alike have an
identical interest in the eradication of sexual exploitation. This
seems to me just as abstract (and so as facile) as the idea that *all*
women share a common interest in the formal equalization of
labour in the productive and reproductive spheres. We had certainly better be sure not to hold our breath as we wait for non-
prostitute women to stand aside alongside their prostitute sisters
in a fight against patriarchal domination, for many non-prostitute
women (even some feminists) buy into the ideologies which construct prostitutes as sexual and social Others, and often actively
police the boundaries of the imaginary community from which

prostitute women are excluded. Prostitute and non-prostitute women are not 'natural' allies. Even when they share a common, highly marginalized economic and political situation, non-prostitute women frequently look down upon and castigate prostitutes.

By the same token, there is no reason to assume that prostitutes will automatically benefit from gains made by other marginalized groups. Yes, there are some commonalties between the forms of oppression which operate on prostitute and non-prostitute women, 'racialized' minorities, sexual minority groups and certain groups of wage workers, commonalties which spring from the fact that many power relations are 'structured by a dynamic of domination/submission' (Hartsock, 1985, p. 155). But identifying domination as a structuring feature of relations between different community members does not imply an identity of political interests among all dominated groups. There are, for example, certain similarities between the powers that fathers exercise over children and those which employers exercise over workers, but it does not follow that political struggles for worker's rights will simultaneously prove liberatory for children. Nor do members of differently oppressed groups necessarily share a subjective sense of affinity or solidarity with each other. Many of the prostitutes I have interviewed have expressed extremely racist and homophobic views, for example, and non-prostitutes who are lesbian or gay, and/or members of a 'racialized' minority group, are no less likely to look down upon prostitutes than are members of powerful majority groups.

One response to such problems is to put campaigns to destigmatize prostitution on the political agenda next to campaigns for legal reform, and most prostitutes' rights do exactly this. Again, such campaigns are very much to be welcomed, but must also be informed by an appreciation of the multiple oppressions involved in prostitution. Imagine prostitution successfully stripped of its stigma. Except perhaps in the case of the most privileged dominatrixes, what actually remains is menial, repetitive, boring, 'caring' work, often hazardous, often involving intimate contact with dirty and/or foul-breathed customers, and almost invariably calling for intensive and depleting emotional labour. Who, faced with equally well-paid alternatives, would choose this? And, judging by the experience of other groups of workers who perform equally menial, 'caring' and non-productive, but non-stigmatized and legitimate, work (such as ancillary nurses, domestic servants, nannies), how likely is it that, even without the stigma, prostitutes would acquire meaningful economic, social or political power? This draws our attention to certain similarities between prostitution and domestic servitude which are relevant to debates on political strategy.

Domestic workers' struggles?

Employers of domestic servants often appear to attach a value to the actual exercise of personalistic power over the person of the servant, as much as or more than that value which they attach to the end product of the servant's labour, and similar patterns of 'employment relations' and enslavement to those found in prostitution can be found in domestic work. Like pimps and brothel owners, third parties who seek to profit from the provision of domestic servants aim to secure a 'cut' of an existing exchange value, that is, the value which employers attach to powers of command over the person of the servant, and are thus constrained in terms of how they can organize the production and appropriation of surplus. Moreover, similar patterns of abuse to those found in prostitute–client transactions occur in the relationships between domestic workers and their employers, as Anderson's (1993) study of overseas domestic workers in Britain all too graphically reveals. Finally, like prostitution, domestic work is not so much central to the reproduction of a mode of production as to the reproduction of a particular status hierarchy within it, and, like prostitution, it represents an economic exchange which takes place in a 'private' rather than a 'public' sphere. Like prostitution, domestic work often falls outside the regulatory framework devised to govern capitalist employment relations in any given country, and it is also the case that the boundaries of the relationship between employer and a domestic servant are imagined in ways which more closely resemble feudal bonds than modern, contractual relations.

To the extent that prostitution and domestic servitude share these characteristics, we can perhaps argue that the success of organizations such as Kalayaan in Britain and Solidar in Belgium in terms of organizing migrant domestic workers offers a ray of hope for the most exploited groups of prostitutes in the West. And yet even this optimism has to be tempered by the fact that, inasmuch as capitalist relations of reproduction in the West include the provision of care for an ageing population, domestic workers perform a recognized and necessary function, and it is this, more than anything else, which gives reason to believe that other European states will follow the example of Italy and begin to make at least some minimal interventions to regulate the domestic worker–employer relationship (Anderson and Phizacklea, 1997). Prostitution does, without doubt, represent a kind of alternative or supplementary welfare system in most countries of the world, and so performs a function for the state. This function is not recognized, however, and, in a period when most Western governments are simultaneously engaged in slashing welfare support to women and children and espousing a commitment to 'family values', it is difficult to envisage any of them abandoning their hypocrisies and bluntly admitting to the fiscal benefits they derive from the prostitution of those who would otherwise require state support. As a catchphrase, 'Welfare to Prostitution' does not have quite the same high moral tone as 'Welfare to Work'.

Since the state rarely acknowledges an interest in the economic arrangements between prostitutes and clients or prostitutes and third parties, these arrangements take on the character of a clients' and employers' 'free for all', and it is this which makes a mockery of the liberal notion of voluntary, contractual consent implicit in prostitutes' collectives' defence of 'free choice' prostitution (see COYOTE, 1988, ECP, 1997). If people are desperate enough, they will 'consent' to enter into contracts of debt bondage or of indenture, or to undertake life-threatening tasks without even the most minimal protection. Contractual 'consent' does not imply mutuality or free choice where the two parties are vastly unequal in terms of economic power, and where one party's freedom to set the terms of the contract is unbounded and the other party's freedom to refuse and/or retract from the contract is limited or non-existent. This is precisely why labour movements and human rights activists struggle to outlaw systems of debt bondage and indentured labour, to compel employers legally to observe health and safety procedures, to ban the use of toxic substances in production processes – in short, to criminalize those who invite others to consent to contracts which will harm them.

Applied to prostitution, this kind of struggle could take the form of pressure for the formal establishment of standard minimum rules for the treatment of prostitutes by clients and third parties, in the same way that organizations such as GAATW (1997) are campaigning for standards aimed to protect the human rights of individuals who have been trafficked across national borders. Governments could, for example, be urged to impose a minimum hourly rate for prostitute use and to outlaw contracts which involve the transfer of particular powers of sexual command over other human beings (for instance, contracting to command unprotected sex, contracting to enact violence against the person of the prostitute), as well as criminalizing any third-party beneficiary of such transactions.

Again, however, such regulation would be largely ineffectual in the absence of measures to address the underlying structural inequalities which drive people into prostitution. Minimum standards would be difficult to enforce in the formally organized prostitution sector and almost impossible to enforce in informal settings such as street prostitution. Drug-using and child prostitutes would hardly be likely to bring charges against clients who attempt to forge illicit contracts with them, and, if they did not report such offences, there would be little chance of them ever coming to light. Also, inequalities between rich and poor countries make it unlikely that universal minimum standards would be enforced around the globe, and their uneven application could well exacerbate the existing tendency for prostitute users to travel to places where prostitutes can be more intensively exploited and for prostitutes to migrate to rich countries where, despite the fact that their immigration status makes them vulnerable to abuse, they can earn more than they could in their country of origin. This draws attention to a final point about the enormity of the problems which confront those who seek to mobilize politically around prostitution.

Prostitutes as a differentiated group

Prostitution not only involves multiple oppressions, but also implies different degrees of those oppressions for different groups of prostitutes. Independent entrepreneurial prostitutes tend to secure (relatively) greater financial rewards and be exposed to (relatively) less risk of violence and intimidation, while prostitutes in cheaper brothels tend to be more intensively exploited and abused. On the streets, independent adults and non-drug-using prostitutes enjoy a greater degree of control over the terms of prostitute–client exchanges than do children, drug addicts and pimped prostitutes, and the same is true in informally arranged, tourist-related prostitution. These hierarchies are typically gendered, classed, 'racialized' and/or segregated along lines of national or ethnic identity, as well as age.

Prostitutes do not constitute a single, unified social group even within a single country, but rather, as Iris Young (1990, p. 48) notes about social groups more generally, 'mirror in their own differentiations many of the other groups in the wider society'. Young continues, 'The culture, perspective, and relations of privilege and oppression of these various groups, moreover, may not cohere. Thus individual persons, as constituted partly by their group affinities and relations cannot be unified, themselves are heterogeneous and not necessarily coherent', and this too is relevant if we are to understand the fact that political gains made by those in one 'stratum' of the prostitution hierarchy can easily turn into losses for those who work in another. Prostitutes' interests are not uniformly served, or harmed, by the same legislation. Decriminalization of brothel prostitution can lead to increased harassment of street prostitutes, for example, and current anti-trafficking and immigration legislation in affluent Western nations does not damage the interests of prostitutes who are nationals of those countries (indeed, since their bargaining position may be adversely affected by the presence of 'cheap' migrant labour, it might even be said to advance their interests), but it neither protects nor serves migrant women in prostitution. As prostitutes, they are necessarily illegal migrants, and this status increases their vulnerability to third party abuse and exploitation (see Bindman, 1997, pp. 57–9, GAATW, 1997, p. 11). Even where trafficked women and children have been forced into prostitution, as opposed to voluntarily but illegally migrating for that purpose, existing legal measures generally mean that, if discovered, they will face prostitution charges and deportation (and so a return to the conditions which first led to their abuse).

Political debate on prostitution has simultaneously to acknowledge the existence of a relatively privileged stratum within prostitution and move beyond a concern with the demands articulated by those in that stratum to accommodate the bleak reality of so many people's lives, a reality which makes notions of consent and self-determination hugely problematic in relation to prostitution. These same points are relevant to child prostitution, for even children who are sexually exploited are subject to different degrees of domination, and the material realities of child prostitution in rich and poor countries are not always identical. If the full horror of some children's lives is countenanced, the array of possible policy solutions discussed thus far appear almost grotesquely irrelevant. In Brazil, for instance, 54 per cent of children and adolescents live in families earning less than US$35 per month, and between seven and eight million children live on the streets, where they are at risk not only of violence from other street dwellers but of systematic abuse and torture by police officers. Death squads operate in poor neighbourhoods, gunning down street children and mutilating their bodies, and Rio de Janeiro justice department statistics suggest that it is predominantly male street children who are murdered in this way. One reason for this is that 'child prostitution is becoming increasingly common throughout the country. A young girl in Recife explained ... "We have got our bodies to sell. We have got something to give them." In return, the pimp or brothel owner provides them with somewhere to live' (Dimenstein, 1991, p. 39). Millions of children around the world face similarly grim life 'choices', and questions about the regulation or deregulation of prostitution, even questions about how to penalize their clients and pimps, do not begin to address their condition.

Moral blame

Prostitute use represents a means of side-stepping certain aspects of the social regulation of sexual life, a way of attaining control over other people as sexual beings without incurring dependencies or obligations, or, in the case of honorific sex tourism, a way of ensuring that one can receive 'love' without making oneself beloved. The client pays to evade the social and sexual meanings that would otherwise attach to his (or her) body or desires; he pays to enact fantasies of revenge and hostility that cannot be realized within 'the community' and/or to avoid the obligations that would otherwise be incurred. His desire is for a walking, talking, flesh and blood body that has been entirely disarmed, that is visible only as a body, as the embodiment of his desire, and not as a full human subject.

Who is responsible for the prostitute's objectification? Certainly the individual client does not have a sense of moral responsibility. He does not force the prostitute to embrace this experience of social death – she does so for economic reasons, or because she is under compulsion from some third party. And, even as a collective group, clients can shrug off moral blame. They do not act in political concert to pursue their ends in the way that capitalists or slave holders, for instance, have acted as classes to secure a supply of labour on favourable terms. They do not even form pressure groups. But then they do not need to, for they are the passive beneficiaries of harm inflicted by other persons and structures. Desiree's clients do not need to prevent her from getting a career as a barrister or a merchant banker or something else equally consonant with her ambitions, intellect and talents in order to secure powers of sexual command over her. Marlene's clients do not need to kidnap and rape her in order to control her. Catalina's clients do not need to hold her baby hostage and threaten to starve it to death unless she submits to their wishes. Men like Bruce Cassirer do not need to abduct fourteen-year-old girls from Burmese villages and imprison them in order to sexually exploit them. All these things have been done already.

Can we therefore conclude that clients, like carrion crows waiting at the roadside, merely feed on the damage wrought elsewhere – on the hurts of individual and institutional abuse, on the byproducts of community exclusion, class inequalities, poverty, racism, sexism and indifference to human suffering? The answer to this question seems to me to be both 'yes' and 'no'. As moral agents, clients must be deemed blameworthy for the fact that the contracts they forge with prostitutes are invitations to harm the self and for the fact that, in so doing, they exploit the misfortunes of others to satisfy their own ends. But clients also act within a given set of structural constraints and opportunities, and they make sense of themselves and their actions through reference to a given set of discourses about gender and sexuality. Their power – as well as their desire – to forge morally reprehensible contracts with prostitutes and their third-party controllers can be explained only through reference to those broader systemic factors.

It follows from this that moral distinctions between clients and non-clients may be finer than many care to think. Clients and non-clients alike inhabit a world in which prostitution is the only thing that stands between millions of people and the absolute indignities implied by poverty (and this is true in affluent as well as poor countries) and a world which offers some of its children a choice only between being starved, beaten, raped, perhaps murdered on the streets and being raped, perhaps also beaten, starved and murdered in a brothel or pimp's shack. Clients and non-clients alike also inhabit a world in which girls and women, sometimes also boys and men, are sexualized, denied access to educational and employment opportunities and excluded from communities as a consequence of abuse or rape or sexual orientation or sexual choices they have made, or by virtue of their 'racialized' or ethnic identity or physical characteristics. So long as these facts are accepted, whether out of indifference or resignation, we all of us carry a degree of moral culpability for the institution of prostitution.

Challenging sexism, racism, homophobia and the ideologies which 'Otherize' prostitutes, forcing governments to recognize, acknowledge and do something about the direct relationship between their own welfare policies and prostitution, forcing world financial institutions to acknowledge the relationship between the structural readjustment programmes and tourist development policies foisted on poor countries and the growth of prostitution, and to take steps to formulate less destructive 'development' policies, is then more than simply an urgent political priority. It is a moral imperative.

A final comment

Gayle Rubin has attempted to incorporate prostitution within a pluralist sexual ethics in which sexual encounters are judged by 'the way partners treat one another, the level of mutual consideration, the presence or absence of coercion, and the quantity and quality of pleasure they provide' (1984, p. 283). But there is and can be no mutuality of consideration, pleasure or treatment in the prostitution contract, the whole purpose of which is to ensure that one party is object to the other's subject, that one party does *not* use their personal desire as a criterion for determining the sexual acts which do and do not take place, while the other party acts on the basis of personal desire. Moreover, because there is no society in the contemporary world in which it is *the norm* to arrange human sexual interaction across a market, prostitutes are invariably made social Others by the fact that their own sexual objectification is traded for money. This is not an essential feature of prostitution – it is quite possible to imagine a society in which people were all brought up to think of their sexuality as a commodity, to think it natural and sensible to pursue rational, economic ends through their sexual interactions, and unnatural and distasteful to engage in sexual relations for purposes of pleasure, romance or intimacy. In such a hypothetical society, prostitution would not imply social death and prostitute use would hold very different meanings.

I cannot see how organizing all human sexual interaction across a market would represent a political or moral advance, however, and as things stand, it seems to me that, no matter how they might subjectively perceive, defend and justify their actions, clients are necessarily social necrophiliacs. If their passion was for the socially living, they would have to enter into *human* relationships with women, children or men who are not constructed as liminal and socially dead beings, and they would then find, in most cases, either that their desire was 'impotent – a misfortune' (Marx, 1959, p. 125) or that it conferred upon them certain obligations and duties. These are not risks that clients are prepared to take.

From my own moral and political perspective, all this makes prostitution a pernicious institution, and firmly marks off prostitute use from non-commercial promiscuous, anonymous and/or public sex wherein *both* parties act on the basis of personal desire and *both* parties are free to retract without economic consequence. While I see no reason to object to individuals indulging a personal taste for anonymous sex involving the exchange of money, very few people's prostitution represents a positive choice over how, and with whom, to have sex. And if, for the mass of prostitutes, prostitution is not a sexual 'orientation' or preference, it cannot be rehabilitated within a new, more liberal framework of *sexual* ethics. But if prostitution implies for the prostitute a form of social death, if it is inseparable from 'the larger surrounding culture which marginalizes, stereotypes and stigmatizes women' (Satz, 1995, p. 80) and people of colour, then nor can it be rendered harmless simply through its reform and regulation as a form of labour.

Because I recognize that, for many people in the contemporary world, prostitution is either the only economic option available or the best of a poor bunch of alternatives, I believe it is vital to think through and pursue realistic reforms which, in any given context, will make it easier for prostitutes to work independently of third parties, increase the degree of control they exercise within transactions, and provide greater protection and support for those who prostitute. But if I were to dream, it would not be of a day when all prostitutes have full rights to self-determination within prostitution. It would be of a day when all people could secure full juridical rights and freedoms without resort to prostitution and when no human being was in a position to use their economic power to transform another human being into the living embodiment of a masturbatory fantasy.

There are many prostitute and non-prostitute activists and campaigners who, through their political struggles against class inequalities, gender discrimination, poverty, 'Third World' debt, racism, existing immigration and welfare policies, and so on, are working towards such ends, as well as many who take action to ameliorate the most destructive effects of prostitution and support those who have been most gravely harmed by it. The odds against which such people battle are immense, and the only comfort I have found in the course of researching and writing this book comes from observing the nobility of spirit of those who do fight against such overwhelming odds on the basis that 'it is better to light one candle than to curse the darkness'.[1]

Notes

Chapter 1   Power, Consent and Freedom

1 There is an immediate and striking difference, however, between organizing the production and appropriation of surplus from wage workers in, say, a factory and exacting a surplus from the prostitution of individuals in a brothel or any other formal setting. Unlike wage workers, prostitutes do not *create* any value through their prostitution. The prostitute does not work in order to produce a commodity which can then be exchanged; rather the 'value' that is exchanged in prostitution attaches to the prostitute's actual person. This has implications for the ways in which third parties can go about extracting a surplus from prostitution. In industrial manufacture the employer can organize the labour process in such a way as to increase productivity, so that, for the same amount of input, a greater number of exchange values are created. This is not a possibility for brothel owners and the like, who are effectively engaged in clawing money from the trade of *existing* exchange values rather than from arranging the production of new exchange values.

   Even in the service sector, where they do not organize the production of exchange values, many employers set in motion a process through which workers' labour power is used to *add* value to existing commodities. Again, this makes it possible (at least under certain conditions) for service-sector employers to enlarge the surplus by rationalizing aspects of the labour process and/or by devising other means of saving labour or cheapening labour costs. If a restauranteur discovers, for instance, that it is cheaper to buy hamburgers mass-prepared by factory workers than to employ a chef to prepare them in the restaurant, then she or he can instigate those changes. This is not the case for third-party controllers of prostitution; again, this is because the value that is exchanged in prostitution actually attaches to the prostitute's person, and not to some end product of her or his labour/services. Customers of a fast-food chain such as McDonalds wish to purchase hamburgers, presumably as a means to satisfying hunger or some other want, rather than because of a specific interest in purchasing the power to command another human being to prepare and serve a hamburger. In reality, it is true that the hamburger represents the congealed labour of a whole chain of human beings, but, from the viewpoint of the customer, this fact is not only concealed but irrelevant. It is the hamburger as a disembodied means of satisfying a want which the customer is willing to pay for.

There is a market for sexual commodities that are disembodied in this same way – people purchase pornographic magazines and videos as well as inflatable dolls and sheep, rubber vaginas which 'really suck', etc. – but prostitutes' clients do not simply wish to purchase the disembodied means to an orgasm. Instead, they attach a monetary value to the power to command the person of the prostitute, and third-party controllers of prostitution cannot therefore increase the amount of surplus value they can appropriate by collectivizing, automating or deskilling the prostitute's labour or by subcontracting some part of the prostitute workforce's labour out to cheaper workers. Brothel owners are thus constrained by the fact that they cannot set in motion a process which creates or adds value, but can merely appropriate a portion of that money which any given client is willing to pay for a transaction with any given prostitute.

2 In this sense, their task is not dissimilar to that of other agents who derive an income from the subletting of human labour power, such as agencies which supply domestic servants (Anderson, 1993), employment agencies more generally, or subcontractors in various other industries (see Austrin, 1980).

3 Some hostess clubs explicitly forbid such contracts, however (see Allison, 1994), while in other cases club owners evade the law by ensuring that customer demand for prostitutes is met by 'independent' pimps/procurers operating on the premises (see Whitehead 1997, p. 111, for an account of such an arrangement in a smart Hong Kong hostess club).

4 At Stephanie's, for example, the receptionist is essentially all that stands between the prostitutes and a violent client or an attacker. Three years ago a man entered the building while the eighteen-year-old receptionist was having a break, lying under the sunbed. The man took her at knife point to an upstairs room and locked her in it. He then went into another room and carried out a horrific knife attack on the prostitute therein and raped her repeatedly. The owner of Stephanie's has done nothing to improve security since this incident took place.

Chapter 2   Patterns of Pimping

1 I am grateful to Joan Van Niekerk of Childline, Durban, for drawing my attention to this point.

Chapter 5   Power and Freedom at the Apex of the Prostitution Hierarchy

1 On one occasion a client did take up her offer, however, and the police arrived. Two officers listened to Desiree's accusation (that the man was

refusing to pay the set appointment fee) and then to his denial that he had contracted to pay her anything at all. They asked him to demonstrate that he did indeed have sufficient funds upon his person to pay the fee, and, once satisfied that he did, they told Desiree that, if she wished to pursue the matter, she could do so through the civil courts. The officers then asked him to give Desiree his name and address so that she could pursue her complaint if she wished to, and, after he had left, explained to her that, if he had not had £20 on his person, they would have been able to charge him with attempted fraud.

Part II   Introduction

1 Take, for example, the regulations in Hamburg, 1909, which ordered that women assigned to stringent police supervision must submit themselves 'to regular examination, twice a week, by the Medical Inspector appointed by the Police Department, at the place ordered by the Police Department, and at the time set by the Police Department', that 'At all examinations they must present themselves in clean clothing and in a condition of sobriety and bodily cleanliness', and that 'They must unhesitatingly comply with the instructions of the medical examiners' (Flexner, 1914, pp. 422–4). These regulations were followed by a long list of public places from which prostitute women were excluded and further restrictions upon their public behaviour, such as not being allowed to appear in public in 'striking apparel' or to 'ride in open carriages'.

Chapter 6   Narratives of Power and Exclusion

1 Some women do emphasize continuities between prostitution and rape once they have exited from prostitution – see Barry (1995, p. 38). None of the women and children I have interviewed who were still working as prostitutes at the time described tricks and rapes as identical experiences.
2 We still live in a world in which people can variously be stoned to death for adultery, executed for homosexuality (see Tohidi, 1991), face prison terms of up to twenty years for consensual 'sodomy' (Goldberg, 1994), beaten by 'queer bashers', executed by death squads for their homosexuality (Lind, 1997), rejected by their family and friends and/or subject to all manner of harassment by their good, God-fearing neighbours if they come out as lesbian or gay or if they transgress 'racialized'-sexual boundaries by entering into 'interracial' relationships.
3 Patterson's (1982, p. 44) remarks on intrusive and extrusive modes of representing social death are also pertinent to both the institution of slavery and prostitution. We could, for example, describe situations in which whole groups of people are denied inclusion in the sexual community because they are 'outsiders' as an intrusive mode of prostitution (as, for instance, in colonized and white racist societies, where all women of colour are objectified as sex; see Guillaumin, 1995, p. 213), and cases in which the prostitute's social death follows internal exile on grounds that the right to community belonging or protection has been stripped away, for whatever reason, as an extrusive mode of prostitution.

Chapter 8   Through Western Eyes

1 Likewise, when the rape of women is ordered in wartime (see Enloe, 1993, Kadjar-Hamouda, 1996), rape serves not only as an instrument of terror and domination, but also further to Otherize the 'enemy' and brutalize the soldier, i.e., to maintain a psychological state among soldiers which allows them to continue to kill.
2 In his war diaries, Jean-Paul Sartre wrote, 'I've been surrounded by women for years, and I still want to meet new ones ... I'm not so sure that I didn't seek out women's company, at one time, in order to get rid of the burden of my ugliness' (cited in Cohen-Solal, 1985, p. 99).

Chapter 9   Diversity, Dialectics and Politics

1 A 'saying' told to me by Bridget Anderson.

References

Aguilar, M., 1994: Alarma corrupcion de menores en Puntareas. *Sucesos* [San Jose], 9 January.

Alexander, J., 1991: Redrafting morality: the postcolonial state and the Sexual Offences Bill of Trinidad and Tobago. In C. Mohanty, A. Russo and L. Torres (eds), *Third World Women and the Politics of Feminism*. Bloomington and Indianapolis: Indiana University Press.

Alexander, P., 1988: Prostitution: a difficult issue for feminists. In F. Delacoste and P. Alexander (eds), *Sex Work: writings by women in the sex industry*. London: Virago.

Alexander, P., 1997: Feminism, sex workers and human rights. In J. Nagel (ed.), *Whores and Other Feminists*. London: Routledge.

Allison, A., 1994: *Nightwork: sexuality, pleasure and corporate masculinity in a Tokyo hostess club*. Chicago: University of Chicago Press.

Anderson, B., 1993: *Britain's Secret Slaves*. London: Anti-Slavery International and Kalayaan.

Anderson, B. and Phizacklea, A., 1997: Migrant domestic workers: a European perspective. Final report to the Equal Opportunities Unit, DGS. Brussels: European Commission.

Archer, L., 1988: *Slavery and Other Forms of Unfree Labour*. London: Routledge.

Asia Watch, 1993: *A Modern Form of Slavery: trafficking of Burmese girls and women in Thailand*. New York: Women's Rights Project of Asia Watch.

Austrin, T., 1980: The 'lump' in the UK construction industry. In T. Nichols (ed.), *Capital and Labour*. London: Fontana.

Baran, P. and Sweezy, P., 1966: *Monopoly Capital: an essay on the American economic and social order*. Harmondsworth: Penguin.

Barry, K., 1979: *Female Sexual Slavery*. Englewood Cliffs, NJ: Prentice Hall.

Barry, K., 1995: *The Prostitution of Sexuality*. New York: New York University Press.

Barry, T., 1991: *Costa Rica: a country guide*. London: Latin America Press.

Bartky, S., 1990: *Femininity and Domination: studies in the phenomenology of oppression*. London: Routledge.

Beauvoir, S. de, 1972: *The Second Sex.* Harmondsworth: Penguin.

Beckles, H. M., 1989: *Natural Rebels: a social history of enslaved black women in Barbados.* London: Zed Books.

Bell, S., 1994: *Reading, Writing and Rewriting the Prostitute Body.* Bloomington: Indiana University Press.

Benjamin, J., 1984: Master and slave: the fantasy of erotic domination. In A. Snitow, C. Standell and S. Thompson (eds), *Desire: the politics of sexuality.* London: Virago.

Benson, C. and Matthews, R., 1995: Street prostitution: ten facts in search of a policy. *International Journal of the Sociology of Law*, 23, pp. 395–415.

Bettelheim, B., 1960: *The Informed Heart.* New York: Free Press.

Bindman, J., 1997: *Redefining Prostitution as Sex Work on the International Agenda.* London: Anti-Slavery International.

Black, M., 1995: *In the Twilight Zone: child workers in the hotel, tourism and catering industry.* Geneva: International Labour Office.

Boyle, S., 1994: *Working Girls and their Men.* London: Smith Gryphon.

Brace, L., 1997: Imagining the boundaries of a sovereign self. In L. Brace and J. Hoffman (eds), *Reclaiming Sovereignty.* London: Cassell.

Brace, L. and O'Connell Davidson, J., 1996: Desperate debtors and counterfeit love: the Hobbesian world of the sex tourist. *Contemporary Politics*, 2/3, pp. 55–78.

Braverman, H., 1974: *Labor and Monopoly Capital.* New York: Free Press.

Brownmiller, S., 1975: *Against our will: men, women and rape.* Harmondsworth: Penguin.

Burawoy, M., 1985: *The Politics of Production.* London: Verso.

Burns, P. and Holden, M., 1995: *Tourism: a new perspective.* London: Prentice Hall.

Butler, J., 1990: *Gender Trouble: feminism and the subversion of identity.* London: Routledge.

Butler, K., 1997: Tricked, beaten and sold as a sex slave – the diary of Mia, aged 14. *Independent on Sunday*, 12 October.

Califia, P., 1994: *Public Sex: the culture of radical sex.* Pittsburgh: Cleis.

Cassirer, B., 1992: *Travel & the Single Male.* Channel Island, CA: TSM.

Chant, S. and McIlwaine, C., 1995: *Women of a Lesser Cost: female labour, foreign exchange and Philippine development.* London: Pluto Press.

Chetwynd, J. and Plumridge, E., 1994: Knowledge, attitudes and activities of male clients of female sex workers: risk factors for HIV. *New Zealand Medical Journal*, 14 September, pp. 351–3.

Chodorow, N., 1978: *The Reproduction of Mothering: psychoanalysis and the sociology of gender.* Berkeley: University of California Press.

Cohen-Solal, A., 1985: *Sartre, a life.* London: Heinemann.

Connell, R., 1995: *Masculinities.* Cambridge: Polity Press.

Cornwall, A., 1994: Gendered identities and gender ambiguity among *travestis* in Salvador, Brazil. In A. Cornwall and N. Lindisfarne (eds), *Dislocating Masculinity.* London: Routledge.

Cornwall, A. and Lindisfarne, N. (eds), 1994: *Dislocating Masculinity: comparative ethnographies.* London: Routledge.

Cox, T., 1993: *The Badi: prostitution as a social norm among the untouchable caste of west Nepal.* Kathmandu: Asian Ethnographer Society Press.

COYOTE, 1988: COYOTE/ National task force on prostitution. In F. Delacoste and P. Alexander (eds), *Sex Work: writings by women in the sex industry*. London: Virago.

Creed, G., 1994: Sexual subordination: institutionalized homosexuality and social control in Melanesia. In J. Goldberg (ed.), *Reclaiming Sodom*. London: Routledge.

Cressey, P. and MacInnes, J., 1980: Voting for Ford: industrial democracy and the control of labour. *Capital and Class*, 11, pp. 5–33.

Crummett, M., 1987: Rural women and migration in Latin America. In C. Deere and M. Leon (eds), *Rural Women and State Policy*. Boston: Westview Press.

Daniel, M., 1994: Arab civilization and male love. In J. Goldberg (ed.), *Reclaiming Sodom*. London: Routledge.

Davies, P. and Feldman, R., 1997: Prostitute men now. In G. Scambler and A. Scambler (eds), *Rethinking Prostitution: purchasing sex in the 1990s*. London: Routledge.

Davis, K., 1961: Prostitution. In R. Merton and R. Nesbit (eds), *Contemporary Social Problems*. New York: Harcourt-Brace.

Davis, N., 1993: Introduction: international perspectives on female prostitution. In N. Davis (ed.), *Prostitution: an international handbook on trends, problems and policies*. Westport, CT: Greenwood Press.

DePaulo, L., 1997: The jet-set hookers. *Marie Claire*, September.

Diana, L., 1985: *The Prostitute and her Clients*. Springfield, IL: Charles C. Thomas.

Dimen, M., 1989: Power, sexuality and intimacy. In A. Jaggar and S. Bordo (eds), *Gender/Body/Knowledge*. New Brunswick, NJ: Rutgers University Press, pp. 34–51.

Dimenstein, G., 1991: *Brazil: war on children*. London: Latin America Bureau.

Dixon, R., 1988: *Production, Distribution and Value: a Marxian approach*. Brighton: Wheatsheaf.

Dunham, C. and Carlson, K., 1994: Sex slavery. *Marie Claire*, June.

Dworkin, A., 1987: *Intercourse*. London: Secker & Warburg.

ECP [English Collective of Prostitutes], 1997: Campaigning for legal change. In G. Scambler and A. Scambler (eds), *Rethinking Prostitution: purchasing sex in the 1990s*. London: Routledge.

ECPAT, 1995a: *Newsletter*, No. 12, May. Bangkok: ECPAT.

ECPAT, 1995b: Report on the ECPAT visit to Southern and Eastern Africa. Bangkok: ECPAT.

ECPAT, 1997: *Newsletter*, No. 19, March. Bangkok: ECPAT.

Edwards, S., 1987: Prostitutes: victims of law, social policy and organized crime. In P. Carlen and A. Worrall (eds), *Gender, Crime and Justice*. Milton Keynes: Open University Press.

Edwards, S., 1993: England and Wales. In N. Davis (ed.), *Prostitution*. Westport, CT: Greenwood Press.

Ekachai, S., 1990: *Behind the Smile: voices of Thailand*. Bangkok: Post Publishing.

Ellison, Ralph, 1965: *Invisible Man*. Harmondsworth: Penguin.

Enloe, C., 1989: *Bananas, Beaches, Bases*. London: Pandora.

Enloe, C., 1992: It takes two. In S. Sturdevant and B. Stoltzfus: *Let the Good Times Roll: prostitution and the US military in Asia*. New York: New Press.

Enloe, C. 1993: *The Morning After: sexual politics at the end of the cold war*. Berkeley: University of California Press.

Ennew, J., 1986: *The Sexual Exploitation of Children*. Cambridge: Polity Press.

Ericcson, L., 1980: The charges against prostitution: an attempt at philosophical assessment. *Ethics*, 90, April, pp. 335–66.

Faugier, J. and Sargeant, M., 1997: Boyfriends, 'pimps' and clients. In G. Scambler and A. Scambler (eds), *Rethinking Prostitution: purchasing sex in the 1990s*. London: Routledge.

Ferguson, J., 1992: *Dominican Republic: beyond the lighthouse*. London: Latin America Bureau.

Flexner, A., 1914: *Prostitution in Europe*. London: Grant Richards.

Foucault, M., 1979: *The History of Sexuality*, Vol. I. London: Allen Lane.

Frankenberg, R., 1993: *White Women, Race Matters*. London: Routledge.

Fraser, N., 1997: *Justice Interruptus: critical reflections on the 'postsocialis' condition*. London: Routledge.

Freud, S., 1912: The most prevalent form of degradation in erotic life. In P. Rieff (ed.), *The collected papers of Sigmund Freud: sexuality and the psychology of love*. New York: Collier-Macmillan, 1963.

Fyfe, A., 1989: *Child Labour*. Cambridge: Polity Press.

GAATW, 1997: *Newsletter*, 7, April–June. Bangkok: Global Alliance Against Traffic in Women.

Geertz, C., 1973: *The Interpretation of Cultures*. New York: Basic Books.

Gibson, B., 1995: *Male Order: life stories from boys who sell sex*. London: Cassell.

Giddens, A., 1984: *The Constitution of Society*. Cambridge: Polity.

Gilfoyle, T., 1992: *City of Eros: New York City, prostitution, and the commercialization of sex, 1790–1920*. New York: W. W. Norton.

Glover, E., 1957: *The Psychopathology of Prostitution*. London: Institute for the Study and Treatment of Delinquency.

Goffman, E., 1959: *The Presentation of Self in Everyday Life*. Harmondsworth: Penguin.

Goldberg, J. (ed.), 1994: *Reclaiming Sodom*. London: Routledge.

Graaf, R., de Vanwesenbeeck, I., Zessen, G., Straver, C. and Visser, J., 1992: Prostitution and the spread of HIV. In *Safe Sex in Prostitution in the Netherlands*. Amsterdam: Mr A. de Graaf Institute.

Greenwald, H., 1958: *The Call Girl: a social and psychoanalytic study*. New York: Ballantine.

Guillaumin, C., 1995: *Racism, Sexism, Power and Ideology*. London: Routledge.

Hall, C. M., 1994: Gender and economic interests in tourism prostitution: the nature, development and implications of sex tourism in South-East Asia. In V. Kinnaird and D. Hall (eds), *Tourism: a gender perspective*. London: Routledge.

Hart, A., 1994: Missing masculinity? Prostitutes' clients in Alicante, Spain. In A. Cornwall and N. Lindisfarne (eds), *Dislocating Masculinity*. London: Routledge.

Hartsock, N., 1985: *Money, Sex and Power*. Boston: Northeastern University Press.

Hengkietisak, K., 1994: A green harvest of a different kind. *Bangkok Post*, 20 March, p. 17.

Hobbes, T., 1968: *Leviathan*. Harmondsworth: Penguin.

Høigård, C. and Finstad, L., 1992: *Backstreets: prostitution, money and love*. Cambridge: Polity Press.

Hollway, W., 1996: Recognition and heterosexual desire. In D. Richardson (ed.), *Theorising Heterosexuality*. Buckingham: Open University Press.

hooks, b., 1981: *Ain't I a Woman?: black women and feminism*. Boston: South End Press.

hooks, b., 1992: *Black Looks: race and representation*. London: Turnaround Press.

Human Rights Convention, 1994: Women's rights, human rights. Report 5. London: National Council for Civil Liberties.

Human Rights Watch/Asia, 1995: *Rape for Profit*. New York: Human Rights Watch.

INSAF, 1995: The needs of children in Goa: towards building an adequate response. Interim report. Panjim: Indian National Social Action Forum.

IOM, 1996: Trafficking in women to Italy for sexual exploitation. Brussels: International Organization for Migration.

Ireland, K., 1993: *Wish You Weren't Here*. London: Save the Children.

Jaget, C. (ed.), 1980: *Prostitutes Our Life*. Bristol: Falling Wall Press.

James, W., 1993: Migration, racism and identity formation: the Caribbean experience in Britain. In W. James and C. Harris, *Inside Babylon*. London: Verso.

Jarvinen, M., 1993: *Of Vice and Women: shades of prostitution*. Oslo: Scandinavian University Press.

Jeffreys, S., 1994: Representing the prostitute. *Feminism & Psychology*, 5/4, pp. 539–42.

Jeffreys, S., 1997: *The Idea of Prostitution*. Melbourne: Spinifex.

Kadjar-Hamouda, E., 1996: *An End to Silence: a preliminary study on sexual violence, abuse and exploitation of children affected by armed conflict*. Geneva: International Federation Terre des Hommes.

Kannabiran, K., 1996: Rape and the construction of communal identity. In K. Jayawardena and M. De Alwis (eds), *Embodied Violence: communalising women's sexuality in South Asia*. London: Zed Books.

Karch, C. and Dann, G., 1981: Close encounters of the third world. *Human Relations*, No. 34, pp. 249–68.

Kelly, L., Wingfield, R., Burton, S., and Regan, L., 1995: *Splintered Lives: sexual exploitation of children in the context of children's rights and child protection*. Ilford: Barnardo's.

Kinnell, H., 1989: Prostitutes, their clients and risks of HIV infection in Birmingham. Occasional Paper. Birmingham: Department of Public Health Medicine.

Kirshenbaum, G., 1994: *International News*, May/June.

Kitzinger, C., 1994: Problematizing pleasure: radical feminist deconstructions of sexuality and power. In H. L. Radtke and H. Stam (eds), *Power/Gender: social relations in theory and practice*. London: Sage.

Kosovski, E., 1993: Brazil. In N. Davis (ed.), *Prostitution*. Westport, CT: Greenwood Press.

Kristof, N., 1996: Special report on children for sale. *New York Times*, 14 April.

Layder, D., 1993: *New Strategies in Social Research*. Cambridge: Polity Press.

Layder, D., 1997: *Modern Social Theory: key debates and new directions*. London: University College.

Le, N. and Williams, D., 1996: Social factors and knowledge of HIV/AIDS in Vietnam. In J. Subedi and E. Gallagher (eds), *Society, Health and Disease*. Upper Saddle River, NJ: Prentice Hall.

Lee, W., 1991: Prostitution and tourism in South-East Asia. In N. Redclift and M. Sinclair (eds), *Working Women: international perspectives on labour and gender ideology*. London: Routledge.

Lee-Wright, P., 1990: *Child Slaves*. London: Earthscan.

Lind, A., 1997: Out of the closet and into la calle. *NACLA Report on the Americas*, 30/5, pp. 6–9.

Long, N. V., 1993: Vietnam. In N. Davis (ed.), *Prostitution*: Westport, CT: Greenwood Press.

Lopez Jones, N., 1990: Guilty until proven innocent. *New Law Journal*, 11 May, pp. 656–9.

Mac An Ghaill, M. (ed.), 1996: *Understanding Masculinities*. Buckingham: Open University Press.

McIntosh, M., 1978: Who needs prostitutes? The ideology of male sexual needs. In C. Smart and B. Smart (eds), *Women, Sexuality and Social Control*. London: Routledge & Kegan Paul.

McKeganey, N. and Barnard, M., 1996: *Sex Work on the Streets*. Buckingham: Open University Press.

MacKinnon, C., 1989: *Towards a Feminist Theory of the State*. Cambridge, MA: Harvard University Press.

McLeod, E., 1982: *Working Women: prostitution now*. London: Croom Helm.

Marlowe, J., 1997: It's different for boys. In J. Nagel (ed.), *Whores and other Feminists*. London: Routledge.

Marx, K., 1954: *Capital*, Vol. 1. London: Lawrence & Wishart.

Marx, K., 1959: *Economic and Philosophic Manuscripts of 1844*. London: Lawrence & Wishart.

Marx, K., 1975: 'The Eighteenth Brumaire of Louis Bonaparte', in K. Marx and F. Engels, *Collected Works*, Vol II. London: Lawrence & Wishart.

May, T., 1993: *Social Research*. Buckingham: Open University Press.

Meisch, L., 1995: Gringas and otavalenos: changing tourist relations. *Annals of Tourism Research*, 22/2, pp. 441–62.

Miles, R., 1987: *Capitalism and Unfree Labour: anomaly or necessity?* London: Tavistock.

Miles, R., 1989: *Racism*. London: Routledge.

Miller, W., 1993: *Humiliation*. Ithaca, NY: Cornell University Press.

Millett, K., 1975: *The Prostitution Papers*. St Albans: Paladin.

Milligan, D., 1993: *Sex Life: a critical commentary on the history of sexuality*. London: Pluto Press.

Mills, H., 1997: Kerb crawlers face lessons in shame. *The Observer*. 30 November.

Mitter, S., 1986: *Common Fate, Common Bond: women in the global economy*. London: Pluto Press.

Momsen, J., 1994: Tourism, gender and development in the Caribbean. In V. Kinnaird and D. Hall (eds), *Tourism: a gender perspective*. London: Routledge.

Monet, V., 1997: No girls allowed at the Mustang Ranch. In J. Nagel (ed.), *Whores and Other Feminists*. London: Routledge.

Moore, H., 1994: *A Passion for Difference*. Cambridge: Polity Press.

Morris, R., 1996: Fair game. *Young People Now*, October.

Morrissey, M., 1989: *Slave Women in the New World: gender stratification in the Caribbean*. Lawrence: Kansas University Press.

Nagel, J. (ed.), 1997: *Whores and Other Feminists*. London: Routledge.

Navhind Times, 1996: Peats found guilty of child prostitution. 34/27, 16 March.

Nelson, D., 1998: Pick up men on video, prostitutes will be told. *The Observer*, 18 January.

Nichols, T. (ed.), 1980: *Capital and Labour*. London: Fontana.

Noakes, K., 1995: Ruff spots and rent-a-dreads. In N. Jansz and M. Davies (eds), *More Women Travel: adventures and advice from more than 60 countries*. London: Rough Guides.

O'Connell Davidson, J., 1995a: British sex tourists in Thailand. In M. Maynard and J. Purvis (eds), *(Hetero)Sexual Politics*. London: Taylor & Francis.

O'Connell Davidson, J., 1995b: The anatomy of 'free choice' prostitution. *Gender, Work and Organization*, 2/1, pp. 1–10.

O'Connell Davidson, J., 1996a: Sex tourism in Cuba. *Race & Class*, 37/3, pp. 39–48.

O'Connell Davidson, J., 1996b. Prostitution and the contours of control. In J. Holland and J. Weeks (eds), *Sexual Cultures*. London: Macmillan.

O'Connell Davidson, J. and Layder, D., 1994: *Methods, Sex and Madness*. London: Routledge.

O'Connell Davidson, J. and Sánchez Taylor, J., 1996a: *Child Sexual Exploitation in the Dominican Republic*. Bangkok: ECPAT.

O'Connell Davidson, J. and Sánchez Taylor, J., 1996b: *Child Sexual Exploitation in South Africa*. Bangkok: ECPAT.

O'Grady, R., 1994: *The Rape of Innocence*. Bangkok: ECPAT.

O'Neill, M., 1996: Researching prostitution and violence: towards a feminist praxis. In M. Hester, L. Kelly and J. Radford (eds), *Women, Violence and Male Power*. Buckingham: Open University Press, pp. 130–47.

O'Neill, M., 1997: Prostitute women now. In G. Scambler and A. Scambler (eds), *Rethinking Prostitution: purchasing sex in the 1990s*. London: Routledge.

O'Neill, M., Goode, N. and Hopkins, K., 1995: Feminist responses to adolescent female prostitution: the experience of young women in residential care. In *Childright: journal of the children's legal centre*. University of Essex. February.

Overall, C., 1992: What's wrong with prostitution? Evaluating sex work. *Signs*, No. 17, pp. 705–24.

Pateman, C., 1988: *The Sexual Contract*. Cambridge: Polity Press.

Patterson, O., 1982: *Slavery and Social Death*. Cambridge, MA: Harvard University Press.

Pattullo, P., 1996: *Last Resorts: the cost of tourism in the Caribbean*. London: Latin America Bureau.

Pério, G. and Thierry, D., 1996: 'Tourisme sexuel au Brésil et en Colombie: rapport d'Énquête'. [unpublished].

Perkins, R., 1995: Alleged trafficking of Asian sex workers in Australia. *Prostitutes Education Network*. <http://www.bayswan.org/Austraf.html>.

Phoenix, J., 1995: Prostitution: problematizing the definition. In M. Maynard and J. Purvis (eds), *(Hetero)Sexual Politics*. London: Taylor & Francis.

Phongpaichit, P., 1982: *From Peasant Girls to Bangkok Masseuses*. Geneva: International Labour Office.

Pilcher, J., 1995: *Age and Generation in Modern Britain*. Oxford: Oxford University Press.

Pitt-Rivers, J., 1977: *The Fate of Shechem or The Politics of Sex: essays in the anthropology of the Mediterranean*. Cambridge: Cambridge University Press.

Plummer, K., 1981: Pedophilia: constructing a sociological baseline. In M. Cook and K. Howells (eds), *Adult Sexual Interest in Children*. London: Academic Press.

Plumridge, E., Chetwynd, J., Reed, A. and Gifford, S., 1997: Discourses of emotionality in commercial sex: the missing client voice. *Feminism and Psychology*. 7/2, pp. 165–81.

Potts, L., 1990: *The World Market for Labour*. London: Zed Books.

Pruitt, D. and LaFont, S. 1995: For love and money: romance tourism in Jamaica. *Annals of Tourism Research*, 22/2, pp. 419–40.

Radda Barnen, 1996: Daughters are worth a fortune in the brothels of Bangladesh. *Barnen Och Vi*, special feature issue. Stockholm: Radda Barnen.

Ren, X., 1993: China. In N. Davis (ed.), *Prostitution*. Westport, CT: Greenwood Press.

Rich, A., 1980: Compulsory heterosexuality and lesbian existence, *Signs*, 5/4, pp. 631–60.

Roberts, N., 1992: *Whores in History: prostitution in Western society*. London: Grafton.

Rousseau, J., 1991: *Emile or On Education*. Harmondsworth: Penguin.

Rozario, R., 1988: *Trafficking in Women and Children in India*. New Dehli: Uppal.

Rubin, G., 1984: Thinking sex: notes for a radical theory of the politics of sexuality. In C. Vance (ed.), *Pleasure and Danger: exploring female sexuality*. London: Routledge & Kegan Paul.

Russell, D., 1986: *The Secret Trauma: incest in the lives of girls and women*. New York: Basic Books.

Sánchez Taylor, J., 1997: *Marking the Margins: research in the informal economy in Cuba and the Dominican Republic*. Discussion Papers in Sociology, no. S97/1. Leicester: University of Leicester.

Sandford, J., 1975: *Prostitutes: portraits of people in the sexploitation business*. London: Secker & Warburg.

SAPS, 1996: Crimes against children. Johannesburg: South African Police Service Statistics.

Sartre, J. P., 1966: *Being and Nothingness*. London: Methuen.

Satz, D., 1995: Markets in women's sexual labor. *Ethics*, 106/1, pp. 63–85.

Sawyer, R., 1986: *Slavery in the Twentieth Century*. London: Routledge & Kegan Paul.

Sayer, D., 1991: *Capitalism and Modernity: an excursus on Marx and Weber*. London: Routledge.

Scambler, G. and Scambler, A. (eds), 1997: *Rethinking Prostitution: purchasing sex in the 1990s*. London: Routledge.

Seabrook, J., 1997: *Travels in the Skin Trade: tourism and the sex industry*. London: Pluto Press.

Segal, L., 1990: *Slow Motion: changing masculinities, changing men*. London: Virago.

Segal, L., 1994: *Straight Sex: the politics of pleasure*. London: Virago.

Seidler, V., 1987: Reason, desire and male sexuality. In P. Caplan (ed.), *The Cultural Construction of Sexuality*. London: Routledge.

Shrage, L., 1994: *Moral Dilemmas of Feminism*. London: Routledge.

Siddique, M., 1993: *Moral Spotlight on Bradford*. Bradford: MS Press.

Silbert, M. and Pines, A., 1981: Sexual abuse as an antecedent to prostitution. *Child Abuse and Neglect*, 5, pp. 407–11.

Silbert, M. and Pines, A., 1982: Victimization of street prostitutes. *Victimology*, 7/1–4, pp. 122–33.

Silver, R., 1993: *The Girl in Scarlet Heels*. London: Century.

Silvestre, E., Rijo, J. and Bogaert, H., 1994: La neo-prostitucion infantil en Republica Dominicana. Santo Domingo: UNICEF.

Singh, S., 1989: *Exploited Children in India*. Calcutta: Shila Singh.

Small, S., 1994: *Racialized Barriers*. London: Routledge.

Smart, C., 1995: *Law, Crime and Sexuality*. London: Sage.

Smart, C., 1996: Collusion, collaboration and confession: on moving beyond the heterosexuality debate. In D. Richardson (ed.), *Theorising Heterosexuality*. Buckingham: Open University Press.

Solomos, J. and Back, L., 1994: Conceptualising racisms: social theory, politics and research. *Sociology*, 28/1, pp. 143–61.

Sparks, I., 1997: Brutal game of life. *The Guardian*, 8 October.

Stanley, L. and Wise, S., 1993: *Breaking Out Again: feminist ontology and epistemology*. London: Routledge.

Stoller, R., 1979: *Sexual Excitement: dynamics of erotic life*. New York: Pantheon.

Stoller, R., 1986: *Perversion: the erotic form of hatred*. London: Karnac.

Stoller, R., 1990: *Pain and Passion: a psychoanalyst explores the world of S&M*. New York: Plenum.

Sturdevant, S. and Stoltzfus, B., 1992: *Let the Good Times Roll: prostitution and the US military in Asia*. New York: New Press.

Sutton, A., 1994: *Slavery in Brazil*. London: Anti-Slavery International.

Thompson, E. P., 1978: *The Poverty of Theory and Other Essays*. London: Merlin.

Tohidi, N., 1991: Gender and Islamic fundamentalism: feminist politics in Iran. In C. Mohanty, A. Russo and L. Torres (eds), *Third World Women and the Politics of Feminism*. Bloomington and Indianapolis: Indiana University Press.

Truong, T., 1990: *Sex, Money and Morality: prostitution and tourism in Southeast Asia*. London: Zed Books.

Twine, F. W., 1996: Heterosexual alliances: the romantic management of racial identity. In M. Root (ed.), *The Multiracial Experience: racial borders as the new frontier*. Thousand Oaks, CA: Sage.

UNAIDS, 1996: *The Status and Trends of the Global HIV/AIDS Pandemic*. Official Satellite Symposium, July 5–6. <http://www.us.unaids.org.html>.

Vanwesenbeeck, I., 1997: The context of women's power(lessness) in heterosexual interactions. In L. Segal (ed.), *New Sexual Agendas*. London: Macmillan.

Veyne, P., 1985: Homosexuality in ancient Rome. In P. Aries and A. Bejin (eds), *Western Sexuality: practice and precept in past and present times*. Oxford: Blackwell.

Walkowitz, C., 1980: *Prostitution and Victorian Society: women, class and the state*. Cambridge: Cambridge University Press.

Weber, M., 1968: *Economy and Society*, Vol. 1. New York: Bedminster.

Webster, J., 1965: The white devil. In G. Salgado (ed.), *Three Jacobean Tragedies*. Harmondsworth: Penguin.

Weeks, J., 1985: *Sexuality and its Discontents*. London: Routledge.

Welldon, E., 1988: *Mother, Madonna, Whore: the idealization and denigration of motherhood*. New York: Guilford Press.

West, D., 1992: *Male Prostitution*. London: Duckworth.

Whitehead, K., 1997: *After Suzie: sex in South China*. Hong Kong: Chameleon.

Willey, P., 1993: *Forced Prostitution in Turkey*. London: Anti-Slavery International.

Wyer, J. and Towner, J., 1988: *The UK and Third World Tourism: a report for the third world tourism European ecumenical network*. Tonbridge: TEN.

Wynter, S., 1988: Whisper: women hurt in systems of prostitution engaged in revolt. In F. Delacoste and P. Alexander (eds), *Sex Work*. London: Virago.

Yavetz, Z., 1988: *Slaves and Slavery in Ancient Rome*. New Brunswick, NJ: Transaction Books.

Young, I., 1990: *Justice and the Politics of Difference*. Princeton, NJ: Princeton University Press.

Young People Now, 1996: Trapped and abused – Britain's teenage prostitutes. *Young People Now*, October.

Zatz, N., 1997: Sex work/sex act: law, labor and desire in constructions of prostitution. *Signs*, 22/2, pp. 277–308.

Index

(Indexer: Zeb Korycinska)